Also by Gene Hull

Slice of Life, Our Ways and Days –
   Short Story Collection

Hooked On A Horn -
   Memoirs of a Recovered Musician

Going to Court, a Tennis Tribute –
   Illustrated Tennis Poetry

CHASING THE MUSE

A Life in Music and Show Business

Gene Hull

Sections of this book appeared previously in "Hooked on a Horn." This new edition, with new publisher and different ISBN, presents revisions, added text, and rare photographs among the more than fifty included.

ISBN: 978-0-9819727-8-7

Library of Congress Cataloging-in-Publication Data available upon request.

Editor: Almut Metzroth

Cover Design: Milkweed Graphics

Published by Fiction Publishing, Inc.
5626 Travelers Way
Fort Pierce, FL 34982

"A day well spent brings a good night's sleep."
Leonardo DaVinci

"A life well spent brings biographies."
Eslaf Eman

"A spent life brings a memoir."
Anonymous

CONTENTS

THE VOICE OF CONSCIENCE

"When you put in good things you didn't do,
and leave out the bad things you did,
that's a memoir."
Will Rogers

The author cites the Will Rogers epigraph because it reminds us that a memoirist can sometimes slide unintentionally into the mush pit of truth-versus-fiction. This doesn't imply simply changing a few names for the sake of privacy. Rather, possibly to capture a wider audience, the writer is tempted to get too creative. Thus, the path toward a slippery-slope of embellishment can begin.

At first the author may add more color to the literary landscape. Since this seems to work, he juices up the facts, little by little; fudges the truth here and there. Eventually, the life story can evolve into gross exaggeration, teetering on the brink of outright fabrication. The writer has let the memoir become a work of fiction, rather than what the reader expected it should be. It has happened.

So what, you say? What harm? A book is a book. Make it interesting. Who would know? The answer is: the author will, and so will someone else.

To be fair, shouldn't the reader be protected from fakery? Wouldn't it be fun if at the precise moment creativity gets out of hand, the conscience of the memoirist bursts in, takes over and cries "foul," thereby setting the record straight immediately. The memoir could be rescued from having a credibility deficit; the reader would be saved from being hoodwinked; and the author might still be a candidate for eternal salvation.

With this in mind, I have been invited me, the author's bigmouth conscience, to have a seat at his shoulder and oversee the writing of this book. From time to time you'll see me rearing my nosey head, just as the going gets irresistibly good, butting into the creativity. This necessitates a bit of author rewrite. But fear not; the real truth turns out to be just as interesting as what might have been passed off as fact.

So help me Will Rogers.

1

STUPIDONE

I wondered if anyone would be there to meet me. I hoped not.

The teak railings had crusted with a gritty layer of salt during the ship's transatlantic crossing. I could feel it on my bare forearms as I leaned against the Lido Deck railing, hands clasped, looking down onto the pier of the terminal. It was eight o'clock in the morning. The ocean liner *S.S. Independence* had arrived in Naples as scheduled, June 10, 1968.

Already the heat of the Mediterranean sun oozed sweat from the bare backs of longshoremen on the pier. The day promised to develop into a swelterer—not unusual in southern Italy at this time of year. For me, however, the day would prove to be everything but usual.

The long, heavy hawser lines, securing both ends of the ship to the quay, seemed almost alive, stretched out like tentacled strands of twisted muscle wrapped around the steel mooring posts rooted in the concrete dock. Everything has a purpose, even squat little mooring posts. We couldn't have docked without them.

From my vantage point, I had a good view of the area. Except for stevedores, who were off-loading baggage with disinterest, the pier was quiet, almost deserted. Good. I didn't really want to meet my Italian relatives anyway. As a matter of fact, I dreaded it. I believed they were probably crude peasants, and I was only doing this for my grandfather. Actually, it was my mother who had asked me, "Please do this for Grampa."

"Aw, Mom, I'd really rather not."

"He's an old man," she said. "It would make him so happy. And he did so much for you when you were little."

"Like what? Give me gruff haircuts and yell at me? I really have no desire to meet his family when I'm in Italy. They don't even speak English."

"Anna does. And they are your cousins. Aren't you even a little curious to know about them?'

"Not really. Why should I want to meet them? I have nothing in common with them."

"Well, they're my family too," she said, "and I think it'd be good for you to meet them."

"Mom, we're in Naples for one day only; and that's my chance to see Italy."

"Well, it's something you should do," she said, "and it's important to me."

I thought about that for a moment ... important to me. She had never used that trump card before. "Okay," I said.

After the dissolution of my 17-piece Jazz Giants band, I formed a commercial, if somewhat eclectic entertainment-oriented trio, GK-3. In order to work steadily, I started to travel again. It had been twelve years since I last gone on the road.

The new group produced a unique sound with electric flute, electric chordovox, and percussion. Ken Duca played chordovox with amazing facility and was my partner in the group. Billy Barrick was our percussionist. I doubled flute and saxophone. Our repertoire embraced a wide range of interesting music, from jazz to pop to classical, all peppered with extemporaneous improvisational inserts. The trio was never out of work. We had been booked to play for this ship's summer Atlantic crossing, its Mediterranean cruises, the return crossing to New York, and a few Caribbean cruises.

The booking afforded an excellent opportunity to meet people and make contacts. I was determined to make the best of it. Now in my mid-thirties, I was in a hurry; I had no time for casual meetings with distant relatives, especially those of my grandfather. They couldn't further my career. Every minute had to count, had to payoff in some way. After all, I had a future to build and a family to support and I was trying to make up for lost, but necessary, time I had spent at home for the past several years. So I figured meeting these relatives would not only be a distraction, it would take time away from doing something I thought was more important. Besides, I just didn't feel like seeing them.

My maternal grandfather, Antonio Persico, came to America from Sorrento seventy-five years before, and now at ninety-seven, had just retired as the barber of his own shop. The whole town of Bridgeport seemed to know Tony the Barber. His shop had been on the corner of Railroad Avenue and Park, for over seventy years. He saved every penny, sending his relatives money every month, never missing, except during the war years of the '40s when mail to and from the 'old country' was iffy at best.

From time to time, various generations of his Italian clan would send pictures to him of what they purchased with the money he had sent them—a new refrigerator, the floor tile they installed, a hot water heater, new toilets, a new iron, a TV. Once they enclosed a picture of a pink pig they had added to the stock of animals actually living for a time on the ground floor of their three-story hillside house.

I could understand why Papa Tony was like a God to their whole village. He had made good in America and hadn't forgotten his family. They worshiped his name. To me, he was just a gruff, little old irritable grandfather who spoke broken English. I remembered how vibration somehow mutated to "volabrash" when he said it. He also slurped his soup, chewed open-mouthed, and picked his teeth at the table. And you could forget about "please pass" the whatever.

When Antonio came to America as a young man in the 1880s, the Italians were at the bottom of the social pecking order. Many earlier immigrants to the Melting Pot had faced similar circumstances and in turn had taken the lowest paying labor jobs, gradually working their way up through the social system. The massive Irish immigrations of the mid-century had produced the same conditions, only worse, especially in the over-crowded cities of the northeast. When it was the Italians' turn, resourceful Antonio, sizing up the situation soon after he arrived, initially passed himself off as a Frenchman to a pretty, young Irish immigrant, Ella Lillis, my future maternal grandmother, who, apparently not knowing the difference between French and Italian, believed him. They fell in love and later were married.

Antonio obviously knew how to survive in a hostile environment and how to get things done. I respected his no-nonsense practicality. But why didn't he speak better English after so many years here? Why did he walk around the house in wintertime in long underwear, wearing a bowler hat and black, high-button shoes? Why did he yell at me so much? Why didn't he ever read books? Why couldn't he be like other people on our street? Why did the Irish neighborhood kids call me "Wop," "Guinea," "Dago," and "Grease Ball," when I was a little kid? I'd always stick up for my grandfather, but inside I blamed him for being so foreign. "Mom," I'd say, "Grampa thinks college is for people who don't know how to work with their hands."

Her response was always the same, "Your grandfather is a good man. He's worked hard all his life and helps others. He's never had an education and doesn't know anything about college."

When she told him I had been elected President of my class, at Notre Dame, he said, "Hmm, how mucha da money he make-a for that?"

He just wasn't an American in my eyes. And after all, how was I ever going to be a famous musician if my grandfather could hardly speak English? Ethnic diversity was not yet chic, certainly not in our neighborhood. I was ashamed of him, and sadly, because of him, I was ashamed of my own part-Italian heritage.

One Memorial Day, at my mother's request, my brother and I had agreed to help our grandfather paint his barbershop. I was a wise-ass college student of twenty at the time and a precocious musician, with somewhat of that screw-you-I'm-a-jazz-player attitude. I dipped the brush into the paint bucket and slapped the thick, fresh white mixture onto the pattern-stamped tin wall-covering, spreading it quickly with long, broad strokes. It splattered a bit. But I didn't care. It felt good. It wouldn't take long. And I liked doing something physical. This would be a kick, I thought.

"No, No! Stupidone! Too mucha da paint!" my grandfather snarled from across the three-barber-chair shop, after only two dips of my brush. "Whatsa matter you? You gotta no brains? Justa washa da face."

He was a frugal, hardworking man, and obviously a thorough paint covering was not what he had in mind for the walls. My brother Duane just chuckled. To me it was more like whitewashing than painting. It wasn't a pleasant day. I never was asked, nor did I volunteer, to paint again. I can still hear my grandfather's gruff rebukes from that day. He had called me stupid, and that galled me.

I never got close to my grandfather. I couldn't relate to his foreign-ness, or the barbershop, or the way he reported to my mother, "Say, Marguerite, *the boy* fell asleep witha the radio on again last night." As far as I was concerned, he was impatient, always needed to control a situation and had to be the center of attention. I also hated the smells in the kitchen when my mother cooked up one of his favorite meals, a conglomeration of smelly onions, green peppers, beet greens, red peppers, peas and potatoes. "Peasant food. It really stinks up the house," I used to say to her.

And all of that is why I had no desire to meet these relatives in Naples.

Looking down from the Lido Deck onto the sprawling concrete pier, four decks below, I saw four people, three women and a man, standing there looking up, searching the faces of the few passengers gathered at the railing to get a morning first look at Naples. The young man wore a tight, brown jacket and a wide, floral tie. He sported a narrow-brimmed old fedora, and he seemed comfortable with that. The three young women were wearing bright print dresses and sandals. Each held a balloon, apparently just as people had done decades ago to catch the attention of a relative arriving as an immigrant in New York from the old country. I was aware of the old custom. My grandfather had told me about it years ago, how immigrants, packed on the decks of arriving ships, searched across the terminal for relatives holding balloons. People hadn't done that in many decades. And yet there they were with balloons, the *only* people meeting the ship. I desperately hoped these weren't my relatives. Balloons, yet.

I tried not to look at them. As a matter of fact, I deliberately turned my head away because I didn't want to make eye contact, in case they were my cousins. But one of the women caught my passing glance, and before I could avoid her eyes, she yelled up, squinting, shading her eyes from the hot morning sun pouring out of the east over the top of the ship, "Hey! You know Jen Hall?"

Wishing they weren't, but realizing Oh my God, they're my cousins, I cupped my mouth with both hands and targeted my reply down to them, "I'm Gene Hull."

With that, the three women began to scream with delight and jump up and down. They joined hands, formed a circle, included the reluctant young man, and danced about wildly happy-faced.

Were they for real? I realized how embarrassing it would be to tell my new friends on board that I had found my peasant cousins, or rather, they had found me, and they were even worse than I had expected.

"I'll be down in a little while," I yelled, and walked away from the railing. Mom, how could you do this to me?

I eased my way back across the deck to the outdoor table where I had left my Waspy friends, the Washington, D.C., crowd. Shaking my head in disbelief, I sat down to finish my breakfast.

"You won't believe the scene down on the pier," I said. "There are only four people waiting for the ship. And guess what? They're my cousins. Well, two of the women are. And they're actually holding balloons! Can you believe that?" I recounted the story of my mother's request. I told them about my grandfather and my distant Italian cousins. (In the course of revealing my personal history, I never did mention that I had eight children. They probably would have said, "What the hell are you doing here? Why are you traveling?" I decided they didn't need to know. At the time I considered the omission to be less than honest. I'm still not proud of that.)

They were amused and kidded me for having such unsophisticated, if colorful, relatives, and even for being part "peasant Italian." I laughed right along with them and allowed as how I was only one-quarter Italian.

Later my cousins explained that the reason they were the only visitors on the pier was that they had to apply at the Maritime Magistrate Offices many weeks before in order to get special passes to go inside the iron gates to meet the ship. Whenever a passenger liner from America was in port in those days, no one was allowed on the docks without special permission. Too many stowaways tried to get on board.

After the contract was signed with *American-Isbrantson Lines* for our group to perform on the *S.S. Independence,* letters flew back and forth between Italy and my grandfather. It was soon agreed that cousins, Anna, Gina, and their friend Marguerite, would meet me in Naples when the ship docked there. My grandfather was overjoyed at the prospect. They would take me for the day to visit his old home near Sorrento, and bring me back to the ship in late afternoon. I spoke no Italian and really didn't know much about my relatives. But what I did know held little interest for me. Certainly not in my league. But okay, it's only for one day. I can do this.

I had made friends easily during the crossing. Each night our lounge was the main gathering place for entertainment and dancing. Our music was varied with a lively potpourri of light classical, jazz and pop tunes. It was a hit with the passengers. By the third day at sea we had developed a following. They began to request arrangements we had played earlier and had already become their favorites.

One of our newfound fans was a former U.S. diplomatic courier, Bob LaPlante, who played flüegal horn, poorly, if with conviction. He loved to sit in with our trio and jam the same two songs every night, flubbing the fourth note of "I Can't Get

Started" with such regularity that it was difficult for me to keep from grimacing. I tried to keep my reaction from showing. His encore was always "When The Saints Go Marching In." This tired evergreen held no interest for me either. But somehow, when he played it, it became fun again. Perhaps it was because he appeared to be living his fantasy, playing with a professional band. Music was pure fun for him. What a concept.

Gretchen, his beautiful young German wife, told stories of the intense days in post war Germany, of how her parents had forbidden her to see him because he was an American with a dangerous job steeped in foreign intrigue and Cold War skullduggery. When he was a courier, a classified pouch was always handcuffed to his wrist until he delivered it, no matter where it had to go. Apparently, more than one courier had been found dead, missing a hand severed at the wrist. It was real-life. Not the movies. I was impressed.

Then there was twenty-eight-year-old Rosie, the shapely redhead, a State Department attaché, returning from a Kansas home vacation to her assignment in Barcelona. She had already attracted the undivided attention of the ship's dashing First Officer.

My new friends also included a Polish Count and Countess, or so they said, Isadore and Ilona Gavlecki, who lived in New York. They were on their way to Italy, visiting friends with villas in Rome, Tuscany and Portofino. Isadore wore a green eye-patch, had one wooden leg, and a huge, warm laugh. The Countess, as everyone called her, was the epitome of old-world charm, always perfectly made up and tastefully dressed with the quiet elegance of the European old riche. They were of that class for which summer was a verb. They fascinated me. I always felt like I should bow when they came by.

Most intriguing was the group of young sophisticates from Washington, D.C., with their cocktail parties, elaborate dinners, and expensive cigars. They danced late every night—the men in white dinner jackets, the ladies in their Emilio Pucci multi-colored long dresses. They were beautiful and handsome and made a fuss over our music. I fell in with this crowd naturally.

To top it off, the passenger list included a handful of movie stars going to a film festival in Nice. Jim Nabors, the well-known TV character Gomer Pile, had hiked the Rock of Gibraltar with me when the ship stopped there a week before. We chatted about his TV life and about his home in Hawaii. He said his best friend, Carol Burnett, was his neighbor. I felt important knowing him.

The whole cruise experience was exhilarating, a far cry from playing in dives, Holiday Inns and roadhouse cafés. I tried to fit in with the worldly and wealthy and became genuinely impressed with their stories, their almost reverent adherence to cocktail hour (something new for me) and the time they had for leisure. I was always doing something to get ahead or pay bills. Their lifestyle seemed so sophisticated and enviable; they didn't seem to *need* anything, and I was afflicted with an entertainer's need for acceptance.

"Gene," said Ned, one of the haughty Staunton twins from D.C., who seemed to have been everywhere and done everything, "Why are you wasting time with relatives? Sorrento is a long drive from here. You might miss the ship. After all, Genie Boy, they're only peasants; you said so yourself. We're all going down to Pompeii to see the ruins, and then have lunch at the Grande Excelsior Vittoria. You're welcome to join us."

I thought about it. I would have loved to hang out with this crowd. I didn't want to appear unappreciative. I did have a hard time saying no.

"Thanks, Ned. I'd like to. But as I told you, I promised my mother." An uncomfortable hole in the conversation developed.

"Oh, it'll be good for a giggle", gushed Trisha, breaking the silence, timing my rescue with the confident aplomb that comes so easily to the privileged. She was a sincere, twenty-two-year-old Washington society debutante, very sweet, with lovely brown eyes, full lips, slender hips, and a genuine, warm smile — Ned's girlfriend, I assumed. *Oh my.* I was rather taken with her.

"You can tell us all about it when you get back, Gene," Trisha added, very upbeat. And then, turning to the others, she cheerily added, "Let's all meet here for cocktails at six, and Gene will tell us about his day. Okay everybody?" How gay. How fun.

"Right," the rest agreed. "At six then."

"Okay. See you later everybody," I said when I left the breakfast table. "And don't worry. I'll be back in time."

I was always on time for everything in those days. In fact, I was usually early. I began to think about the day ahead of me. Ned was right; it probably would be a long drive. I knew Italy didn't have Interstates yet. I wondered if I would make it back before the ship sailed at 6:00 p.m.

Missing the ship for an employee was serious; it had said so in the Maritime Articles when I signed-on to the ship. What if I was late and got fired? What about my luggage? My clothes? My instruments? And the money? What would happen to the musicians in the trio? Most likely I would have to pay their fares back to New York at the least. Yes, missing the ship was out of the question. I looked at my watch as I made my way down the six decks to the crew gangway, determined not to let the time get away from me.

Once on the pier, I was surrounded and warmly hugged by my cousins Anna and Gina and their friend Marguerite, as though I were a long lost prodigal whatever. Anna, who was around my age, spoke English fairly well. Introductions followed. The guy in the tight clothes was Franco, Marguerite's boy friend. Since he owned a small, once-green, four-door Fiat, he had been cajoled by the girls into driving them to Napoli to meet "Cousin Gino from America, Papa Tony's grandson." I sensed a proud indifference from Franco, as if he really didn't give a hoot for Gino or America. He would rather have been taking a nap, I guessed, probably with Marguerite, who was fun loving, ripe, and twenty-one-ish, threatening to spill out of her low-cut summer dress at any moment. The possibility of this kept Franco's attention. Mine, too.

As we approached the waiting Fiat, the four of them circled around it, bumping each other like Keystone Kops, trying to decide who would sit where. It was finally settled with Franco and Marguerite in the front seat, and Gina, Anna and I squeezing into the back. Franco took off his jacket and tie and rolled up his shirtsleeves past his elbows, as if preparing for physical labor. He handed his hat to Marguerite.

Once underway, he was in his element. He knifed and zigzagged through the chaotic madness of Naples traffic with its din of beeps and honks, weird midget cars, buzzing hoards of Vespa scooters—the kamikaze motorati—and a multitude of trucks of every description, all racing wildly, like the start of a land purchase stampede, from one traffic light to the next. Once halted at a light, drivers ignored each other but revved up motors in preparatory challenge for the next takeoff.

I saw that crossing the wide city thoroughfares of Naples, Italy's second largest city—home of the pizza, Sophia Loren, *O Sole Mio* and Mt. Vesuvius—could be a death-defying experience for pedestrians, who automatically thumbed their noses or flipped a bird at drivers who had barely missed them. Drivers often shared such pleasantries, adding an unabridged, one- or two-word piece of their Italian minds. But such encounters never seemed to bother anyone for more than a moment.

Franco was no exception. He swore and gestured excitedly at other drivers, none of whom, including him, seem to take it personally. With her flowery frock pulled up well past her knees, Marguerite sat next to Franco. After all, it was a hot day and the car had no air conditioning. Franco was in heat himself and couldn't keep his eyes or his hands off her. In the narrow back seat the two other women and I squished together like an upright stack of folding chairs—Gina on the left, Anna in the middle, with me on the right. Elbows tightly drawn in against our chests, deep breathing—expanding our corpus—was something not to be taken for granted and required some instinctive compromising.

The car cleared the city and headed out to the two-lane highway that led down the coast to Sorrento, the famous town perched scenically on the edge of the Mediterranean about thirty miles away at the southern end of the great Bay of Naples.

Once on the road, Franco accelerated the Fiat to full-gale velocity, obviously enjoying the trip—windows open, hair blowing, on-coming traffic whizzing past us. The narrow road wound along the perimeter of the magnificent Bay, cut into the side of mountainous terrain that rose steeply from the sea. From my seat I could look almost straight down the 100-foot cliff on my right into the blue Mediterranean below. Incredibly beautiful. *But oh my God, this road is narrow.*

Anna could see my concern. "Gino," she said, "Franco has-a drive dis-a road many times. Eat's okay. Notta to worry."

"Okay, Anna. But we're going pretty fast. And this is a very curvy road."

Placated for the moment, I looked at my watch again. She repeated this exchange in Italian to the others. They laughed and smiled at me, and patted my arm--or wherever they could touch me, as if to say, "That's okay, we'll take care of you, little Gino." Even Franco thought it was funny and turned around to reassure me, shaking my hand while steering with his other.

"Look out," I yelled, as we lurched around a curve and headed straight for a slow, oncoming truck full of chicken crates in the other lane. Franco swerved suddenly back to his side of the road, swore, and yelled out his window at the other driver as the vehicles barely missed each other, adding an Italian gesture which probably translated into What the hell's the matter with you? As the truck lurched to a halt part way up an embankment, several crates slipped off the back and soon chickens were squawking all over the road.

And so went this frenetic drive to Sorrento. Anna continued to converse with me in English then repeat in Italian to the others what had been said. They in turn would nod understandingly. Several times Franco turned around and said something in Italian to me, whereupon I would yell and point wide-eyed at an oncoming vehicle, which somehow Franco managed to miss. I'm going to die. I know it. I stared at my watch. An hour had already passed. This is not good.

Anna had spent a year in the United States when she was thirty, and she told me she didn't like the phoniness and the fast life in the States. "People in America don't know how to live, Gino. Run, run. Always run. No relax. No enjoy. That's no living. The only thing they do right, is know how to make money!"

She had a point, and of course she repeated it to the others. They agreed with knowing nods, which I took to mean Yeah, that's for sure.

They respected the fact that Americans seemed to know how to make money, and I didn't contest it. Someday I hoped to make plenty myself—when my music was recorded and I was famous.

By 11:30 a.m. we were on the outskirts of Sorrento. I looked at my watch and made a mental note: we'd better leave by 3:00 p.m. at the latest in order to be back in time. To the right I could see the Isle of Capri just off the coast, gleaming like a soft, green, hilly jewel in a mid-day Mediterranean golden glow. What a sight, mountained, lagooned, terraced, treed, and flowered. It looked so inviting and dramatic with its tall cliffs rising right out of the sea. I could understand why Roman emperors and gods of Roman mythology had lived there.

"Ca-pri," said Anna, pointing out the car window past me, accenting the first syllable. "I have-a boutique there, but I tooka today off to be with you."

"You do? You did?" I said. She nodded, and we continued into the busy, picturesque, narrow streets of Sorrento. Kids were playing everywhere, oblivious of the real world. Neighbors leaned out of windows and chatted across alleys. Vendors sold fruits and vegetables from their carts with the machismo of serious bankers. And everywhere waves of music from radios and record players crossed paths with double and triple aural exposures, morphing into a musical tapestry that I found at once enchanting. Sorrento was charming, an easy little town of incredible beauty. And despite its un-pretentiousness, I could sense the people were proud and took themselves seriously.

There was a gentle, uncomplicated quality about the place that relaxed me. A mélange of aromas wafted past my nostrils: fresh flowers, mint, sauces, garlic, fish, breads, pastries, smells that make you feel alive and comfortable. And hungry.

The trusty, rusty Fiat crept along steadily. I checked my watch again. About that moment Marguerite began hugging Franco around the neck, practically sitting on his lap. "Franco, Franco, *mi amore!*" she said. I could understand her being grateful to him for using his car. After all, the four of them had arisen at 4:00 a.m. to drive to Napoli so they would be there when the ship arrived. And this was probably her way of rewarding Franco, for the time being at least. Or maybe her hormones were just responding impulsively to the romantic Sorrento environment. Soon her hugs were followed with loud kisses, a long, wet-tongued one slurping into his right ear. And as she apparently slipped a hand between his legs, Franco hit a goat. Ka-thump! Someone screamed. Everything stopped, including the car.

People who were going about their business poured out onto the narrow side street, yelling and pointing, all of them running to see what was going on.

More shouting and *mamma mia's* followed. Some of the old ladies in the swelling crowd held their heads in both hands. A round, gray-haired matron railed at Franco, who was still sitting in the car, regarding her with indifference. After all, *he* had a car. Another woman, short and plump, with all the tact of a drill sergeant, scolded Marguerite, who had jumped out to pet the poor goat lying injured on the ground. Children started to kick the car and beat against it with a switch of twigs, as if it were a bad car. Anna and I managed to wriggle out of the back seat. It was an Italian street scene from a Rossini opera and getting more commotional by the moment. A butcher came out of his shop with a cleaver and stared at Franco. A man who looked as if he could be a farmer threw up both his arms and cursed in the local dialect, "Ba fenabala". Suddenly Anna cried out, "Stazitto! Solito! Silenzio!"

Quiet descended on the place. When she was sure she had their attention, Anna explained dramatically that, "This", turning to me, gesticulating with an out-stretched arm, "is Papa Tony's grandson from America, our cousin Gino, and we are on our way to our village, Massa Lubrenza, just two miles away." She added that she would gladly pay for the goat.

"Ooooooh," they said, nodding slowly in unison. "Ahh, ce, senorina, ce, Papa Tony." They nodded toward me and backed away.

It seemed to me that they were unusually respectful. And then I remembered that Robert Kennedy had been assassinated only a few days before while walking through the kitchen of a Los Angeles Hotel with his entourage. The world was shocked by the event. Another Kennedy killed. Italians, who especially loved the Kennedys, took the news extremely hard. To them the Kennedys were larger than life, the world's royalty. It was as if they had lost a beloved star of their own. Many sobbed openly when our ship had stopped at Sardinia the day before. American passengers were greeted solicitously and received heartfelt condolences from the people. Most residents wore black armbands in sympathy, and pictures of the Kennedys with black ribbons on the frames were posted outside many of the local shops. A large condolence book to be sent to Ethel Kennedy was displayed for all to sign. Their warmth and concern for us touched me.

Anna had said the right words: Papa Tony and America. It worked. She gave some money to the lady of generous circumference who immediately stopped complaining. We got back in the car. Franco steered around the fallen goat—some barefooted kids were trying to milk it—and we rumbled out of town at about five-miles-an-hour onto a dirt road that led to the little village just ahead.

As our car approached Massa Lubrenza, I saw a crowd of several hundred people gathered at the base of the fifty-or-so steps that led up the grassy hill to the Persico compound. The village had a population of about four hundred. Apparently most, including the parish priest had turned out to see Papa Tony's grandson. Everyone cheered as I stepped out. My grandfather's ninety-three-year-old sister, the surviving matriarch of the clan, Emiliana, was standing at the head of the group in a place of honor, a wrinkled, wizened figure wearing a long black dress, high-button black shoes and a black shawl draped over her head and shoulders. She blessed me then held me at arm's length to get a good look. "Antonio, Antonio," she said, as she hugged me and wept, apparently thinking I was her long-lost-to-America brother. It embarrassed me.

Anna took my hand and led me to the steps. I kept looking around in all directions. I could see Sorrento and beautiful Capri out in the sea. To the north, a few miles off, loomed Mt. Vesuvius, a smoking giant, hovering over its dominion like a mythic monster warning the wary not to ignore it. I could even see Pompeii, where life had stopped instantly in 73 AD, buried in a blizzard of molten ash from the Vesuvius eruption. Ahead, at the crest of the hill, stood what used to be their farmhouse and now was an impressive, large, three-story stone house with two pink marble pillars straddling the front entrance way

We didn't go right in. By-passing the entrance we walked around to the back. The hilly acreage there was filled with trees—lemons, figs, pears and peaches. Grape arbors drooped, burdened with purple bunches. Adjacent to the flower gardens huddled a small barn for the few cows, goats and pigs, which obviously were no longer welcome in the house. Three other substantial houses nestled comfortably among the tall pines on the ten acres of hilltop land. I stood there and looked around, and thought about what I was seeing. My grandfather's family lives in this private compound of big houses, atop a beautiful spread of land across from the Isle of Capri, overlooking Sorrento and the blue Mediterranean, with a breathtaking view of Mt. Vesuvius. They're happy and loving and gracious. This place is a paradise. It's unbelievable. And I'm looking down on them, regarding them as peasants?

We walked every step of the land, escorted by the whole entourage who clearly wanted to show their respect for Papa Tony and for me. They behaved as if they were following dignitaries, with slow strides, hands clasped behind their backs, nodding to each other each time I reacted to whatever Anna pointed out to me. She explained who lived where, pointed out the tree that Papa Tony himself had planted more than eighty years before, and the grape vines and fruit trees he had cultivated. I marveled at the oversize, luscious-looking citrus — unplucked prizes. Anna led me to the wine cellar my grandfather had dug into the side of a hill where he made wines from the grapes he had grown.

I was impressed and humbled. As a matter of fact, I was beginning to feel ashamed. I realized how wrong I had been about my Italian relatives and my grandfather. I really didn't know them, yet I had pre-judged them. I had no idea of how giving and warm these people were, how they felt about my grandfather and how much they honored him this day by showing me such respect.

Then suddenly it struck me. I can't be late for the ship. I looked at my watch. It was almost 2:00 p.m.

"Shouldn't we start back to Naples now, Anna?"

"Oh no, Gino. We have a bigga luncha for you. Notta to worry."

Notta to worry? Hmm. We went into the house. A long, polished veneer wooden table with a green oilcloth cover had been set up in the large, pink-tiled kitchen on the second floor. Its generous space indicated it was the most important room in the house.

I was asked to sit at one end of the table. Anna sat next to me. Emiliana was at the opposite end. My cousins and other important members of the families joined us at the table, twelve in all. They had taken the day off from their jobs to meet Gino. Several of the clan's younger women, who did not sit at the table with us, served course after course of superb dishes—pastas with red sauce, tender beefsteaks with succulent mushroom gravy, pork chops stuffed with spinach, sensuously seasoned chicken legs and breasts, fresh green vegetables, casseroles, salads, fruits, and creamy potatoes, all nurtured and grown on their land, served with a red wine they had made from grapes they had cultivated. Everyone sipped the wine cut with soda water. A tall blue vase filled with a colorful mixture of fresh garden flowers decorated the table.

Anna told them about her conversations with "Gino on our ride from Napoli" and her comments that Americans didn't know how to relax but did know how to make money. They loved it and voiced their strong agreement. *"Ahhh ... Ceeee"*.

All through lunch the people of the village lined up outside the house. In single file they entered through the front door into the kitchen, walked around the table to the place where I was seated and were introduced to me by Anna. I stood for each introduction, shook hands warmly with each person, then sat down again. Between greetings I managed to chew a few more mouthfuls of the delicious foods. I estimated that about three hundred people passed through the kitchen in two hours.

TWO HOURS! Oh my God. I checked my watch again. I looked around at the others and said, "Okay, Anna, what's everyone laughing at?"

"What do you mean, Gino?"

"Come on, Anna. I can see everyone at the table looking at me, snickering and giggling. What's so funny?"

"Oh, Gino, I'm sorry, but you're just like all Americans. You can't relax. You're always looking at your watch." She repeated this in Italian for the others and they all laughed warmly. I smiled. It was a tension-breaker.

When things quieted I said, "Anna, you say that Americans know how to make money. Right?" She translated this for them. They nodded in agreement with Italian Oh yes sounds. "Well," I said, "how do you think we make money?" They all looked at me, sensing my seriousness. "By looking at the watch," I continued. I raised my wrist and tapped my index finger on the watch for emphasis. Anna translated. Their faces dropped. It was as if they had just heard the secret of life.

Ahh's and ooh's resounded in the kitchen as if a theater audience had been shown a magic trick. Each one came over to hug me, thanking me over and over. I could hardly believe it. It embarrassed me. Were they putting me on? But then I realized that they really were simple folk who were even more unsophisticated than I had thought. Their response had been open and honest and completely unaffected. I began to understand that it might be they who knew the secret of life.

Franco drove me back to Naples in his same wild Italian cowboy shoot-em-up style. But I hardly noticed. I sat in the backseat, not even looking at my watch. I was thinking of what had happened during the day. Soon we were only a few miles outside of Naples.

POW went one of the tires! The car careened from one side of the road to the other, then back again. I fell against the right door, unable to right myself, and held on trying to lean toward the middle. Franco struggled to get control, but the rear end fishtailed when he applied the brakes too hard, and the little car spun around several times in the middle of the road, finally bumping and stuttering sideways, before tipping up one side and bouncing down again on its four wheels, coming to a dead stop.

We weren't hurt. Franco sat there behind the wheel and swore—first at the car, then at the tire, then Anna, then me, probably, then at God, the road, the heat, and finally, I assumed, the goat he had hit back in Sorrento.

We got out of the car. He bent down to look at the left front wheel and what remained of the blown tire. Twisted remnants wrapped around the wheel rim, emitted the pungent acrid odor of burned rubber. More cursing followed as Franco kicked at the tire with the form that would have done justice to a soccer player's tie-breaking penalty shot. I walked to the back of the Fiat to get the spare out of the trunk.

Franco shook his head balefully from side to side and shrugged. "No, Gino," he said, indicating there was no spare. Together we then pushed the car off the road onto the shoulder. Franco took out a cigarette, lit up, puffed away as if accepting our fate, and turned toward the sea to enjoy the view.

"Excuse me. Franco. *Scusee?*" I said pointing at my watch. "The ship. Barco. Ship. Boat." Franco just looked at me. He gestured toward Naples with one arm, palm up, smiled ironically, shrugged his shoulders, and waved at the boat with his other hand, a gesture that I took to mean What can we do? Good-bye, boat.

"No, no, Franco. Ship. I must go quick. Pronto," I said in a sweat.

"Ah, Gino, sorry, sorry." Franco shook his head and shrugged toward the car as if to say, "Nothing I can do about it now … look at my car." He pointed to the mangled tire. He had given up the fight. I recovered the packages I was bringing to the ship out of the back seat. I set them down on the shoulder of the road, looked at my watch again. I had lost a precious half hour, and held out my thumb to hitch a ride.

Seeing this, Franco, understanding my intent, dramatically held up his hand, a reminder that he was in charge. Stepping out into the middle of the road, he waved with the officious grandeur of a *poliziotto* directing traffic, crossing his arms back and forth at the on-coming vehicles heading north toward Naples. Pretty brave, I thought. When a car finally stopped, Franco went over to the driver, pointed to me, then to Naples. The driver shook his head no. Franco gave him one of his personalized, special finger salutes and a ready curse, both of which the driver returned in kind before driving away.

After ten minutes Franco managed to flag down another car. The driver wore what appeared to be a black cap like a military hat with a red medallion just above the beak. They talked. They laughed. They talked some more. They gestured. Finally, Franco pointed toward me. More talk. The driver nodded. "Quanto, quanto?" Franco asked him.

"Cinquante septe mille lire," the driver said. He would take me in his taxi the rest of the way for "fifty-seven thousand lire". He said this in English and repeated the number for me.

"Fifty-seven thousand lire?" *How can I pay that ... there goes my job.* Then I started to figure. At 1800 lire to a dollar, that would be, ah ... just a minute ... about thirty-one dollars. "Yes," I said. "Okay. Okay. Thirty-one dollars. Let's go."

After Franco helped me load the packages into the taxi, I shook his hand warmly. "Thank you, Franco. Thank you. *Grazie. Grazie.*" In return, Franco hugged and kissed me hard on both cheeks and said something that sounded like it meant Hurry, hurry. I pressed a ten-dollar bill into Franco's hand, at which he smiled a huge smile and waved goodbye. The race was on. I could only hope.

"You know Teddy?" said the driver after a few minutes.

"No," I said, assuming he meant Ted Kennedy.

"Oh," said the driver. "My name is-a Pietro. Whatsa yours?"

"Gene ... Gino."

"Ah, Gino ... that's-a nice. My brother is-a name Gino. He live in United States, too. What part U.S. you from?"

"Near New York."

"Ahh, my brother is-a live in-a Brook-a-lyn. You know Brook-a-lyn?"

"Sure," I said, trying not to be chatty, so he would sense my urgency.

"I love-a-Brook-a-lyn. I love United States. God bless-a you."

"Thank you. *Grazie.* Could you please hurry? I have to make it back to my ship."

"We make. Notta to worry. What-a time?"

"The ship sails at six. I'm supposed to be onboard no later than 5:30 p.m." I checked my watch. It was already 5:15.

"Hmm," the driver said. He pushed down hard on the accelerator and the taxi lurched ahead.

I watched as we came into Naples onto a six-lane main artery, three of which headed into the center of the city. A truck loaded with metal pipes sped past us on our left in the middle lane. Suddenly it veered to the right, cutting in front of us, and careened violently into a side street on the right. Clangity bangity bang went piping all over the street, bouncing every which-way, as the taxi swerved to the left to avoid them. Screeeeeech, went the police car's brakes behind us, followed by a loud thud as it whumped the rear of our cab just as metal pipes smacked into our front end.

The taxi driver had done a good job of avoiding a serious pile-up. But a pipe post had wedged into our right front wheel and jammed the steering. The *poliziotti* strutted out of their car, assessed the situation and talked to the taxi driver. Another police car soon arrived, its siren whooping. Pietro was calm, considering the circumstances. He explained he was cut off and that he was urgently trying to get "Gino to the American ship, which was sailing in just few minutes." Traffic was stopped in both directions. Horns honked. The two *poliziotti* in the second police car then motioned to me to get in. Paying the taxi driver, I grabbed my packages and plopped them onto the back seat of the police car. Off we raced with its whoop-whoop siren blaring. The flashing blue strobe light on top of the *machina della polizia* warned all Neapolitans along the way that this was serious police business. I held tight to the back of the driver's seat as we maneuvered in and out of traffic with intrepid skill and determination.

We were close now. It was two minutes before six. As the police car approached the port, I heard the ship's deep horn, blaring like a giant tuba, sounding its ominous announcement of imminent departure. *Shit.* The police car pulled up to the gate at the pier entrance. It was closed. No one was there. The driver blared the siren, leaned on the horn until two stevedores and a security guard came out of a shack and swung the gates open. Whereupon the police car dashed down the pier toward the ship, squealing to an abrupt stop at the crew gangway, which had been pulled halfway up. Too late. I didn't make it. And so close. The lines of the ship had not yet been cast off. Both *poliziotti* jumped out of the car and yelled up to the deckhands to lower the gangway back down. Shouting ensued. The ship's horn blasted again. Heatedly, the two *poliziotti* repeated their orders. The port pilot, seeing the scene from out on the fly bridge of the ship, called down to the deckhands, and after some commotion the gangway was reset in place. As my uniformed friends helped me with my packages, one said to me in very clear English, "Tell-a Teddy ... please notta to be President. He coulda be shot like his-a two brothers."

The D.C. crowd, all six of them, watching the bizarre scene from A-Deck, cheered as I stepped on board carrying several bulky bundles wrapped in newspaper and tied with twine, all of which elicited good-natured laughter from them. I smiled but couldn't manage to laugh with them.

"Please, don't anyone say anything," I said. "Come with me to my cabin." They followed, helping me with the packages. Once there, I opened each bundle slowly, carefully covering the bed with delicious surprises. Each package contained extraordinarily delicious fruits, homemade cheeses, pastries, desserts, breads, cookies, candies and treats that the girls had stayed up at night for weeks making for my visit. Two bottles of homemade red table wine promised instant happiness.

I told them the story of my day and about my remarkable relatives, how generous and kind they were, how they had treated me with such respect, like a cherished celebrity, and so had honored my grandfather. I added that I would never, ever, deny them or my partial heritage again. When I recounted my wild trip trying to get back to the ship, no one laughed. They listened, drank the wine and sampled all the foods with gusto.

"Welcome back, Gene," said Ned. "But in view of what you've just told us, I think you owe us an apology."

"I do?"

"You put your relatives down. Called them peasants. That kind of cranked us up, Genie Boy. Made us sound like a bunch of snobs, and we were only agreeing with you."

"Ned, I apologize. I'm really sorry."

I knew he was right. I had jumped to conclusions. Fortunately for me, I had done what my mother had asked me to do.

"We thought you weren't going to make it back in time, once they started to pull the gangway. That's cutting it pretty close," he said. "But what a grand entrance," he added lightheartedly. "We're sure glad to see you."

"Thanks. I can't believe I'm here."

That night in the Empire Lounge, on Sunset Deck, the atmosphere was warm and friendly with guests sharing experiences of their day in Naples. We were playing light cocktail music, show tunes, easy-listening stuff, background music. Shortly after my friends arrived, along with the rest of the formally dressed after-dinner crowd, I picked up my Selmer alto sax, turned up the microphone a bit, and made a special dedication. "Ladies and Gentlemen … a toast to Italy. Cin Cin!" I played the most soulful saxophone rendition of "O Sole Mio" I could muster. In looking back on the scene, this may have been hammy and sentimental. But something had changed in me that day. People stopped talking. They listened, sensing an unknown message. Word had gotten around about my being escorted back to the ship by police, but most of the passengers didn't know why.

When I finished, the crowded room of guests applauded politely. Young Trisha made her way across the floor to the bandstand and hugged me. *Umm. How sweet.*

Bob LaPlante caught my eye and nodded his wise, worldly approval. Ken Duca, whose fine young wife Carolyn was traveling with us, shook my hand. Sometimes he was a moody guy, especially when he drank, but he was a musical genius. "I hear you, man," he said.

Many weeks later, seated in his favorite wicker chair on the front porch, my grandfather wept as I presented him with a small jar of black dirt from his boyhood home. Memories of a place he left over seventy-five years before, nearly overwhelmed him. "Thanka you, thanka you, Genie," he said over and over, sobbing. "You-a gooda boy."

No longer the grumpy grandfather of my youth, he listened and nodded when told about the trip and how everyone had treated me with such respect, and how, thinking I was her brother, Emiliana had called me Antonio. He looked into the distance as I spoke, his eyes full of yesterdays. And when I described the luncheon feast, he said in a weak voice, almost a whisper, "Ahh, it was-a-like Chrisymoos for them."

And for me, too. He died two years later at ninety-nine.

*

Well, you reported that story truthfully. But why not start at the beginning?

(Just wanted to see if you were paying attention.
First, here's an early photo of my maternal grandfather.)

**

The Beginning

Grandfather, aka: Grampa, Papa Tony, Antonio Persico
♫ circa **1896**

2
_____

_____

ROOTS

Every family is unique. Ours was a musical family, quantifiably at least. At nine years old I began taking clarinet lessons—more instruments were added later. My sister Barbara was a piano student, and my brother Duane played accordion and trumpet. My mother was a professional pianist

Grampa, who came to America to Bridgeport from Italy around 1892 at the age of twenty, played accordion and a handcrafted mandolin he had made himself. It was a beautiful instrument with a polished acoustic belly chamber of inlaid fruitwoods. When he settled down in his upstairs kitchen chair for an hour or two of evening practice, the term "musical" became a more than generous description. And referring to him as self-taught gave us reason to question the definition of that phrase also.

He saw no reason to alter his Columbus Method when searching for the right note: *find it and land on it.* This was difficult for us to listen to. Three of us were taking lessons and practiced more or less seriously, and my mother was a music teacher. For my grandfather, however, accuracy was the least important requirement for his own participatory enjoyment. His hit-or-miss approach never seemed to affect his personal satisfaction. He must have lived by the maxim 'The act of doing is its own reward.'

If Grampa heard us practicing, he would often announce mistakes. "Dats-a wrong-a note," as if he were the duly recognized authority on the subject of accuracy. His own playing, exempt from self-criticism, was a flight of stairs less than perfect, even if it was ardent. We all knew it, smiled and shrugged it off. Hell, he was our grandfather.

My father, though not a musician—nor did he pretend to want to be—was a self-appointed critic. He didn't listen to our practices; most likely he overheard them once in a while when reading the newspapers. But when he did, he sensed when our playing wasn't right, though he didn't say what was wrong. You could always tell by the way he winced when he heard obviously wrong notes; *clinkers*, he called them.

Even though music wasn't his passion—he had two: the Flag and the Brooklyn Dodgers—his pained reaction to clinkers was his way of letting us know he was aware of what was going on in the crazy household around him. This was particularly evident whenever my grandfather plowed through music in the kitchen of his upstairs flat at night or on Sunday mornings, a particularly painful ritual for my father.

The sounds of Grampa's persistently fractured music, with little regard for consistent tempi, left-out beats, or added beats, and with a chaotic collage of clinkers, wafted inexorably downstairs into the ears of the unprotected. "Jeez. Is he deaf or what?" my father would call out to us. Tolerance and patience did not come easily to Pop.

When I practiced my clarinet, I often set up my music stand in the kitchen so my mother could listen, hearing mistakes, squeaks and all, as she prepared a meal. For a son there is nothing like maternal attention and approval. And because my mother was a musician, I appreciated the audience all the more.

I hated practicing, but she always encouraged me. One day in particular, when, after just twenty minutes she saw I was ready to give up, she said it was okay to stop. We sat down at the kitchen table. First she explained that if a person wanted nice looking teeth he had to brush them every day, even though it wasn't fun to do. And to learn a musical instrument, well, he had to practice every day, even if he didn't want to. There was no shortcut. "No progress without practice," she said. Another patch of family dogma.

She went on to relate how it was when she was a little girl learning to play the piano. She said her father, her first teacher, was very tough on her. One day she practiced longer than ever before. That night she couldn't wait for him to get home from his barbershop so she could tell him of her first-time accomplishment.

"Poppa, guess what?" she said proudly. "Today I practiced four hours."

"Hmm. You should-a practice a-five," he said.

She wanted to cry. But she didn't. She said it only made her try harder. When I told her I thought that was pretty mean, she said, "No, Poppa wasn't mean. He was just trying to teach me the only way he knew how. If it hadn't been for him, I never would have become a musician. It takes discipline to stay focused on learning music. He just made me stronger."

Still, he sounded crude to me. I could see that criticizing him was something my mother just would not tolerate. So as I got older, I dropped my duty-like attempts to inform her of Grampa's rude ways, something she most likely knew better than I did.

My mother said that when she was thirteen, her father decided it was time for her to be a professional and took her to the neighborhood theater to play piano for the silent movies. He walked with her the five blocks to the Parkway Theater, a small movie house across the street from his barbershop, He knew the manager, gave him haircuts. The kids called the movie house The Garlic Hall, most likely in reference to the elegant flavoring apparently used generously in the diets of many of its patrons. Grampa would leave her at the door and come back after the film was over. Upon returning, each night he'd collect her money and give her a quarter each week, which she was expected to save. I wondered what happened to the rest of her earnings. Most likely he saved that, too.

When she had accumulated a dollar, he took her downtown to the bank. They always walked to save the streetcar fare. She deposited her money in a savings account. She told me she hated the bank because she could never spend her money, not even a nickel for ice cream or anything else, as other kids in the neighborhood did.

When her father took her to play at the movie house the first time, she said, "But Poppa, what will I play?"

"Justa play whata you wand when you watch-a da picht ," he said and left her there to figure it out.

So every night she sat in the pit, looking up at the screen, making up music as she watched the movies unfold, playing slow, sad pieces when the movie was sad, and peppy selections when it was happy or when there was action.

She told me that one night there was a very sad scene in which a pretty little girl was dying of pneumonia, so said the sub-titles, breathing weakly in her bed, her family and dog around her. The actors in the film were crying melodramatically. People in the movie house were crying also. Even my mother was crying. She didn't know what to play but had to think quickly. Then she remembered a song she had heard somewhere. And although she didn't know the words or the title, she played it because of its tender melody. When my grandfather came to pick her up later, the manager, clearly displeased, told him she had played "The End of a Perfect Day," and the audience knew it.

Even though Grampa didn't quite understand, he knew it wasn't good. Cuffing my mother's head, he said, "Whatsa matta you, Marguerite?"

After much practical experience and practice, my mother became a well-known bandleader in New England during the depression years of the 1930s—Marge Hull and her Melody Boys—ten men and my mother. Whenever she told me how well the musicians in her band played, I wondered what it would be like to play in a band.

My sister Barbara and I took dancing lessons every week. Tap and ballroom. We became quite accomplished, and most every week we performed our routines at clubs, halls and theaters. My mother accompanied us on piano. Our act was billed as Little Fred Astaire and Ginger Rogers, and earned five dollars for each performance, my start in professional show business.

I remember an incident years before our dance-act days, when my sister and I were much younger. A tall, heavy-set young woman, a mother's helper named Irma, used to take care of us at home whenever Marge was away traveling with her band. My father was out of work most of the time, so he'd usually travel with her. We didn't like Irma. She was mean and hollered at us, and she spoke with a heavy accent. She was Hungarian, I believe. However, at that age I really couldn't tell for sure. Suffice it to say she was foreign, and I could see by her face she wasn't Chinese. Anyway, she developed a habit of slapping my little sister's hand if she wet her pants.

"How are my little sweethearts?" my mother asked one day when she came home from a one-week tour. I must have been about four. I remember she always kissed the top of our heads then picked us up and held us close.

"Mommie," two-and-a-half-year-old Barbara said with a pout, "nurse spank hand much." And she turned up her reddened palms for my mother to see.

It wasn't long after that my mother gave up her band, and we never saw Irma again. My mother stopped traveling and began teaching piano and accordion at Harry Hawley's Studio in Bridgeport. She had so many pupils that eventually she established her own studio, which became the largest in Bridgeport. My mother was always trying to do things bigger, and this often irritated my father. "Why the hell do you have to have your own studio, anyway?" he said. "It's always something." He honored the status quo like a true Republican.

My guess is that my mother would have been quite famous if she had kept on being a bandleader. She had the drive, energy and vision. But then she wouldn't have been home with us. Obviously, being a good mother was more important to her than anything else. It was a good thing, too, because we missed her terribly when she was away.

It can be difficult to give up something you love for someone you love. But I doubt my mother ever gave it a second thought, even if that something was music.

It would take me a long time to learn that kind of love.

*

Sounds like a noisy house. So far, so good.
But remember, I'm watching you.

(Go right ahead. I'm cool.)

Bandleader Marge 🎵 circa **1931-1935,**
for whom all things were possible

Father, Naval Reservist
"Marge, don't make waves."

Marge at 60 years old

3

AT THE LYRIC

It's February cold. Depression cold. But no one in the long line is grumbling. In fact, the mood is high-spirited, buzzing, festive, carefree. Waiting with his mother and father, the ten-year old boy wonders about "the surprise." What is it?

He watches the group of boisterous young adults in line clapping hands rhythmically as a short, scruffy, dark-haired man starts to dance on the sidewalk doing some kind of free-form jitterbugging the boy has never seen before.

He tugs at his mother's coat. She is a petite, pretty woman, with brown hair, a good figure. She dresses with flare, to say the least, as befits her image of herself. Today she's wearing a long, bright red, spring cloth coat, even though it's cold; black rubber galoshes cover her high heels. A squirrel boa is draped around her neck. On her lapel a large grand piano rhinestone pin glistens. She sports a black, broad-brimmed Easter hat highlighted by a white faux gardenia. Usually avoiding conventional dress-of-the-season, any season, she knows she's different and always manages to look it. She's supposed to, she thinks. After all, aren't former entertainers always in show business, even after they've left it?

"What's he doing, Mom?" the boy asks. "I never learned any steps like that."

The crowd is noisy. His mother doesn't hear him. She's watching, too.

The man is wearing a shabby, heavy brown overcoat with a large tweed cap pulled over his ears. The coat is too long, almost touching his shoes. He bends and swoops like a big bird, brushing against the slush-stuccoed sidewalk when he does. An unlit cigarette dangles from his lips. It falls. Before his parents can stop him, the boy dashes out and picks it up. He holds it up to the man. The man waves him off. The father takes it and throws it away.

More people join in, clapping louder and louder, standing back to make a large circle on the sidewalk. The man is twisting and jumping about wildly. His face reddens; his dark eyebrows seem to touch each other in effort. He grunts intermittently, as the crowd encourages him. "Yeah, yeah. Go, Crackers, go!" The father reaches out and with one arm partly shields his son. The man slips, falls down on all fours but quickly rolls over onto his back, kicks his legs high up into the air, wriggling them wildly. It's like he's being electrocuted, the boy thinks, just like in the movies.

When he finishes, the man jumps up and bows to the crowd. Everyone cheers. The boy doesn't understand.

The sky threatens snow again, a typical Connecticut winter day, damp and gray. But for the boy there is nothing typical about this Sunday afternoon. For one thing, he's wearing his good plaid mackinaw coat over his best Sunday pants and sweater. Why did his mother tell him to dress up? He usually has to do that only for church.

"Aw, Mom, do I have to?" he had said. "Just to see a movie?"

"Do what Mommy tells you, honey. It's a surprise."

And now there's this guy dancing all wild like … what's going on, thinks the boy.

"Why was that man dancing like that?" the boy asks, as everyone resumes a place in line. The episode was a refreshing divertissement for all, an impromptu moment that captures the crowd's attention, just the thing to warm them up on a frigid afternoon. "He looked like he was crazy, Mom."

"Wasn't it fun?" she says with a calm and poised expression. "I think he's just excited about coming to see Benny Goodman."

"Who's Benny Goodman?"

"That's the surprise! He's a famous musician, one of the best in the world. And he plays clarinet, just like you."

"Is that why everybody's here? Not just for a movie?"

"Uh-huh. Daddy and I thought you'd like to see his stage show with us. Benny Goodman is the King of Swing and he's never come to Bridgeport before. It's a big day today. He has a wonderful band."

"You mean a band like you had when I was little?" the boy says.

"Oh, much better than that. Wait till you hear it."

The boy wonders what it will sound like. He has never heard a live big band before. He's small with a wiry build and expressive blue eyes that do not miss much. His brown, bushy hair wants to go in different directions. His mother has put Pomade on it. Pomade hair gel is the hair dressing of choice for men and boys in the 1930s and 40s. At least it is in Bridgeport. It smells fruity. His mother doesn't put much on him, just enough to keep the straggly ends in place. It makes his hair shine.

"How long are we going to stand in line?" he asks. "It's cold."

"We're almost there, sweetheart," his mother says, reassuring him. She rearranges the scarf around his neck, snugs it up, pulls his hat closer to his ears, and pats his head.

"It won't be long now."

"Do we have to do this today?" the boy asks her. "I'd rather go ice skating at Seaside Park Pond."

"You'll love it," she says. "Be patient."

He kicks at some snow. "Mom," he says, "why does Duane say I'm a dreamer? I'm not, am I?"

"Your brother is only kidding. Don't pay any attention to him."

But the ten-year old knows what his older brother says is true. Sometimes he does go to an imaginary world. For instance, right in the middle of tying his shoes when getting dressed for school, he'll stop and stare off at something without focusing. But it doesn't seem to him like dreaming; he's just thinking and wondering about stuff.

"Hey daydreamer, I'm not waiting for you," his older brother will say, and leaves for school without him.

(These are Depression years. Like most other areas, Bridgeport, a blue collar, industrial city in southern Connecticut, is hard hit. For millions of people the United States is a nation with little. Unemployment, big bands, and movies are the most frequent subjects discussed. Movie theaters are jammed ... an inexpensive escape. And palace-like dance halls are packed as music of the Big Bands captivates the nation.)

On an entertainment scale of one to ten, today's attraction at the Lyric Theatre is a solid ten, a not-to-be-missed event. And all Bridgeport seems to know it. The Theatre's shows are a sell-out.

Since getting a clarinet for his ninth birthday, the boy has a lesson every week and practices regularly. His mother finds an excellent instructor for him, a musician who used to play clarinet and saxophone in her band and tells her he thinks the boy has talent.

The boy isn't thinking about music right now. He's still wondering about the strange dancing he has seen the odd-looking man doing. It wasn't at all like the tap or the jitterbug steps he learned in his dancing lessons with his sister.

Gradually working their way forward with the line, the family is now about fifty feet from the Lyric's box office. The boy notices the marquee's white lights chasing one another relentlessly around the edges and tries to follow them with his eyes to see where they start. But there's no beginning and no end. He looks at the big black letters on the white background and reads aloud, "On Stage, Benny Goodman and His Orchestra with Helen Forrest." Underneath, in smaller type, he reads, *The Grapes of Wrath* with Henry Fonda."

Benny Goodman and His Orchestra will play five sold-out stage shows this day in a theater that holds thirty-eight hundred people. The Lyric's policy is to play a movie alternating with a live big band stage show.

Finally, they reach the box office at fifteen minutes before two o'clock. The boy watches his father pay for the expensive tickets.

"That'll be fifty-five cents for each adult and thirty cents for the child," says the woman behind the glass.

The boy doesn't see any other kids in line. Maybe it's a show for grownups, he thinks. He feels special, proud that his parents have brought him, even though he'd still rather be ice-skating. He hopes seeing the band will be worth it. But he doesn't think so.

They push along into the lobby with the hurrying crowd. Almost smothered, he looks down and sees the floor's large white and black marble squares—like a big checkerboard, he thinks. Above people's shoulders he can make out the tops of posters on the walls that say Coming Attractions.

Everyone bunches together at a doorway where ushers are taking tickets. People are calling out to one other, joking and laughing as they wait to have their tickets ripped in half. Once through the bottleneck, they funnel out into a spacious, fancy inner lobby with its high ceiling. It has thick gray and red carpeting, the kind you sink into a little when you walk. Big golden-framed mirrors hang from the red cloth-covered walls. What a fancy place, he thinks.

Most people do not stop at the candy and snack counters. Instead they surge forward directly into the auditorium, rushing down the aisles to get seats close to the stage. There is no reserved seating. By this time the main orchestra section is already half full. The boy and his parents find three seats together fairly close to the stage and settle in.

The boy looks up at the ceiling and all around. Never has he seen such a beautiful theater. It's the biggest one he has been in. As a matter of fact, it's really the biggest place he has ever been in, bigger than his school and way bigger than Sacred Heart Church. This has two large balconies. There are sculptures of *bare people* all around and a big red curtain with tassels hanging on it in front of the stage. A gigantic, lighted, crystal chandelier is suspended from the middle of the ceiling.

He's been to other theaters, like the Parkway and the Cameo, but they're small compared to the Lyric. He wonders if that's because the Lyric is downtown. He notices that many of the young ladies are dressed in pretty dresses, but not the same as his mom's. She looks better. But they look beautiful, too. He stares at them. They don't notice him. Some men wear ties. So does his father. He still doesn't see any other kids.

"Dad, how high is this ceiling?" he asks.

"Pretty high, I guess," his father says.

"But how high?"

"Oh, I don't know. What difference does it make?" He turns away to put his coat under the seat in front of him. The boy looks up and ponders the ceiling height. *Bet you'd get killed if you fell from there.*

The boy's father is a short, thin man, with dark curly hair. He has a strong, chiseled face. He dabbles as an actor and subs as a sort of stage electrician or something like that in the Park City Community Theater. He used to be in the Naval Reserve. Now he's an airplane mechanic, whenever there' is work at the factory. But when he comes home from work he mostly falls asleep on the couch. The boy thinks his father would rather be an actor or in the movies. He's smart and knows lots of things, even if he does get impatient easily. He knows the good actors and the good movies and says movies he doesn't like are corny. The boy wonders why they're corny; they seem okay to him.

His mother always says, "Yes, dear," and "No, dear," when she and his father have a discussion. His father acts like the boss of the family. But the boy knows his mother is actually the leader, the one who has ideas and is always thinking of things.

Maybe his father resents this. The boy has thought about this before. He figures this might have something to do with his father getting mad at nothing, usually when his mother has an idea to go somewhere or do something different. Like, "Let's go downtown and see the lights tonight."

He's glad his father isn't upset today. *It must be awful to be mad so much.*

It's two o'clock. The theatre house lights dim. It's time for Coming Attractions, after which comes Movietone News of the Day. The news is mostly about the War in Europe.

"Dad, Dad!" the boy says. "Why are there airplanes? And soldiers? And who's on the stretchers?"

"It's a war," his father says.

"But why is there a war?"

"Because of Hitler."

"Who's he?"

"A dictator."

"What's a dictator?"

"Shush," says the father, "the movie's going to start."

The boy watches *The Grapes of Wrath* and fidgets. He's restless. His feet are cold. He doesn't understand the movie. It's too long and slow. But he can see that his father likes it from the way he seems to be concentrating, staring at the screen, mouthing words with the actors, now smiling, now frowning.

"Dad, I thought we're going to see Benny Goodman today," he whispers loudly.

"We are," his father says, "right after the movie."

"Why is it called *The Grapes of Wrath?*"

"That's a long story."

"I don't see any grapes."

"That's because there are no grapes."

"Why not?"

"Shush."

"Why don't they have a cowboy movie instead?"

"Hush," his mother says. "Leave your father alone."

At the end of the movie the main curtain lowers. The house lights come on. The chandelier lights up. Immediately, people start whistling and stomping feet, chanting, "We want Benny. We want Benny."

"That's for Benny Goodman, right, Mom?"

"Uh-huh. They can't wait. Isn't this exciting?" she says.

The boy nods. But so far he's not as excited as he was when the man in the long coat was dancing on the sidewalk. Now he's not sure what to expect. He hopes he won't fall asleep, like he almost did during the movie. A drum rolls. He hears music coming from behind the curtain, and the audience begins to cheer—like they know what's coming.

The house lights dim, and the main curtain opens. But wait. There's a second curtain, a filmy one, bathed in a bank of colorful lights. It looks purple and silver and shimmery.

"That's a scrim," his mother says, pointing to the stage. He can see the band through the curtain, but not clearly, and he can hear the music. He waits. *When will the scrim open? Why is the band behind it? Maybe it doesn't open.*

Finally the scrim curtain rises slowly, teasing the audience; and as it does, the sound of the band gets louder. Finally the whole Benny Goodman Orchestra is revealed, with Benny himself standing in front in a dark blue suit. He's wearing horn-rimmed glasses, *like Father Healy wears*. White spotlights shine on him and he waves ... a little.

The crowd cheers and whoops. Benny turns around, faces the band and makes some kind of hand signal. The trumpets and trombones stand up, and the sound they make smacks the boy full in the face with a musical force that pushes him back in his seat. It's a fusillade of brass notes, a wall of sound. The boy has no idea music could be so powerful.

Benny smiles at the audience, not a big broad smile, just a small one, then picks up his clarinet and joins in with the band. He solos at the microphone. His clarinet sounds alive to the boy, like a person talking fast and making jokes and almost telling a story. *A clarinet can sound like that?* Behind the solo, trombones slide and punctuate riffs, getting louder and louder as Benny plays higher and higher, until a point where the whole band is producing rich-sounding chords that keep getting bigger and broader. *It sounds like they're going to explode.*

Then, as Benny climbs to the highest clarinet note the boy has ever heard, the band hits a final gigantic chord and holds it while the drummer plays freely all around the drum set until the final cutoff. The crowd screams in delight.

A song called "King Porter Stomp" comes next, and the brass attacks again. *It's like they're biting at the air.* The boy feels a strange thrill moving up through his legs, like the time Gertie Collins kissed him at her party. Yeah! ONLY THIS IS WAY MORE. The sax section stands up and dazzles him. How can they play so fast? And so together? The drummer's beat seems to make the whole band excited.

More players come down in front. They go to the microphone and play jazz solos, like Mr. Goodman does. They're not reading music either—*making it up as they play!* First one trumpet player solos, then another, then the tenor sax player,. then Benny again. The audience applauds. So does the boy.

By this time people are dancing in the aisles. The ushers let them. The boy doesn't know where to look next. He's smiling so much his face hurts. He loves the way clusters of light color the stage with blues and golds and reds and purples. He squeezes his mother's hand. She smiles at him. She seems to know it is the most amazing thing he has ever seen or heard.

Suddenly Mr. Crackers jumps up on one side of the stage, still in his old overcoat and hat, and starts doing flips and wriggles on the floor.

"Mom, Dad, it's him!"

The man whips off his coat and throws it out into the audience. They cheer. The boy looks wide-eyed at his mom. A spotlight swings over onto Crackers. Benny Goodman moves to the other side of the stage and watches Crackers dance. He tucks his clarinet under his arm and starts clapping his hands in time to the music. The crowd loves it and whistles and yells, "Go, Crackers, go!" The boy joins in. After the number is over, ushers escort Crackers off the stage. The crowd cheers him. He waves at everybody. For the rest of his life he'll probably be remembered in Bridgeport as the guy who danced on stage when Benny Goodman came to town.

Without warning, the music seems to fade to a distant undertone in the boy's head, as if his ears are plugged, and he sees himself on stage, out in front of the band, playing wild notes on his clarinet. The spotlight is on him. People are clapping in rhythm. The men in the band cheer him. "Go, Gene, go!" He sees his family from the stage. They're smiling. They're so proud of him. He feels wonderful!

Slowly the live music floods back into his ears; he's back in his seat. The effect of the stage lighting and the incredible pulse of the music are almost too much for him. He holds his mother's hand so tightly that a thousand words couldn't tell her any better how he feels.

"Oh, Mom, thank you," is all he can manage to whisper.

"Someday you'll be up there," she says clearly. And he knows she believes it.

"What are you telling him that stuff for?" his father growls.

She doesn't answer. Instead she gives the boy's hand a secret little squeeze.

Just before the band plays its closing theme, "Goodbye", Benny steps down from the stage, comes up the aisle to the row where the boy is sitting. He gestures to the boy. The boy can't believe it. "Go on," his mother says." He leaves his seat, goes to the end of the row. Benny shakes his hand, asks his name, and brings him up on stage. The crowd applauds.

Benny announces, "I've been watching this young lad all through the show. He hasn't missed a note we played." (Applause.) "Are you a musician, by any chance?"

How did he know? Did my mother send a note up to the stage during the show?

"Yes, I play the clarinet."

"Are you good?"

"Well, my mother thinks so. I practice a lot. I can play 'SWEET SUE' pretty good."

Benny hands the boy a clarinet. The boy is bewildered. *What'll I do?*

"Ladies and Gentlemen, Gene is a musician and is going to play 'SWEET SUE' with us. Hit it, guys."

Again the crowd cheers. The band intros, the boy plays the melody. Benny jams around him. The crowd loves it. They play another chorus. The band stands up at the end and applauds the little boy. Benny hires him on the spot for the next show. His mother and father stand up and cheer. His picture is on the front page of the paper the next day. *A star is born.*

*

Ahem!

(Oh … right. It isn't quite like that.)

As the band plays its closing theme, the boy listens until the very last note. The curtain lowers. The house lights go up full and the Lyric starts to empty. People are happy, singing, and bouncing along up the aisles. Band notes swirl in the boy's head.

Darkness has replaced daylight by the time he and his parents leave the lobby. It's snowing. They cross Main Street and wait at the corner for the bus that will take them home to Black Rock Avenue in the South End. The bus ride costs ten cents. But for twenty-five cents you can get three tokens. The boy knows that his father will get the tokens.

While the family waits, head-lighted cars and buses splatter freezing slush in both directions along Main Street. The boy looks at the long line of people on the other side of the street. It continues around the corner. He gazes up at the marquee. It's brighter now in the twilight and transforms the falling snow into twinkling colors. The words blur out of focus, as once again the boy is on stage, playing in Benny Goodman's Band. *The crowd applauds him. He's famous. He smiles graciously. He bows.*

"Genie, for God sakes, wake up! Watch your step!" his father says, as the boy half stumbles up the two high steps onto the bus. "Pay attention to what you're doing. Tsk, tsk."

"Oh, right. Sorry, Dad."

Seated on a cold leather bus seat, the boy stares out the window into the quiet snowy night, not focusing, losing himself in the future.

*

That's better. I guess Mr. Crackers was break-dancing fifty years before the rest of the world caught on?

(Come to think of it, that's probably what it was.)

**

Dancing in the aisles was *de rigueur* when Benny Goodman
and other big bands came to America's theaters like the Paramount in
New York and the Lyric in Bridgeport. Circa ♫ 1938
Courtesy: *JAZZ, A History of America's Music*
Geoffrey Ward and Ken Burns

4

MAYBE SOMEDAY

I think my mother knew when she presented me with a clarinet for my ninth birthday that someday she would find a way to buy a saxophone for me also. From the way I had reacted when my parents brought me to see Benny Goodman—hardly able to contain myself—she must have sensed the possibility of a music career in my future, which I'm sure was fine with her. If I were ever to be a professional reed musician in a big band she knew it would be necessary for me to play saxophone as well as clarinet.

Of course at the time I had no idea she was planning this. I don't think my father did either, because if he had, he would have said no, like he did with most schemes my mother would "cook up"... as he called her plans. His negativity never seemed to deter her. She'd just go ahead and set about doing whatever it was she had in mind, then tell him about it after the fact. Or sometimes he'd just find out for himself. She was an irrepressible doer who believed it was easier to get forgiveness than permission. This saxophone story illustrates the point.

On my twelfth birthday, my sax birthday, I call it, we were still sitting at the kitchen table after supper—my father, mother, brother, sister and I. The dishes hadn't been fully cleared yet, but some of us had already started on the ice cream before the cake was served. As usual, I'd managed to spill ice cream on my shirt. My brother giggled. My sister, embarrassed for me, offered her wide-open blue eyes in sympathy. My father shook his head with the impatience of one who suffers when witnessing the bumbling of others.

"Sorry, Dad," I said.

"Here, Gene, use this wet dish towel," said my mother.

Through an open window I could hear the neighborhood kids playing in the street. During Daylight Savings time, August nights were always the best for long games of Kick-the-Can or touch football in the street. So after we all sang "Happy Birthday," I said, "Can I go outside now?"

"Not yet," my mother said and proceeded to bring out a big, weird-shaped package covered with sections of different pieces of leftover wrapping paper and tied with red string. She wasn't exactly a natural-born present-wrapper, a detail that never seemed important to her.

"Happy Birthday, honey. This is from Daddy and me."

I tore through the paper and uncovered a gleaming golden alto saxophone, actually brass. "Wow! It's beautiful. I love it."

"We'll get the case for it later," my mother said. "Just keep it in a pillow case for now. You'll have to be careful."

I was ecstatic. On the other hand, I knew it must have been very expensive. "Mom, where did you get the money for it?"

"Yeah, Marge," my father said. "Where did the money come from? The boy's already got a clarinet. What the hell's he need a saxophone for?"

"I sold a few things," my mother said quietly. "Besides, you know the doctor said playing a larger wind instrument would be good for little Gene's asthma."

"Christ! You and your ideas again. Damn it." He slammed his hand down onto the kitchen table. A dish jumped up, did a flip and splattered on the red, yellow and gray linoleum floor. Creamed corn left on a plate splashed all over. "You could have told me," and he stormed out of the kitchen.

I watched my mother. She looked down at the broken dish and the splatter-dashed floor, then said quietly, "Kids, finish up your desert. You can go out after clean-up."

Al Sency and Richie Gavlick were my best friends since we were five. We played ball in the street almost every night in the summer. I couldn't wait to show them my new sax. Later in life Al became the most revered biology teacher Stratford High has ever known, for thirty years exciting young minds with the wonders of dissected frogs, plant phylum and the anatomy of beetles and bugs. Richie became the successful owner of a large machinery importing company.

This was August of 1941. America was recovering from the long Great Depression. The ominous clouds of war were sweeping closer to our shores. Factories had reopened, gearing up for the country's impending entry into World War II. In retrospect, prosperity was coming. But to me, completely unaware of the outside world, it seemed that most families in our neighborhood were poor—except maybe for the Sencys. They had emigrated from Hungary many years before and owned a small meat market and grocery store across the street from our house. I think we always owed them money. They extended credit to just about every family on our block. Even though Mr. Sency grumped about it, Mrs. Sency always insisted. She was a gentle lady who wore her graying hair in a bun.

"Here, Genie," she'd say softly, as she wrapped the pound of ground beef and five pork chops, my mother had ordered, into two packages of shiny white butcher paper, tying them with white string. "Tell your mommy I'll put this in the book."

"Thank you, Mrs. Sency."

Anyway, back to the birthday supper. I can see why my father was upset. Money was always in short supply. And of course, my mother had not consulted with him.

"I'm sorry, Mom," I said, after he had left. "Is it okay to keep the sax?"

"Of course," she said, "You know how Daddy is sometimes."

"Can I join a band now? That's what I really want to do."

"I know, sweetheart. But you'll have to have lessons first."

I had a private lesson every week. I didn't like to practice, but I did every day. After several months Ernie Czanski invited me to join his band. Once a week, after supper, I took the Bridgeport East Main Street bus over to Pulaski Street for a rehearsal at Ernie's house. The neighborhood was heavily populated with first-and second-generation immigrant families—Polish, Russian, Lithuanian, Slovak, and Hungarian.

Ernie's flat was on the second floor of a yellow three-story house, above Wasco's vegetable market, which stayed open late at night. Every time I walked up Ernie's hallway stairs, the initial scents of fresh fruits and vegetables gradually gave way to heavier odors of pirogues and cooked cabbage Mrs. Czanski made for dinner on Wednesday nights. The pungent smells became overpowering as I neared the top. When I knocked at the door and Ernie let me in, I'd be almost overcome with a cabbage attack. To this day I avoid cooked cabbage.

Neighbors jammed into the living room and dining room to listen to our rehearsals. We made many mistakes. They didn't seem to mind; it was a neighborhood happening. Two other kids also played saxophone in the band. They were older than I was, but I played a bit better, so Ernie made me first sax.

Besides Ernie, there was another trumpet player, a pudgy looking Jewish kid named Ralphy. Shy and polite, he always wore a clean white, ironed shirt and a tie. His playing wasn't a strong player, but he didn't make many mistakes.

Danny, the drummer, perspired profusely when he played, as I recall, even in wintertime. So cabbage wasn't the only smell that permeated the room. But I smelled mostly like cabbage when I got home.

Larry Plessinger played piano. The Czanski's had an old brown upright, topped with a blue vase of fake flowers. Red-haired Larry was short, like I was, so he had to put a cushion on the stool to reach the keys and pedals. He wore glasses and had big ears. He played very well, and he was smart, too—he knew how to transpose at sight. I liked him (Larry grew up to be a research engineer at General Electric).

We all read music and took lessons, including Danny, even though he was just the drummer. Ernie played lead trumpet pretty loud. It hurt my ears when I sat in front of him, but it was better than sitting next to Danny the Stinker. Ernie was the oldest, sixteen. He had big husky shoulders and a crew cut—we called them zip haircuts back then. My brother also had a zip. In fact, that became his nickname.

I remember thinking Ernie must not brush his teeth very much, because they looked yellow. My mom always told me to brush my teeth every time I went out, even before I'd play touch football in the street. It was a thing with her.

"Movie Stars all have perfect white teeth," she'd say to me. That gave me something to think about. Maybe when I grew up I'd be a movie star. Well, why not? I thought about it sometimes when I went to the movies and saw all those pretty actresses. It seemed like a good idea. So I brushed my teeth often and with great gusto, until one day the school's visiting dental hygienist told me I was brushing too hard and would injure my gums.

From what I could see, Ernie had no chance of ever being in the movies when he grew up.

Ernie's father helped us when we practiced—he played upright bass with a polka band. A large friendly man, he always smiling, joking, and talking. His tightly cinched belt, the end of which dangled loosely, seemed to hold up his big stomach. His shoes were the biggest I had ever seen, probably size fourteen. When we rehearsed he'd sit in a chair and stomp his foot in time with the music. Sometimes the thumping was louder than the drums.

By the second rehearsal we started playing stock orchestrations, music that Ernie's father had bought at Gilman's Music store. We always played from written music, because none of us knew how to improvise.

I still carried my sax around in the pillowcase. No one seemed to notice; at least they never asked me about it. My mother said we'd get a case as soon as we could afford it.

One of the things I liked about rehearsals at Ernie's house was that everyone applauded after we played even half a song. It made me feel special. And at the end of a rehearsal, his mom always had pastries and Nehi sodas for us. What a nice lady.

Following rehearsals, Mr. Czanski drove Ralphy and me in his old four-door Chevy to our corners on the other side of town. I'd take the music home with me so I could practice it. We were pretty serious about being a good band. But of course we didn't sound anything like Benny Goodman. At the time I figured that would take a while, maybe a year or so. Nothing seems impossible at that age.

After six months I was playing in two bands, Ernie's and Frank Wasko's. Later, I started my own band. We all played in each other's bands. Today they're called garage bands, but not many folks had garages in those days. Whoever had the music could be the leader. I saved up money and bought my own stock arrangements.

My band had four saxes, three trumpets, and Freddie Harris played trombone. He didn't play very well, but he did have a trombone, and every once in a while he landed on the right note, and it sounded good. My friend Larry was the piano player. Of the three bands, mine was the biggest.

Soon I was playing weddings most Saturday afternoons, either with my band or someone else's. Sometimes we'd get hired to play for a dance on a Saturday night at the White Eagles Polish Hall. We'd make a dollar or a dollar and a quarter each. Often we played just for tips—it didn't matter. I was almost a professional, getting paid, and earning money playing my sax. Ah, the sheer euphoria of it.

The blissful bubble burst when one night the White Eagles people complained that they couldn't dance to our music and refused to pay us. It never occurred to me that grown-ups would do that. They seemed mean to me and I felt helpless. I remember being insulted when they criticized our music. But more than likely we sounded rather out of tune and probably missed more than a beat or two here and there. In any case, I realized then that life wasn't always fair, so I decided to get even by getting better. I also resolved that if I played there again, I would ask them to pay us first, before we started to play.

Ernie's band broke up suddenly. One morning Mrs. Czanski, carrying a full laundry basket, fell down the long flight of stairs and tumbled to the bottom. She must have been there all day. Ernie found her when he came home from school. She died a couple of days later. There were no more rehearsals at Ernie's house after that.

My band improved rapidly. I was always looking for kids who could play better than I did. We rehearsed as often as I could get everyone together.

People said we sounded good. In fact we got so good that we started rehearsing in the back yard so more neighbors could come and hear us. Soon the yard was packed.

The next week my father started charging ten cents admission, but still the people came. It was magic. Our music was just what the neighborhood needed. People danced and had a great time. After a few months we had so much money my father bought a new car, an Oldsmobile, I think. It was our first car. The newspaper sent a photographer and did a big write-up on our band. Local dignitaries started coming to hear us. The Mayor asked us to play a concert at City Hall and invited school kids from all over the city to come hear us play. We were famous already. It didn't take as long as I had thought.

*

Uh-huh. And two and two are five. I know what really happened. That's not it. And how about some of those names?

(Okay, so I changed some names. Picky, picky. Big deal. But you're right; the story did end a little differently.)

People said we sounded good. Of course that was the opinion of the neighbors, always excellent and impartial judges of talent. But I began to see that becoming as good as Benny Goodman might not be so easy. Being really good at music was a lot different than just playing for fun. I realized that becoming an accomplished musician might take a lot longer than I thought. But when I got there, I guessed I'd be famous then. After all, my mother said I'd be famous someday. It was sort of taken for granted.

She was always saying things like, "Someday when you're famous," this; or "someday when you're famous," that. So I kept on practicing. I brushed my teeth every day, too, just in case. Fame might come either way.

I couldn't wait to grow up.

It takes forever when you're thirteen going on fourteen.

**

"Thirteen going on fourteen"
(Note the plastic bow tie)

5

THE RITZ

World War II dominated the news every day. Big Bands didn't come to the Lyric Theatre anymore. If you wanted to see name bands you went to Pleasure Beach Ballroom on Sunday nights during the summer. In wintertime it was the Ritz Ballroom.

It seemed everyone in town loved the Ritz, Bridgeport's social center, the place young adults gathered to hear great music, dance, and meet each other. My mother said I was too young to go there. "It isn't a place for kids."

By the time I was fifteen I figured I was old enough. I had been playing sax for three years and thought I knew everything about it. So I figured I could learn more quickly by listening to the famous bands live at the Ritz.

"It's an older crowd," she said, "and there's drinking downstairs in the lounge." Her band had played there many times. "Besides, you'd have to take the bus. You'd be out late and you have school the next day."

I explained that was no problem for me. "I don't drink; I'll take the early bus. I'll be home early. Please can I go?"

In the interest of my having a positive learning experience, I believe, she gave in. "But make sure your homework's done first. And be careful. Call me when you get there."

That wasn't quite all there was to it. I had a plan that I didn't tell her about. I was planning to take my saxophone with me.

Most every Sunday night thereafter that's just what I did. The bus that took me to the Ritz was always jammed. Each week I'd board at Park and Fairfield Avenues with my sax protected in its pillowcase. I still hadn't gotten a real case for it, but that didn't matter. If my plan worked, I'd soon be able to afford one. I sat up in the front of the bus right behind the driver, cradling the weird-shaped pillowcase, pretending to look out the window at something important. I could tell that other people were looking at me and snickering. I made believe I didn't notice them.

Admission was ninety-five cents to see the biggest name bands and seventy-five cents for the not-so-famous ones. Movies were twenty-six cents in those days, and gas was seventeen cents a gallon. The older girl at the ticket booth always said, "Good evening, Gene," giving me my ticket, smiling down at me through the glass, leaning forward so I could hear her through the half-circled hole at the bottom. She had dark hair and a very pretty face. I liked the fact she knew my name, but I wished she wouldn't have been so obvious in greeting me like a little kid with all the adults standing in line. It just attracted attention to me and my pillowcase.

Each week when I entered the ballroom the sound of the band's brass section hit me full in the chest and made my rib cage vibrate. I loved the feeling. The manager kept an eye on me. My mother must have called him. Once inside, my ritual was to walk around the ballroom, then call my mother and tell her I was fine (the pay phone cost a nickel). Then I would find a place right next to the bandstand, opposite the entrance, and sit there with my sax on my lap, listening to the music, and wait for the "announcement." After remaining there for two hours, until intermission, I would take the 10:05 p.m. bus home.

To me, the Ritz Ballroom was a magical place. I could be close to world-famous big bands and hear their sounds in the closest ring of audience. I liked the jazz-oriented big bands best, especially Stan Kenton, Boyd Rayburn, Claude Thornhill, Gene Krupa, Charlie Barnet, Benny Goodman, Harry James, and Woody Herman (he was my favorite). Once a month great colored bands like Jimmie Lunceford, Count Basie, Earle 'Fatha' Hines and Duke Ellington appeared. I never went to see them. My mother said it wouldn't be a good idea. I never asked why.

The Ritz was a long, white, wood-frame building with a low ceiling. It had a sunken dance floor and capacity for over 3,000 people. That was if they were dancing. But most fans stood, packed in front of the band, absorbing the excitement. Dancing was necessarily limited to the extreme ends of the dance floor. One night the crowd actually reached over 4,000 for Guy Lombardo—not my style of band, too schmaltzy.

From the outside the Ritz didn't look like much. But inside it was elegant, with its huge polished hardwood dance floor and glittering chandeliers. Blue and red carpeting covered the elevated promenade, which surrounded the sunken dance floor. A white balustrade-low fence, topped with a varnished oak railing, bordered the promenade.

Above the floor, accordion-pleated red drapes gathered from the top of the sidewalls, swooped up to the middle of the ceiling over the dance floor, and terminated around the chandeliers. The drapes reminded me of the inside of the coffin I had seen at my grandmother's wake in our house when I was a little boy. I thought the coffin was beautiful. Some things leave a lasting impression. I can't recall my grandmother's face, but I can remember the interior of the coffin.

Voyeurs and dancers, who sat resting, flirting, or just watching between dances, often occupied the red velvet cushioned benches along the walls.

Downstairs had a noisy bar with a separate soft-drink service area and a jukebox. I checked it out but never spent much time there. I came to the Ritz to listen and absorb. Besides, everyone else there was much older than I was. That in itself was kind of intimidating.

The elevated bandstand was situated in the middle on one side of the ballroom. You could walk completely around the ballroom along the promenade, even behind the bandstand, so it was possible to look over the musicians' shoulders and see the sheet music they were playing. Local musicians always gathered behind the bandstand and smoked cigarettes and talked boisterously, as if they knew everything. They acted as important as the famous musicians up on the bandstand.

I sat right alongside the bandstand each week, waiting, holding my sax and hoping. This was my plan: someday, it could be tonight, there would be an announcement on the public address system. An important voice would say, "Your attention, ladies and gentlemen, attention, please. The band's lead alto saxophone player has been taken ill. Is there an alto saxophone player in the house?"

I would be right there. I'd take my sax out of the pillowcase and be ready to play for thc famous bandleader who needed me. I'd save the day. I would be discovered, soon to be famous. This was a real possibility to me. People get sick all the time. So each time I went to the Ritz, I'd say to myself, tonight may be the night. *I'm ready.* The possibility of the glorious fame of it all gave me more incentive to practice and improve each week.

Faithfully, month after month, I kept the Sunday night vigil. By this time everyone who worked at the Ritz knew me, and people on the bus recognized me. I knew it was just a question of time before the important announcement would come. And then I would be up on the bandstand playing my sax with all those wonderful musicians.

But no sax player ever took ill, at least not ill enough to stop playing. I listened carefully each Sunday night, but the announcement never came. I even told the manager I was available and had my horn with me. "Thank you, Gene," he said. "I'll keep that in mind." He must have been amused.

After several months of bus riding to the Ritz almost every winter Sunday night, I realized that my plan, albeit ill conceived with the optimistic logic of a dreamer, wasn't going to happen. I wasn't going to be discovered in this way. My mother had the wisdom to let me find out for myself. I stopped going to the Ritz.

Soon after, I got my long-awaited case. It could carry both the sax and my clarinet. With it I adopted a new outlook. I thought of myself as a budding professional, not a kid anymore. After all, I had a case now. No more childish dreams about being discovered. I decided not to waste a moment and hunkered down and prepared seriously for the big time.

I dove into personal practice with renewed vigor. By the time I went to college, my daily practice sessions were three to four hours. I was determined to be ready when the right opportunity came along. My sight-reading skills sharpened till I could gobble up written notes like splattered breakfast cereal. I formed the official University of Notre Dame dance band, a big band called "The Lettermen." We played functions, proms, and events like the Saturday night Victory Dances during football season. In those days Notre Dame didn't lose football games very often, so we had plenty of work. I'll always cherish those Golden Dome years. It was an inspiring time. I met some fine men. How lucky I was to go to school there.

During those four years I was able to cover much of my tuition costs with earnings from the band. I was a concert band saxophone soloist and a first clarinetist in the marching band. Following graduation I spent a year in Chicago studying with

Santy Runyon and gigging with various big bands there ... Billy May, Lou Breeze and others. I also recorded with Duke Ellington at Universal Studios before returning to Bridgeport to settle in and raise my family.

One wintry Sunday night, about ten years after my Ritz daze, I was at home watching television with my wife and our three young children. We had finished dinner and were cozy in the living room of our rented apartment watching the Ed Sullivan Show. Señor Wences had just finished his hilarious talking-thumb act. I remember the kids holding up thumbs against their fist moving their thumb knuckles up and down like a lower lip, imitating Wences: "Saw right? *Sawright.* Sawright? *Sawright.*" We were all laughing. Ed introduced the next act, "Topo Gigio." Circus music brought him on.

The phone rang. "For you," my wife said. Ray Colonari, still the manager of the Ritz Ballroom, knew I had become a professional musician, since my bands now frequently played in local clubs and for dances and special parties at the Ritz. He remembered me from the days when I was a polite little kid going to the Ritz on Sunday nights with my sax and a dream in a pillowcase.

"Gene," Ray said, "how are you? You play sax, right?"

"Sure do, Ray."

"You play baritone sax, too?"

"Yes, I do. Why? What's up?"

"Claude Thornhill's band is playing here tonight."

"I know. It's a fine band. Heard him years ago."

The bells were ringing. Could this be the night? Was it possible? After all these years was I finally getting the call to play with a name band at the Ritz? But on bari sax, not on alto? So what. It didn't matter. It was the Ritz. And it was a name band. This was my chance.

"It's happening!" I called out to my wife, putting my hand over the phone.

"Huh? What's happening?"

Ray continued. "Something's happened here at the Ritz tonight."

"Uh-huh," I said. I couldn't wait. I could hardly believe it. Oh, thank you, God.

"You know Gerry Mulligan, the baritone sax man with the band?"

"Yeah, sure. He's famous. A fine player. One of the best."

"Well, there's a problem. Maybe you can help us out tonight. Jerry and the lead alto player just got into some kind of an argument with a drunk when they were setting up. The alto player took a sock on the lips. And Jerry's horn got banged up."

"Sorry to hear that, Ray."

"Can you come out here and take the lead alto player's place tonight and bring your bari for Gerry to play? It might be a big break for you."

I don't remember driving out there, but I was there in twenty minutes. My heart was pounding as I took my horn from its case and stroked it a few times. Dry-mouthed, I swallowed several times until I could whistle. I sat down in the lead alto chair without being introduced to Thornhill or the guys in the band. A nod and smile was the proper protocol required. Musicians shaking hands on a bandstand made customers and venue operators uneasy. They would wonder, "Is this the real band or a pick-up bunch?"

During the fourth arrangement, I nailed the alto solo beautifully. It just felt right. Pent-up feelings, accrued in years of struggling, let go with exuberance. Thornhill seemed amazed. On both sides of me I heard. "All right, kid. Too much! You play!" Frankly, I played the best I ever had. Before my next solo Thornhill introduced me to the crowd as "a fine guest artist from

Bridgeport." They gathered around the bandstand and cheered each time I played any kind of a solo during the rest of the night.

Thornhill asked me to join his band for its current tour until his regular alto player was well. At last I had broken through. I was on my way. This was the opportunity I had hoped for. The feeling was unbelievable. Excitement. Pride. Anticipation. Gratefulness. It's amazing how sometimes your dreams can come true when you least expect them to.

*

Oh yes, speaking of dreams, that was an interesting ending to the story. I'm sure you're going to change it. Right?

(Okay, okay. So Ray actually, said …)

"You know Gerry Mulligan, the baritone sax man with the band?"

"Yeah, sure. He's famous. One of the best."

"Gerry's horn isn't working right, some key is broken. And I was wondering…. Could we borrow your bari tonight? You know, for Gerry to play?"

Suddenly I deflated and became depressed. No, that doesn't come close to what I felt. I was crushed. Just when it looked as if the moment might finally be and was dangling right in front of me, poof, it was gone. I suppose it was one of life's little ironies. Everybody gets teased once in a while. It was just my turn. Get over it, I said to myself; you're not a kid anymore, even if you are a dreamer.

"Sure, Ray. I'll bring it right over."

I felt like kicking something. I couldn't believe this was happening. It was actually funny, when you think about it. But I was too numb to laugh.

"Ha," I managed to say as I hung up the phone.

"What so funny?" my wife said.

"Oh, nothing. I've got to go out to the Ritz and let someone borrow my horn. I'll be back in a little while."

I drove to the Ritz in my ten-year old blue Plymouth, the bari snug in its case on the back seat. I handed the horn to Ray and never let on how I really felt. I was too proud. I sat alongside the band in my old familiar spot—habit, I guess—and listened to the great Gerry Mulligan play my baritone sax brilliantly.

Time flashed back to many years before, when I was a kid. I remembered the excitement and the anticipation and how hopeful I was. Now as I gazed around the ballroom, I saw that I was older than many of the patrons. Local musicians weren't enclaved behind the bandstand anymore. People no longer gathered *en masse* in front of the band as in former years, cheering and applauding each individual soloist. They were dancing. The charged atmosphere was gone. The era of big band mass hysteria was in flux, changing to what, I didn't know. But I didn't like it.

After a few tunes, I couldn't listen any more. I got up, found Ray and said, "I'll pick up the horn tomorrow, Ray."

"Fine," he said, "I'll have it right here. And thanks a lot, Gene. You saved the day. I won't forget it."

"Sure. Glad to help. Anytime."

I went outside and moped in front of the Ballroom. I stood there, kind of blurred out. It was snowy and cold. The green and white bus came by and stopped. People got off. I got on. It was brightly lit and almost empty. The floor was wet where snow had been tracked and melted. We bumped and bounced our way back to town. I thought about all the times I went to the Ritz as a kid with my horn. I thought about the music and the fine band I had heard that night, and the telephone call, and my family, and playing my sax, and never playing in a name band ... or even being a movie star, which was not as important.

Twenty minutes later I got off at my stop and walked home.

"You okay?" my wife said.

"Sure." Then I told her what happened.

"Well, it just wasn't meant to be this time."

"Yeah, I guess so."

The next morning I went outside to get in my car. It wasn't there. I shook my head, a little puzzled. Then I remembered it was still parked out at the Ritz.

So was my saxophone.

**

Crowds gathered around bandstands when famous big bands
came to America's ballrooms like the Meadowbrook in New Jersey
and the Ritz in Bridgeport, both favorites on the tour.
Glen Miller, trombonist in tan jacket.
Tex Beneke, tenor sax upper left corner
Circa ♫ 1940
Courtesy: *Jazz, A History of America's Music*
Geoffrey Ward and Ken Burns

6

ME AND MY SHADOW

"No, damn it! What do you think you're doing? That's the way I play. Nobody plays the way I play. Only Ted Lewis plays that way!" I wouldn't forget those words.

I had taken my first full-time traveling gig as lead alto saxophonist with the Ted Lewis Show a few years before the Claude Thornhill incident at the Ritz. Our third child, Peter, was born the day after I left on tour.

Ted Lewis's band was not really jazz oriented, although it may have been in years past. But it offered steady work and a chance to gain professional experience. The pay was okay, if less than remarkable—but so was I. This was a welcome growth opportunity.

A lean, striking man of medium height, in his late sixties, Ted Lewis wore a craggy, ruddy face, seriously interrupted by a prominent nose. His wavy white hair, always carefully groomed, was swooped back perfectly on the sides with just the right flair. He commanded attention whenever he spoke in his inimitable, booming theatrical voice. He was one of those people who knew he was important and made sure everyone else did too, even if he were saying, "Please pass the butter." Every utterance was a platform to impress.

Billed as the Tragedian of Song, Lewis presented a stage and floorshow revue with his band, dancers, singers, a novelty act—Irving Shatz, playing "Hot Canary" on a miniature violin—and a ten-piece band. The show featured Ted singing, presenting acts, telling stories and playing his clarinet. His monologues were mostly nostalgic tales of "the old days, when life was simple, people were polite, and bread was five cents a loaf"; or was it when life was polite and people were simple? They were romantic tales of yesteryear, all recounted by Ted in grand style, every verb emphasized, every adjective milked with shameless disregard for subtlety of any sort. And yet somehow it worked, mesmerizing his fans.

Ted's theme song was "When My Baby Smiles at Me." But more famously, he was the one who originally created and performed the classic dramatization of the tune "Me and My Shadow." This was the highlight of his show and artfully presented. Putting down the clarinet, he would pick up a walking cane and stroll back and forth across the stage, gesturing like a Shakespearean thespian, like an old-time vaudevillian, like himself, all the while singing the title song with the controlled fragility of a much older man. *"Me and my shadow, strolling down the avenue ..."*

The stage was dark except for a spotlight on Ted, accoutered as usual in tux and tails and a weathered old collapsible top hat. But a second spotlight, one of lesser lumens, would capture the movements of another person on stage, Ted's shadow, dressed the same as Ted, except totally in black. The shadow mimicked every one of Ted's gestures, every step, every movement.

Stopping mid-stage, with a grand flourish Ted would tuck the cane under one arm and light up a cigarette, then puff perfect smoke rings which undulated up through the bluish light, morphing into larger hoops, vanishing into the darkness. He'd pause then, as if savoring the moment, as the violinist carried the plaintive melody of the song.

Sensing the right moment, Ted resumed his stroll and sang the rest of the song, doffing his battered top hat to the audience with the aplomb of a gallant Maurice Chevalier. His shadow duplicated the movements with perfect timing.

Just before leaving the stage, Ted would pause at the wings, gaze out into the spotlight and invoke the familiar wistful phrase the audience was waiting for. "Is <u>eve</u>-ry-body hap-py?" The act was total theater. And primarily because of it, Ted had become a show business legend. Later in the show, some of the band members (playing trombone, trumpet and clarinet) would come downstage and join Ted and his clarinet in recreating a jam session from "Rector's Restaurant in 1910 back in Old New York," as Ted always announced it. Johnny (I never knew his last name) played the jazz clarinet solo in this number.

During the second month of the tour, on Johnny's first night off, the manager told me I was to play the jazz solo in his place. I was called to Ted's dressing room before the show, a private audience with the star. This felt strange, particularly since he had never spoken directly to me before. It must be important. Maybe he likes my work. Maybe he's going to give me a raise. As I entered his small dressing room, there was the maestro seated at a small dressing table in his boxer shorts, black patent leather dress shoes, garters hold up his socks, with his top hat on, patting pancake makeup onto his face with a small, damp sponge. At regular intervals, he took off the hat, checked the mirror, dabbed a little more makeup here and there, then put the hat back checking in the mirror for the right jaunty angle.

"Yes, Mr. Lewis?" I said from the doorway.

"Let me hear the solo you're going to play in the show tonight, kid," he said without looking around.

"You mean you want to hear my improvisation?"

"Yes, yes. Right now. Play it for me."

"But then it wouldn't be an improvisation."

"Damn it, I want to hear it now!"

"Okay, sure." I hadn't thought about what I was going to play on stage. But it occurred to me that since I had been listening to Ted play his clarinet for several weeks now and had a pretty good idea of his style, he might be flattered if I imitated him. So I launched into my *improvised* solo, playing a rather coherent collection of his favorite stylized licks. Not bad at all, I thought.

"No, damn it!" he boomed in his W.C. Fields voice, whirling around on the bench. "What do you think you're doing? That's the way *I* play. Nobody plays the way *I* play. Only *Ted Lewis* plays that way!"

"Okay, Okay. I'll play something different."

"You better! And let me hear it right now."

I played some standard old Dixieland kind of phrases. Nothing too hip. Nothing creative or inspired. I was just sort of kidding. But he approved. I couldn't believe it.

"That's better. That's more like it. That's what I want to hear tonight. That's what my audience wants."

Later, in the show, after my backstage audition, I played a stunning new improvised solo, nothing like what Lewis expected. Lewis went ballistic. He didn't know what to do. His face reddened. I thought he was going to throw me off the stage. But the crowed cheered madly when I finished. Lewis stopped the show and introduced me to the audience. More thunderous applause. That night after the show he gave me a raise and asked me to play my own creative solo every night for the rest of the tour.

*

My, my, what a fertile imagination. A raise? From Lewis?
No way.

(Well, that's the way it happens in the movies.
So there was no raise.)

Later in the show, after my backstage audition, I repeated the same solo Lewis had approved, note for note as close as I could, in what was supposed to have been an authentic impromptu jazz jam session. I resented having to do it. I was young enough to be idealistic about that sort of thing. But in the context of the show it was appropriate, and Lewis had been right. I still didn't like it.

Much later I realized that the Ted Lewis experience had taught me the meaning of a maxim well worth remembering. In show business, people pay to be entertained, not to be educated, especially by someone who thinks he should be trying to elevate their tastes.

They don't teach you that in music school.

**

Ted Lewis
"The Tragedian of Song"

7

IS EVERYBODY HAPPY?

Several weeks had gone by since Pittsburgh, where I played the *fake* clarinet solo for Ted Lewis. We had moved on and were booked for an extended engagement in Memphis.

One sultry summer night during this booking, I was feeling particularly restless. The separation from family was getting to me. If anything was bothering me, it usually surfaced in this kind of weather. There was something about the heavy, static atmosphere that always seeped into my irritation slot. Why am I here anyway? Is it worth it? I questioned whether the road would bring me closer to my goals. I didn't have the answers. But I was asking the right questions.

After we finished playing our two shows at the Peabody Hotel that night, Lewis announced to the band and cast that we were invited to a private party in his hotel suite. I was in an antsy mood and not too anxious to attend. I hadn't forgotten the way he had demanded that I play my jazz solo for him in his dressing room weeks before. I had felt insulted then and was still smarting like an adolescent.

So instead of going to the party, I went out, walked to an all-night eatery and had breakfast. Surprisingly, the stroll in the dampness of the early morning refreshed me. Nature's nightly thermostatic adjustments were well under way, as another warm Memphis evening had cooled and the inevitable nocturnal invasion of Mississippi mist began. Intermittent fog rolled off the river and billowed into downtown, colliding with hours-old sidewalk heat, wilting forgotten flags, cooling oaks and moistening car windows till they dripped. A captivating event, if you had time to notice. I did. I liked it. No cigarette smoke. No noise. No people.

I gave more thought to attending Lewis's gathering. It occurred to me that even he if was overbearing, I was taking myself too seriously. I resolved to redirect my energies and not let my personal feelings keep me from getting on with making a living as a musician.

It was late but once back at the hotel, I decided I should go up to his suite and put in an appearance at the party. So maybe he's taking attendance? You never know. No sense in taking a chance. One of the other musicians let me in.

The gathering seemed quiet enough, strangely so. Just a little subdued talk here and there. Many people stood around holding drinks … a few guys from the band, the show people, and several others I didn't recognize. Soft music from a record player filled the void between casual conversation and the clinking of cocktail glasses. Someone handed me a glass of Chablis. I sipped; it was bitter. I preferred beer, but sipped again. I stood there holding the glass and looked around. The lights were low, but I noticed that several people seemed to be focused on something of interest on the far side of the spacious, floral-carpeted room. Seated on a large couch, two partially clad young women and one young man, wearing nothing but boxer shorts, were getting better acquainted. That got my attention.

Another young woman, this one in black panties, emerged barefoot from a bedroom with a black ostrich boa draped around her neck. Extraneous accoutrements were lacking, but her personal attributes were anything but limited. Sashaying over to the couch, she extended both ends of the feathered serpent from her outstretched arms, stepped gracefully up onto a coffee table, and commenced performing slow, sensuous gyrations in sync with the music.

Someone turned up the stereo until the sound of "Harlem Nocturne" bounced off the walls. The couch tomatoes, and carrot, proceeded to remove remaining garments and appeared to begin passionate samplings of each other's offerings. I couldn't quite be sure. All the while the boa-draped one slithered around an invisible pole. That, I could see plainly.

Amazed, aroused, embarrassed, yet curious, I could feel my face getting warmer. The watchers stared, transfixed. This was the 50s and a pretty weird happening. The impresario himself, clad in tux and silk smoking jacket, sat in a large easy chair across the room watching intently. As the action steamed ahead, he frowned, nodded rapidly, then bellowed out to one of the musicians, "Get the camera! Get the camera!" It wasn't a request. The scene had mesmerized me ... until he spoke. Suddenly I was embarrassed. Unpleasant vibes crept in. I didn't know why at the time. After all, Ted Lewis was world famous and this was his party. I was an employee. Besides, one's choice of recreational activity is a personal matter and has little bearing on professionalism.

Of course, the 50s was the age of innocence and the scene seemed to be outside the kind of public behavior I wanted to be associated with, even if it was a private party. I wasn't a prude or particularly fragile, but I left the party and considered leaving the band and going home, when I could afford to. Something about his voice got to me.

Perhaps the years spent in a Catholic prep school and Notre Dame had left at least some moral impressions on me. I would hope so. At least at times. They're supposed to. However, it had to be more than that. These were adults, productive, talented and successful in a business that traditionally is open-minded and free-spirited. The scene was really no big deal. So what really bothered me? Why did I react like that? Was I really that embarrassed? It was something in Lewis's manner—dismissive, insensitive and belittling. I recognized the bully-and-intimidate syndrome but didn't realize why it made me see red.

Why was I being so sensitive? Whatever the reason, before the tour ended, even though I was working with talented people, I decided not to renew my contract for another tour, if asked to do so.

When writing of this event, years later, I was able to put into focus why I might have been so agitated. Somewhere in Lewis's voice I had heard the scolding tone my father used when, as a kid, I would trip or drop a glass or break something accidentally, or misplace his hammer, or forget a chore. Often I'd hear him yell on and on at my mother, too, indulging in out-of-control tantrums. I cringed when he unloaded with one of his red-faced tirades. And when he yelled at me, I did nothing except apologize. I knew he loved me and cared for me and didn't intend to hurt. He just couldn't help it. I also knew it wasn't good for me.

On the other hand, my mother was always telling me how wonderful I was, and how I was going to be a success when I grew up, and that I was thoughtful and kind and talented. No doubt her constant reinforcement helped to give me confidence. Perhaps it also led me to seek others' approval too much. I always seem to need to replenish a leaky supply of self-esteem.

More than anything else, this need, and my father behavior probably keyed my desire to achieve. I'm sure his anger dented me at the time, certainly not his intention, but it also likely impelled me to try harder.

But there was more. Not only had Lewis' voice reminded me of my father's darker moods, it also awakened unpleasant memories of my grandfather, who had ranted at me for something foolish I would do when I was little: like when I moved my head the wrong way while he was giving me a haircut, or fell asleep with the radio on, wasting electricity. It was just his way.

I know my occasional dreaminess irritated him, too. He never thought I'd amount to anything. I can still hear him hollering at me, even when I was a young man of twenty, because I didn't begin painting the walls of his barber shop the way he wanted it done.

I loved him, but I just didn't like the bullying then, and I still don't. Sometimes people with power, whether they are bandleaders, bankers, secretaries, CEOs, schoolteachers or kids, regard subordinates as inferior. They focus on what they perceive as a person's deficiencies. In my view, their attitude toward others doesn't change. Early on, I resolved to distance myself forever, if I had a choice, from anyone who belittled me, talked down to me, bullied me, or made me feel less than a man. Lewis qualified as a prime villain in my book

In retrospect, most likely ghostly echoes of the past had spooked me and influenced me to leave the party. Poor, sensitive me. Obviously, I wouldn't have made good army material.

In an effort to solve the problem, the next night I sat down to talk with Lewis after our show. Hearing how offended I was, he understood and apologized, said it would not happen again. The rest of the tour was delightful.

Lewis apologized? Oh really? Lewis!?

(Would have been nice if he did. I like happy endings.)

Too bad for you. The facts, please.

Lewis and I never did reach an understanding. I'd like to think that leaving the band at the end of the tour was a decision based on integrity and strength of character; it wasn't. His manner had gotten to me, even though it didn't seem to bother anyone else. Besides, I didn't like playing that old-fogie music.

Twerp.

**

8

THE AUDITION

"When are you leaving?" she asked.

How do you tell your wife you're desperate? That you're quitting your job at the department store? That you're leaving home for the second time in a little over a year? That you're taking another traveling job, this time with a name band?

You're twenty-six and life is passing you by.

You're a young father with three kids. You have responsibilities and dreams. What do you say to them? Daddy wants to play his saxophone? Daddy can't stand working in the store? Daddy hated working in the factory? Daddy hated being a census taker? Daddy can't make enough money playing weddings and bar mitzvahs to support his family? Daddy is dying inside? Daddy feels like a failure? Daddy doesn't love you as much as he does music? Of course not.

What do you tell your family, who loves you, and only wants you to be with them? How did it all ever get to this point? When the Ted Lewis tour was over, I returned home and worked a succession of day jobs, anything to keep from going on the road again, even if the road meant steady work, especially with the kind of bands that played commercial cornball stuff. I had had enough of that. While it was music and served a purpose for older people, it was watered down, had no edge, no swing, and it wouldn't bring me closer to attaining professional goals. So if I had a choice, I decided to avoid playing that kind of music.

I continued the practice regimen on sax, clarinet and flute, taking lessons in New York, playing every kind of gig I could find in the Connecticut area and working part-time day jobs. But it wasn't enough to pay the bills. I had to find a better way to support my family without traveling. There just wasn't enough full-time work in music to sustain us. Unlike so many young artists-in-waiting who sometimes wait on table, I sought work that might offer a permanent career change.

I took a job in the Executive Training Program at Holland's Department Store in Bridgeport, part of the Allied Stores chain. I started as a part-timer, running the Lionel Railroad layout in the toy department. Seeing me there shocked some friends. I was four years out of Notre Dame, where I had been president of my class one year and was already a known bandleader in the Bridgeport area. I'm sure hometown people expected bigger things of me than running toy trains in a department store. I did, too.

I experienced some sensitive moments. Dorothy, an elegant ex-girlfriend from high school days, whom I hadn't seen in years, walked past the far side of the toy department one day. She recognized me, did a double take, but quickly covered her mouth with a gloved hand and turned away as if concentrating on a nearby mannequin—obviously an instinctive reaction to prevent our eyes from meeting. She was embarrassed for me. I couldn't blame her. There I was, wearing a gray and white striped engineers cap with a red bandana around my neck, tooting on a wooden, three-toned train whistle, trying to attract shoppers to the Lionel train display, a clownish but definitely necessary activity.

After that incident, whenever shoppers recognized me, I'd smile and give them a big wave and call out, "Hi," a maneuver that usually headed off awkward conversations. People usually managed a weak smile, a little nod, and a whatever-happened-to-Gene look, before hurrying on. I understood. I was embarrassed, too.

From toy trains, I was promoted to full-time, first to Children's Shoes, then to Ladies' Shoes and on to Assistant Shoe Buyer. In a few months, I was promoted to buyer in the basement annex for Budget Ladies Coats, Suits, and Dresses. It seemed I had finally established an economic beachhead. I attended all the training courses and company seminars. I was an up-and-coming young executive-in-training on a fast track. Store management and employees seemed to regard me with deference. But putting on a different hat doesn't change who you are and I never let the job define me. Apparently, I was still a musician.

Quite unplanned, a chance meeting diverted the course of my career in retailing forever.

Each week I took a train ride into New York City to shop the market for next season's budget fashions. That spring I was looking for ladies fall coats. It was Wednesday about noon, late March, on Seventh Avenue in the Garment District. I splattered through the slush from a spring snowfall and made my way into a corner drugstore to warm up, have a sandwich and a hot chocolate.

The place was crowded with lunch-hour people, its narrow aisles packed with clutter, displays, bookracks, and cardboard boxes. A maze. Mice must have enjoyed their nights alone when the store was closed. As I made my way toward the lunch counter in back, I bumped into my old roommate buddy from the Ted Lewis Band, Al Verst. I hadn't seen him in over a year.

Al played alto sax and was a good man. Handsome, about thirty-five, dark-haired, always smiling, a mellow kind of guy, he was a dead ringer, only shorter, for Tony Martin, the famous singer married to Cyd Charisse. Cyd was a tall, exquisitely statuesque movie-star dancer. When Al and I were on the road together, I used to kid him as if he actually were Tony Martin, the husband of Cyd.

"So, Tony," I'd say, "do Cyd's legs really start at her armpits?"

"Sure."

"She must like midgets, huh?"

His comeback, in warm Jewish Brooklynese, á la Jackie Mason, was always, "So wadded think, my hands are small too?"

Al saw me first, just before I reached the lunch counter. "Geeeeennnn. It's so good to see you, man. What a surprise! What are you doing in New York?"

I told him about my new job and about shopping for fall coats for the store, trying to sound like a solid business retailer. Al wasn't wearing an outer coat, so I took him for a store employee. "So what's with you? What are you doing here?"

"I'm working, man. I manage the place for my uncle."

"No kidding. You'll own the store someday. Playing any?"

"Naw, not any more. That's history. I'm getting married. The music business is dead. How about you? Still married to Connie?"

"Sure. Four kids now. Two boys, two girls. Beautiful family."

"Still playing your horns?" he asked.

"Weddings and club dates at home, but I'm pretty much out of it now." (I lied.) "I've got a career going in retailing, and I'm home with my family

"Uh-huh," he mused. "Still practicing and taking lessons with Joe Allard in the City?"

"Oh sure. Something might come up. Maybe a record deal or something."

"Uh-huh, I see. You know, I heard that Tex Beneke is in town auditioning for a lead alto player today up at Nola Studios."

"Really? Ah, that's not for me. I'm not interested." (I lied again.) "I'm settled now. I'm a clothes buyer. Besides, even if I wanted to try out, just to see if I could cut it, I don't have my horn with me." I was off the hook.

"You could borrow Joe Allard's horn. Just call him up and tell him about the audition. You're one of his better pupils. He'd let you use it."

"Aw, I don't know." Slipping gradually into a what-if mode, I started thinking about the possibilities. Opportunity was knocking at an inconvenient time.

"Well, if you want to audition," said Al, "the band manager's name is Eddie Matthews. Call Nola's and ask him if they're still looking for a man. What do you have to lose?"

"Hmm, I don't know, man. Gotta run, sorry. Al, it was great to see you." We shook hands warmly. I never saw him again.

I turned and retraced the circuitous route back to the front door. Didn't eat lunch. Once out on the sidewalk, I realized that I just couldn't walk away from this opportunity. What harm would it do just to see if I could make it? ... to see if I were good enough to play lead sax in a real name band? What would it matter if I just auditioned? Who would know? I wasn't going anywhere, anyway.

I stood there musing with myself on the crowded sidewalk, getting bumped into by people who seemed to know where they were going and were busy trying to get there. I escaped to a pay phone booth on the corner and called Joe. Yes, I could use his sax.

Then I called Nola's and spoke to Eddie Matthews. "Yeah, sure," he said, "If you study with Joe Allard, we want to hear you. Come over in an hour." Momentum was gathering.

Nola's was on the corner of Broadway and 54th Street. It occupied the entire second floor loft of a large building and had several rehearsal rooms of various sizes. The outside studios had floor-to-ceiling windows that could swing open. In summertime, you could stand across the street on Broadway and hear great bands rehearsing at all hours, day and night. When a famous band was rehearsing, you'd see many people up there sitting and standing along the windowsills inside. A year before, I had gone in with a friend to watch Dizzy Gillespie's big band being rehearsed by Quincy Jones for a State Department Cultural Exchange Tour to the Middle East and Latin America. Phil Woods was one of alto players. Extraordinary music. Awesome musicians, way beyond my level.

At precisely two o'clock, I walked into Nola's and immediately got an eerie feeling, as if famous notes were still echoing in the halls. Almost numb, I made my way to the largest rehearsal hall, Studio A, the same studio where I had heard Dizzy's band.

Studio A had faded yellow walls and a high ceiling whose dingy paint was muted by brightly lit suspended florescent lights. Several floor radiators were busy hissing, trying to smother the room's March chill. The Tex Beneke band, fourteen musicians, was set up at one end of the long, rectangular room. *Wow, there they are. And there's Tex himself.* He was standing in front of the band, facing them, listening intently. He wasn't as tall as I had thought. I was psyched.

On three sides of the room about thirty wooden folding chairs were set up in a single row. In each chair a nervous looking guy sat facing the band. Different ages. Some dressed in shirts and ties. Some in sweat shirts. A few had beards. A couple sported berets. But each cradled an alto saxophone on his lap waiting to audition. I wore a business suit.

As I entered and took in the scene, one fellow was auditioning, sitting in with the band. I stood by the door and listened. He played a solo. I could tell in an instant I was a much better player.

Apparently the band had been auditioning players for about an hour. They still hadn't found what they were looking for. If they had, they would have stopped auditioning.

"Eddie Matthews? I'm Gene Hull," I said, when the song was over.

"Yeah, the guy from Joe Allard's, right?"

"I guess," I said.

"Good. Get out your horn. We'll hear you next."

Before the others who are waiting? Hmm. I blew a few notes, wiggled a few keys, and sat in the vacated audition seat, the lead alto chair in the center of the sax section. Tex stood right in front of me, facing me.

I was pretty relaxed. I didn't need the job. But sitting there, I realized how much I wanted to show him I could play. In fact, I wanted to show everyone there, and my friends and family and the people back at the store. Suddenly I wanted everybody in that studio and everywhere else to know who I was, that I was a good player, ready for the big time. I wanted the job. I wanted to be the lead alto man with Tex Beneke. The adrenaline kicked in.

He counted off a ballad that had a tricky but beautiful alto solo. I flubbed a note. He stopped the band. "That's an A sharp," he growled, looking down at me.

"Oh, right." I didn't look up.

We played it again. I played it perfectly this time. Tex didn't say anything to me, instead he called out to the band, "Guys, pull out American Patrol."

This arrangement featured plenty of ensemble sax section work, with the lead alto right out there in front, charging ahead.

It swung. I played it pretty well. Tex strolled over to Matthews and murmured something to him.

"Let's take five, everybody," Matthews announced. He and Beneke talked head to head. I figured that with thirty guys yet to audition, they wouldn't be taking a break yet, unless I was the one they wanted. Immediately I put the horn in its case—yes, I had a case for my own sax at home now, too—and walked out of the studio into the hall. Before Matthews could get to me, I found a phone booth and put in a dime.

"Yes, operator, collect to anyone from Gene Hull. Thank you."

My wife answered.

"Connie, guess what? Tex Beneke is auditioning today in New York. He's looking for a lead alto player for a tour."

Silence.

"Well, just for kicks, I borrowed Joe Allard's horn and auditioned. Just wanted to see if I could make it. Ya know?" Still no response from her.

"You there, Con?"

"Uh-huh."

"Well, I'm sure I've got the job if I want it. But I'm telling them No thanks. No way I'm leaving you and the family and the store job just to play a road gig, name band or no name band. Just thought I'd call and tell you. I'll catch the five o'clock home from Grand Central.

*

Oh, how unselfish. Are you sure, sure, sure that's what happened when you called your wife? Doesn't sound right to me.

(Now that I think of it, the conversation went like this)

"Well, just for kicks, I borrowed Joe Allard's horn and auditioned. Just wanted to see if I could make it. Ya know?" Still no response from her.

Matthews was pounding on the phone booth door. "I need to talk to you," he mouthed.

"Just a minute, Con." I opened the door, held my hand over the phone and said, "Eddie, when does the tour start?"

"Friday."

"You mean the day after tomorrow?"

He nodded.

I shut the door on Eddie. He paced back and forth.

"Connie? Sure is crazy around here I, a...actually, I, I'm sure I've got the job, if I want it."

A long silence. Then, a sigh. "When are you leaving?" she said quietly. Too quietly.

"Two days," I said sheepishly, feeling like a heel. "It's really a career move."

"I know," she said. "Come home."

"Right. I'll get the five o'clock from Grand Central."

I was so excited I could hardly speak.

My wife was crushed. I could hear her disappointment. She must have realized her hopes for my staying home to pursue a stable career in retail management were being vanquished by an infrangible force she had come to recognize in our marriage but felt powerless to resist.

She was a saint.

I wasn't.

You rat.

(Ow.)

**

9
––––––––––––
––––––––––––

SATURDAY NIGHT IN TEXAS

"Remember guys, it'll probably be the same tonight as it always is here. So be ready when the time comes." Tex Beneke was standing in front of us with his back to the dancehall audience. It was a few minutes before we were to start playing. Some of the musicians chuckled, apparently not concerned about his remarks.

"What did Tex mean by that?" I said, wide-eyed and innocent, leaning over to Sante Russo, the veteran saxophonist sitting beside me. Sante always seemed to know what was going on.

"You'll find out," he said with a wry smile. We searched through our music folders and pulled out the arrangements for the first set.

What was that all about? Why all the mystery? Be ready for what? Because I was new with the band, I didn't ask any more questions.

Just the usual 1956 Saturday night in Longview, Texas, I guess—now a year after the Ted Lewis tour. The Brooklyn Dodgers would eventually loose the World Series to the

Yankees—Don Larsen would pitch a Yankee no-hitter. The New Look was in; skirts were long again. And I was the lead alto saxophone player with the famous Tex Beneke Orchestra. We were on a spring-summer tour of one-nighters throughout the Midwest and South.

Bandleaders like Beneke, who had built famous reputations during the Swing Era's halcyon days, were now touring more and more to "Flyspeck, U.S.A.," performing live for pockets of fans who knew them from so many hit recordings. Since Tex had taken over the Glenn Miller Band at the end of World War II, his music library had many memorable hits, like "In The Mood," "Tuxedo Junction," "Moonlight Serenade," "String of Pearls," "Little Brown Jug," "Kalamazoo," "Serenade In Blue." And here I was, playing in his band.

I was proud to be in the band, but I did have mixed emotions again. I was excited and thrilled to be there, of course. Yet I wanted the experience to be worth the decision I had made to leave my family for another tour. I was happy, sad, anxious, hungry to learn, afraid to fail, and all too well aware this was a chance to validate myself as a professional musician, an opportunity I couldn't afford to waste.

Longview, Texas was a busy little town of ranches, farms and a few oilrigs. Post-war urban expansion and commercial development was on its way but hadn't yet taken hold. Neither had the interstate highway system. The railroad, however, ran through town. With a population of about 25,000, and 120 miles east of Dallas, it was still a cowboy town in spirit. You could see cattle being driven by cowpokes on horseback near town, crossing a road here and there to get to the railroad yard.

People generally minded their own business and worked hard in Longview. And, as I would soon discover, they played hard too, especially in their dance hall.

The Beneke band was booked to play for one night at Longview's Longhorn Ranch Dance Hall. It wasn't a ranch, and it wasn't exactly a hall but rather an almost-a-building structure, half the size of a football field, mostly open-sided, situated on a scruffy prairie about five miles from town. The Longhorn's wooden bandstand, a two-foot-high, tiered platform, sat on the concrete floor at one end of the hall. Obviously, the night air probably cooled the place. But when there was no breeze, whew!

We arrived at Longhorn Ranch on our chartered Greyhound bus at 5:00 p.m. that afternoon in June, after an eight-hour, bumpy, 300-mile haul from Tulsa. The sun was still overhead. The driver maneuvered the bus up behind the building, close to the bandstand back entrance. Once we left our air-conditioned bus and stepped outside, the first thing that hit me was the strangling heat reaching from the ground, stored up with a full day's download of Texas sun. Every time I took a deep breath I could feel the heat pouring into me. It was hot — Texas hot, June hot, Saturday night hot, sticky hot, Jack Daniels hot.

Miles of parched land stretched off into the distance, dotted with shrubs that were probably tumbleweeds in the making. I wondered why anyone would want to live out here in this dismal dirtscape.

Since we weren't staying in a hotel that night but would be traveling on the bus to the next town right after the gig, we didn't unload our bags, just our instruments, equipment, and the usual shaving cream, toothbrush and razor.

The typical one-nighter bus tour pattern was: travel all day, get to the dancehall, set up, get dressed, play the gig, get back on the bus, travel all night, arrive at the next town early in the morning and check in to a hotel, sleep till late afternoon, set up, play the gig, go back to the hotel, sleep there that night, get up the next morning, get back on the bus and start the process all over again. I adapted to the routine easily. Booking into hotels every other day and spending alternate nights traveling saved money—always a plus because band members paid for their own hotel rooms.

After setting up the music stands, lights, wires, and unpacking the music that day, Eddie Matthews, who rode with us on the bus wherever we traveled, went about the business of checking the PA system. Eddie took out Tex's gold-plated microphone to begin the sound check and connected it to a cable already in place. He did the same with the girl singer's mike. A few of us stood around to watch and listen.

"Testing, testing, one, two, three. Check, check. One, two," Eddie said. "Check, check, testing, testing ..." etcetera, etcetera. Boring.

I wondered why, just for once, someone didn't say something different during a sound check. Like maybe throw in some Shakespeare, just for laughs.

> *Is this a dagger I see before me?*
> *the handle toward my hand?*
> Testing.
> *Come, let me clutch thee.*
> One, two, three.
> *I have thee not, yet I see thee still.*
> Check.
> *Art thou not fatal vision*
> *sensible to feeling as to sight...?*
> Check. Check. Check.

Why not?

The younger musicians in the band all agreed the place sounded like a barn. Hell, it was a barn. I wanted it to sound like Carnegie Hall and expected that it should. But the musicians who had played here in past years were indifferent. They had more important things on their minds, like finding a pay phone, reading newspapers, catching up on stock market quotes, writing music, practicing and sniffing out the locals.

Two of them already had their eyes on the young women who had gathered around to watch the band set up. After all, this was a name band, a sufficient flame for some of the local moths.

Duke Bellaire, the drummer, and Nick Cavas, one of the trombone players, both from the Providence area, had struck up a friendly conversation with two lovely young local cowboyettes, pretty as butterflies in their Saturday-night pastel dresses. It seems that Duke had met one of them the previous year when the band had passed through. Knowing the importance of advance planning to enhance possibilities of testosteronian success in the fast-paced, here-today, gone-tomorrow life of a road musician, Duke had called ahead to let her know the band would soon be in town. The man was motivated, always thinking ahead. Seems like every band had at least one dedicated musician like him.

The scene reminded me to call my wife, which I did every other night. The separation was rough on the family. I ran up a hellava phone bill on that tour.

The musicians felt pretty gritty after the long, hot ride. There were no showers, so after set-up, we used the sinks in the men's room to wash and shave.

"Hey, guys," I said, "there's no hot water."

"Welcome to the road, man," one drolled, as he cruised his electric shaver across his face.

"What was Tex talking about when he said to be ready?" I asked Sante.

"You'll know soon enough."

"Come on, man. What's up? We going to have to march, or something?"

"In a manner of speaking, yes," he said.

I really didn't get it. But I didn't want to appear too curious. I shrugged it off. We ate boxed sandwiches and had cold beers and soft drinks before going back onto the bus, which was air-conditioned, thank God. We changed into our uniforms: black tux pants, black patent leather shoes, powder blue dinner jackets with shawl collars, blue cummerbunds, white shirts and matching blue bow ties. Tex wore a midnight blue tux. This was Saturday night in Texas and Tex was a favorite son, so it was dress-up night.

I felt important wearing the band uniform. Looking back, we were playing the kind of music that seemed worthy of getting dressed up, and the crowd expected it. Of course, times have changed. If a contemporary band went on stage dressed that way today, they'd probably look like a wedding party on Prom Night.

We strolled onto the stand fifteen minutes early to get ready for the first set. I noticed a few ceiling fans sparsely spaced overhead, whirling around lazily, not pushing much air. Two floor fans, set up at the sides of the bandstand, aimed at us. If they were supposed to keep us cool, somebody was a dreamer, or a salesman.

Finally we were set up, tuned up, and ready to go. It was eight o'clock. But just before we started, a chicken wire curtain, the width of the bandstand, was unfurled, lowered from the rafters in front of the stage and secured to small hooks in the concrete floor, the bottom angling out a few feet onto the dance floor. It was like we were caged animals for everyone to look at. It turned out to be the other way around.

"Really, Sante," I said, "that's wild. I never saw that before. What's the chicken wire for?"

"You'll find out," he said, busy making adjustments to his octave key with a tiny screwdriver. Sante was a man of few words. As usual, our first tune would be Tex's signature theme song, "Moonlight Serenade," probably the most recognizable Big

Band theme song of the era. It had been Glen Miller's theme, the first and last tune we played every night.

The band drew a big turnout. After all, it was Saturday night in Longview. The famous Tex Beneke Orchestra had come to town to play all the Glenn Miller hits. No self-respecting citizen could stay away, even the mayor. He introduced us with a big "Ladies and Gentlemen, as your mayor it is my distinct pleasure to present the pride of Texas, Mr. Tex Beneke himself, and his fabulous orchestra!" The crowd cheered like the freshmen bleacher section at a college football game.

"Wow," I said, "this is really something, huh, Sante? Listen to them. They love us already."

"Yeah, sure," said Sante, nodding casually.

Women looked festive in party dresses; men wore chinos, shirts and cowboy boots, some in jeans with short sleeve shirts. Others donned fancy western garb with string ties. Most kept their cowboy hats on. Some wore jackets and regular ties.

Everyone had brought liquor, and everywhere coolers were stashed full of beer. Long wooden tables with pipe legs lined both sides of the hall, facing in toward the huge dance floor like out-of-bounds markers. Each table, covered with a shiny white paper tablecloth, sported a plastic bucket of ice.

When it was "Moonlight Serenade" time, well over three thousand good citizens of Longview invaded the dance. No one was shy. No one waited for someone else to go first. They swept *en masse* out onto the concrete like a flood and immediately began dancing. After all, that's why they had come, so why waste time.

The sparkling overhead mirror ball began its slow, glittery rotations right away. No waiting to be introduced as a special effect at some appropriately romantic moment later. Hell, no. Shoot the works right away. The crowd was warmed up and raring to go. The night had started at an energy level usually not reached before the halfway point.

By nine o'clock, the place was rocking like New Years Eve at an Elks Club in Erie. The din became a roar and kept climbing. The booze was flowing. The Good Times were rolling. And boy, was it hot.

After the first forty-minute set, we took a twenty-minute break. Off came our jackets. We were all sweating so much that I wondered if the crowd could smell us. Vinny, the t-bone player, immediately put on a clean shirt and spent the break next to the bandstand chatting up one of the local lovelies he had met before. While the girl was ooing, cooing, giggling and fondling his tie, a couple of big young dudes, really big—I mean, these guys must have been 6'6" at least, wearing Stetsons, boots, and jeans, with tee shirts rolled-up to their shoulders—were moving toward Vinny. As they got closer, I could see them glowering with tough-guy looks that definitely didn't convey brotherly love. Evidently this was their territory and Vinny was poaching.

I also noticed that Duke, the drummer was missing, and so was Miss Pastel Dress Texas-ette number two.

Fortunately, just about then Tex called the musicians back onto the bandstand to start the next set, and the big galoots walked off. I was on stage first, ready to go, since I had a solo coming up and was silently woodshedding the notes on my horn. Duke came hustling in through the back door and ran up onto the bandstand, pushing back his hair. Oddly enough, he didn't have his shoes on. Not the best thing for a drummer, I thought. But, hey, what did I know. Anyway, he just made it behind his drums as Tex counted off.

We opened the set with one of Miller/Beneke's biggest hits, practically a household name, "Chattanooga Choo Choo." The crowd loved it and cheered as we began. The dance floor swarmed once again with eager, sweaty flesh.

After the eight-bar intro, complete with train whistle effect, and the initial sax section first chorus, Tex began singing the tune's memorable lyric, just as he had on the original Miller recording, with his distinctive throaty, nasal style and wide vibrato. Compared to singers like Sinatra, he had the romantic appeal of a lumberjack singing "Tenderly" while sawing down a Redwood. But the crowd loved him.

I never understood in those days why Tex was personally such a hit with audiences. He had a rough, unpolished voice. But he was truly one of the vocal originals of the big band era. Now I can understand how he made fans feel at home and relaxed as if he were a regular guy. Because he was.

"Pardon me, Boy, is that the Chattanooga Choo Choo?
Track 29. Well you can give me a shine."

The dancers sang right along with him. It was a fun tune with an infectious beat. During Eddie Zandy's trumpet solo I noticed that both the local lovelies, looking like dolls, were dancing with their too-tall Texans, all smiles, probably sweet-talking their men. But all the while they were looking past them, over to the band, making eyes at their two musician dandies, who, noticing they were being noticed, began playing with an extra bit of showmanship. There's nothing like the attention of admirers to make you feel appreciated and want to perform with extra spark.

"Sante," I said, leaning over to him, "Vinny better watch out, or he's going to get popped." He shrugged. It was none of his business.

The next tune was "Skylark," a beautiful ballad by Hoagy Carmichael, composer of "Stardust." It had a challenging solo that really showed off the alto sax ... and me. I loved playing it and played it well. Nobody cheered when I finished, but a quiet "That was nice," came from Sante when I sat down again. Thanks, Sante.

Six more tunes followed. By the time we got to the set-closer, "American Patrol," the crowd was practically levitating. In a whoop-it-up party mood, fueled by alcohol and by just plain pent-up energy, they demonstrated an aspect of group dynamics I hadn't observed before.

We had just finished Patrol when the fight broke out. And what a fight it was.

CRASH. SMASH. BAM. WHACK. Yelling. Fists connecting. Bodies colliding. Everyone seemed to be involved. It was a mass melee. But I swear some people were laughing.

When the first bottle hit the chicken wire in front of us with a sudden wangggg, it scared the hell out of me. I was sitting, right in the middle of the front row. More bottles followed. Wangggg, wangggg—empties, I surmise, judging from the state of the crowd, though the thought didn't occur to me at the time, I was too busy trying to duck. We were caught in the middle of a good ole Texas Saturday-night brawl.

"This is it, huh, Sante," I said. "This is what Tex meant?"

"You got it, man."

Each bottle that hurtled toward us bounced harmlessly onto the slack chicken wire screen, before rolling down, and clanking onto the concrete.

"That's it, guys," Tex said calmly. "Pack it up."

I froze, open-mouthed. I thought for sure we might be killed. Maybe the crowd would charge the bandstand. I clutched my beautiful Selmer Alto close to me and ducked. But Tex was cool and matter-of-fact, as if it were a rehearsal. We had played only half the time for which we had been contracted, since the dance was supposed to go till midnight. But the old-timers on the band were already grabbing their horns and music and beating it out the back door onto the bus—which, I discovered, was warmed up, cooled down, and ready to roll.

Most nights it took us about an hour to strike the set, putting away horns and equipment, hanging around and loading up the bus. And that was if we were in a hurry to get on the road to make it to the next town, check in, and get some sleep. Musicians don't move too fast after playing a gig. They like to mill around and unwind.

On this night it couldn't have been more than fifteen minutes before we were out of there. All the while, the brawl continued inside with merry abandon. We changed out of our tuxes on the bus. No one seemed to be too upset, but I was shaking my head in disbelief. A crazy scene. So this is the road.

That's when Sante told me this happens every year the band plays in Longview.

"You're kidding," I said. "Then why does Tex play here?"

"Because every year they offer him more money to come back. And they always pay in advance. It's the best-paying date on the tour. And we never have to play more than half the gig before the fight starts."

About that time we heard some insistent pounding and yelling on the outside of our Greyhound. "Laurie! Missy Mae! Laurie!" The giants were stalking along the outside of the bus, actually looking *down* into the windows.

"Laurie. Come outta there!" one of them, yelled. "I know you're in there!"

"You too, Missy Mae," said the other. "Come out now, gol-damit, 'fore I turn this shit bus over." He probably could have.

It seems that the butterfly girls had accepted invitations from Dandy Duke and Nick and managed to flit onto the bus during the big brawl and were now hiding. The two bruisers were prowling back and forth outside the bus like hound dogs stalking quail. Most likely they were sniffing for Duke and Nick also—probably to rearrange their noses—pounding their fists against the side of the bus as they walked. I was getting anxious, but I decided to keep my mouth shut and see how the scene played out. As it turned out, this was one of my more prudent decisions.

Suddenly an angry face topped with a Stetson, was staring through one of the closed windows at Duke, who was slumped in his seat, bent over laughing, while the sweet, young lovely named Laurie, was on the floor in front of him, apparently massaging his crotch, giggling.

Catching sight of Duke, the mad-faced Stetson guy yelled, "You little sonovabitch. I'll break your ass!" He smacked his fist against the window. It didn't break. Duke wasn't laughing any more. He slid down onto the floor between the seats.

"Oh, honey," one Texas bimbette said to Duke, "don't mind Hank. He's just jealous."

"No shit!" said Nick, sitting across the aisle with Missy Mae on his lap. "You girls better get off the bus," his words confirming, as I suspected, that he was the more practical of the two musicians. Clearly, he didn't want his mouth re-arranged.

The fist pounding got more intense. The Giants were mad as hell and swaying drunk. A couple of Jacks had climbed the Beanstalk and were making off with the golden eggs.

Tex Beneke, the great white Texas oracle, who might have interceded, wasn't there, having already left in his '55 yellow Caddie convertible well on his way by now to whatever town was next on the tour. He didn't travel on the bus with the band; neither did his wife. She drove a red Thunderbird. The two of them bantered back and forth on the road via their CB radios.

"Jesus, let's get out of here," said Zandy, who had been with the band for over five years. He wasn't known for risk-taking. The guys respected him. I guess he didn't want his embouchure adjusted by some crazy cowboys either.

Eddie Matthews spoke up. "You girls gotta get off now. I mean you have to leave the bus right now. We gotta go, and you can't come. Come on now, girls. Out! Now!"

With that the driver swung the door open. The girls gave the dandies long sloppy, liquor-soaked, lipstick-smeared smooches. Uck.

"Hurry up, for crissakes," Eddie said.

The big guys were making their way around the front of the bus toward the door.

"Come on girls," Eddie yelled. "Out. Now!"

Calling out, "Bye, fellas," the two femme fatales alighted, apparently unfazed, then faced their awaiting cowboys.

"Now Hank, honey," the one named Laurie said. "We was just havin' some fun, some harmless fun. So doncha' go gettin' yourself all upset now."

Seymour slammed the door shut and gunned the motor a few times, just to let everyone know we were leaving. The two "trees" were shaking serious fists toward where they figured Duke and Nick were sitting. The girls clung to their guys' arms, doing their we-got-to-soothe-our-stupid-but-necessary-men tap dance. It appeared they knew the steps well.

The time had come to *move*. As we drove off in a cloud of Texas dust, Frank Huggins, the carefree lead trumpet player, yelled, "Hi Ho Silver! Away!"

Duke and Nick sat together and chuckled over their escape from the jaws of justice. Duke got out his little black book and started discussing possibilities for the next town. The man was dedicated.

Hermie opened a book to read. Zandy and some of the guys started a card game in the back. Frank was sipped a pint of gin through a straw while reading aloud to no one in particular from *Downbeat* magazine. Eddie Matthews sat up front schmoozing the girl singer, telling her how he could get her a record deal after the tour was over.

I was a slim 130 pounds at the time, and five foot seven. I climbed up into the shallow overhead luggage rack, flattened a small pillow, stretched out on my back, and settled in for the all-night drive to wherever. Studying the ceiling, inches away from my nose, I asked myself if this was the glamorous career I imagined traveling on the road would be, making memorable music with a famous name band.

I listened to Duke and Nick compare notes and to Frank read aloud, laughing with sheer enjoyment at *Downbeat's* penchant for hyperbolic descriptions of idolized jazz musicians. I could overhear Eddie working his I'm-really-an-important-guy routine on the girl singer. Random jokes from the poker game filtered up to me as the bus lurched down the highway into the night.

How lucky I was to have made it. I was playing with a name band. Finally. But though I appreciated the opportunity immensely, something was missing. I figured this was not the way to fame and fortune, and certainly not the way I wanted to spend my life, especially with a family. The road leads nowhere. Sooner or later you're right back where you started. I would have to think carefully before touring again.

'Think carefully?'Hmm. It's about time.

(Arrugg ...)

TEN

RHAPSODY IN BLUE

He banged the baton repeatedly until it shattered against the conductor's music stand. "Goddammit, who's playing the clarinet solo?" he growled.

A hush swept over the orchestra, as if fanned by a silent wind. "I am," I said, ears burning at being singled out, heart pounding. *Who does he think he is, Toscanini?*

Its guest conductor, the famous Paul Whiteman, thus interrupted the afternoon rehearsal of the Connecticut Symphony Summer Pops Concert.

The summer after the tour with the Tex Beneke Band I was asked to play the outdoor Pop series with the Connecticut Symphony. I was primarily an alto saxophonist, which was the reason they hired me. In classical circles I was called a doubler, that is, I doubled on sax, clarinet, flute and piccolo, something that's par for most pop/jazz woodwind players. But for many symphony musicians, who focus a lifetime on perfecting facility on a single instrument, the term carried with it the implication that a doubler, ipso facto, could not be outstanding on any single instrument. The doubler, however, might be considered acceptable on the instruments doubled.

Even though the term's negative connotation was fading, there was still a *sub rosa* stigma attached to it, as in, "Oh, he plays well enough, I guess, but of course he's a doubler."

I was sensitive to this and frankly didn't like it. Although I never had the discipline to practice hours and hours perfecting the technique required to be a polished classical performer, I knew about swing and rhythm, sight-reading, intonation, phrasing, style, tone, how to blend with an ensemble, and improvisation. I knew I was an experienced and competent professional. So when I got the call, I was anxious to show the classical guys just how well a doubler could play. I took it as a challenge.

The afternoon of the concert, I drove to rehearsal at Fairfield University Field in high spirits—windows down, warm wind blowing in my face, singing along with the radio. I felt good after the stint with Beneke. I had attained a major career goal and that was encouraging.

The outdoor facility could seat more than 8,000 people, not including the blanket crowd. Folding chairs were set up on the mown grass in hundreds of converging rows facing toward the stage. The roofed music shed stage, trimmed in dark green wood, was framed by tall pine trees. Flower boxes full of chrysanthemums decorated the front on the stage floor. On the ground in front of the six-foot high stage, tall potted ferns swayed in a gentle breeze. To the audience the symphony musicians must have appeared suspended, framed in a garden of greenery.

The opening half of the program featured Paul Whiteman, an American music icon, conducting the works of George Gershwin: A Gershwin medley followed by *An American in Paris*, and finally *Rhapsody in Blue*. Johnny Mathis was the featured performer for the second half of the concert.

When I sat down behind my music stand and thumbed through Whiteman's music, I saw that the solo clarinet cadenza, which opens *Rhapsody In Blue* —starting with a trill on a low G and followed by a long, glissando to a high D—was scored in this arrangement to be played on clarinet by the lead saxophonist (the doubler) and not by the orchestra's first chair classical clarinetist.

Now I was even more excited. It would be a welcome challenge. And what an honor it would be to play the clarinet solo conducted by Paul Whiteman, the man who had actually commissioned the original work. The Rhapsody had been premiered in 1924 by Whiteman and became an enduring classic, known worldwide; the clarinet glissando opening was like the signature of the piece. And to think this was happening right in my hometown area with the Symphony. How many pop musicians get to do something like that in their lifetime? I was psyched.

But the feeling didn't last long. Right at the start of the rehearsal, as Whiteman (with a theatrical overhead flourish) attempted to give the initial downbeat for the Gershwin Medley, he slipped off his high stool, knocking his music stand from the podium. The score went sprawling, as he landed on his corpulent butt. *What happened? Maybe he's sick?*

Whiteman was a large, graying, bald man, baggy-eyed and pear-shaped. With his tired eyes he had the sanguine look of a man trying to squeeze a few more years out of past glories. His pencil-thin black moustache slimmed the length of his upper lip and resembled the look of an old-fashioned movie actor. The stash was like a dark latitude marker across the middle of his high fore-headed map.

He shook off his fall without comment and recovered his composure. We began again. A couple of minutes into the medley he stopped the orchestra abruptly and began to rail at the drummer, getting redder and redder by the second.

"Dammit, drummer," he snarled, "What's the matter with you? Can't you read notes?"

I could feel the orchestra getting uneasy. We knew then it was going to be a long afternoon.

"Play it again," Whiteman groused. "And this time play it right."

We started over, only to have him stop again almost immediately. "Jesus," he said shaking his head, "that's not it, what do you think you're doing, buddy? Take it again from the top. And play it like it's supposed to be played! Understand?"

Silence from the drummer.

After stopping us a third time, he turned on his stool and yelled over to the stage manager, "Get on the phone and get my drummer Johnny up here from New York right away."

This guy's going to blow a serious fuse, I thought. That kind of anger isn't good for you. We didn't rehearse any more of the Gershwin medley. The truth was, no one could follow his direction. He couldn't manage to give a recognizable downbeat or count off in time. Nor did he conduct with authority or clarity; tempo changes, at best, were a guess. It was as if he expected the orchestra to know the arrangements. We tried to be polite, even though he showed us little respect. After all, he was Paul Whiteman. We wanted to respect him. At one time he was known as the "King of Jazz" and he had been a great innovator. Then, too, he was old. But why did he need his own drummer? I thought maybe he just couldn't conduct.

We managed to get through the next piece, *An American in Paris,* without incident, though he continued to make a sour face when tempo changes apparently didn't seem quite perfect to him. The orchestra played beautifully, but all around me the feeling was tense.

Rhapsody in Blue was next. I had never played the famous clarinet short cadenza before, but I was vaguely familiar with it. Short. Nothing to it. A possible intimidating factor, however, is that the clarinet starts the Rhapsody all alone. You're there completely exposed, with your bare tone hanging out.

I wasn't quite sure what Whiteman wanted when, while he was looking off to the side of the stage, he sent out an off-handed wave in the general direction of the woodwind section. There was no cue, no downbeat. So nothing happened. No one played anything. He looked back, grimaced and yelled, "All right, PLAY!" With that he waved his baton wildly at the woodwinds, apparently indicating that the solo clarinet cadenza should start NOW. So I began playing it, note for note, exactly as it was written on the manuscript.

That's when he threw his second tantrum, banging his baton repeatedly against his stand, long after the orchestra had stopped, until it broke into pieces, one of which landed in the hair of a lovely young cellist seated directly in front of him. He was really out-of-sorts. I almost felt sorry for him. I shouldn't have.

"Goddammit," he bellowed, glaring at the woodwind section, his hands on his considerable hips. "Who's playing the clarinet solo?"

I could feel eighty pairs of musician eyes swing toward me like converging mini-spotlights. They knew who was playing the clarinet solo.

"I am, " I said, trying to sound relaxed, like it didn't matter. I wasn't going to let him bully me, as he had done to the drummer. I was a little sensitive to that kind of treatment.

"You ever hear my recording (hic) of *Rhapsody in Blue?* " He slurred loudly, trying to stare me down.

Now I understand. He's …

"No, I haven't," I said clearly. I was polite, but a far cry from being humble.

"Well, for Crissakes, go out and buy it!"

"OKAY, " I said, matter-of-factly. The situation was clear to me, as I'm sure it was to the other musicians. He had a problem.

Even so, I was embarrassed. I felt that my reputation as a good musician was in jeopardy, and I couldn't let that happen. At the same time, I had no idea of what he really wanted to hear.

Following a break, we rehearsed with Johnny Mathis. His arrangements were fine and he was a perfect gentlemen. He was most appreciative, and so were we. After rehearsal I immediately drove to Zera's Music store in Fairfield, with my clarinet and the music, and asked if they had Paul Whiteman's recording of *Rhapsody in Blue*.

I took the 12" LP into one of the audition booths and listened several times to the cadenza. Aha. So that's the way it should sound—a long glissando. In my music the notes were written out with no indication that they should be connected into one long upward slide. The tie-slur mark was missing. Maybe a copyist error. I should have known better. I corrected the part, took out my clarinet and played along with the record several more times until I had it. I'd show that has-been turkey tonight.

Fifteen minutes before concert time I was seated on stage in my white dinner jacket, silently fingering the clarinet solo. Other musicians were warming up. A couple of them said to me, "Everything okay, Gene?"

"Yeah, sure. No problem," I said. See? I knew some of them would be concerned over whether I could play it right. Doubler, they probably thought.

The July night clearly showed a starry roof of heaven. Though the field had been sprayed that afternoon and again an hour before the concert, some of God's little bugs were hovering around the lights. Soon the lights dimmed. Time to begin the concert.

When Whiteman walked on stage to applause, he seemed to have recovered from the afternoon's disaster. I could only hope. Surprisingly, the program went well. Before his final number, *Rhapsody in Blue*, he went to the microphone, resplendent in his size 48-long white dinner jacket, red bow tie, and red cummerbund, and told the story of how he had asked "George to compose something different for his orchestra, a composition that would be both classical and jazz."

"The result, ladies and gentlemen," he went on to say with grand pomp, *Rhapsody In Blue*, a composition that I had the privilege of premiering at Aeolian Hall in New York City over thirty years ago. Of course the rest is history." He paused. The audience applauded warmly. You would have thought he had composed the Rhapsody himself.

When he turned around and faced the orchestra, my clarinet was already at my lips, waiting for his downbeat, or gesture, or whatever sign might come my way. I could feel the tension in the orchestra building. The audience hushed. He raised his baton.

At that precise moment there was a terrifying scream from a woman somewhere out in the crowd. It cut the night like lightning slices darkness. She kept screaming, running wildly though the audience toward the stage, apparently hysterical. The audience stilled. Her screams smothered even the silence. Ushers froze where they stood. Special police ran to her aid and carried her, still screaming, to an ambulance that was kept parked behind the stage.

It was terrible. What had happened? The crowd was now buzzing. I was supposed to be ready to play the cadenza. I tried to re-focus my concentration.

Whiteman had stood to the side of the stage, partly facing us, watching the interrupting drama unfold. When it was over, smiling graciously to us and then to the audience, he shrugged with understanding, as if to say, "Oh well, what can you do?" then returned to center stage. The crowd applauded. They were with him.

When he turned to the orchestra, I made it a point to look right at him, so he'd know I was ready to go. I wasn't going to screw up this moment, screams or no screams. He smiled broadly at me. Huh? He indicated that I should stand up for the solo. When the audience had quieted completely, he gave me a little nod, a raised eyebrow, an expression that said, "Ready?" I affirmed with a serious nod. He tapped briskly on his music stand two short ticks with a new baton, raised his arms, then gave me a precise downstroke to begin.

I hesitated for a millisecond.

In that instant I could sense panic grip the musician next to me. Sometimes my mind does wander. He nudged my arm with his elbow just as I was starting to play. I guess he was afraid I would be late playing the cue. I blew into my horn at the same time I was jostled. A terrible squawking squeak came out. Whiteman became enraged. He must have thought I was making fun of him. The audience amused themselves with snickers. He came over to my stand and ordered me off the stage. I got up and left, totally embarrassed. It was six months before I'd play again. Eventually I moved to a different city.

*

Oh my, you really do have a flair for the dramatic.
A "squawking squeak?" Get real.

(Heh, heh, just kidding; you know.)

Do me a favor. Tell it like it was.

I hesitated for a millisecond, disregarded the impact of the screams and proceeded to deliver the cadenza with conviction, exactly the way Whiteman wanted it. From the first note I could feel the tone I was producing resonate with sureness. Even though the moment was brief, I felt at one with the music. You live for such moments. You dream about them. They complete you like no other exultation can. I was helping to create a first-rate happening. And nothing beats the realization of creative accomplishment.

When I finished, Whiteman smiled a raised eyebrow. "Thank you," he nodded, and conducted the rest of the piece comfortably. His regular drummer was playing in the orchestra, and that relaxed him.

With a gracious bow he took the generous applause of the audience, swept his arm back to the fine piano soloist, who took well-deserved accolades and then gestured over to me before recognizing the orchestra with a gallant sweep. I was proud of myself. I had done a professional job.

He had put us through hell that afternoon, but by evening he had gathered himself together and performed with the control and charisma the audience expected of a man of his reputation.

It was an enlightening experience, and I was glad I had done well. I still thought he was an ass.

The next day we found out that the screaming young woman, still in hospital, had reason to be upset. A buzzing Japanese beetle had crawled deep into her ear canal.

Poor woman; she never got to hear my little solo.

**

Clip from a Hollywood film bio about Paul Whiteman
"The King of Jazz" - *Rhapsody in Blue*, circa ♫ 1930
Whiteman, center top, with baton.
Foreground, unidentified
featured clarinetist and show girl

11

THE MUSICIANS CLUB

"You don't sound so bad for a white guy," Tiny said after I finished playing a few jazz choruses on "Comin' Home Baby." I appreciated the compliment. Tiny was a bass player and organized the jam sessions at the Musicians Club. Short, very wide—a "Mister Five by Five" type—dark-skinned, red-haired, he had a calm way about him that was easy to like. I liked him even more after his compliment.

The Musicians Club was a dive, but it was a great place to jam once in a while, especially at this time in my life. I was pleased with my development as a lead alto saxophonist and multi-reed professional, and was getting a respected reputation in the business. However, I wanted to improve my improvisational skills, which are, after all, the heart of jazz.

When you're learning the unfamiliar, you have to let go of what you feel secure with in order to grow, especially when you're trying to develop a new musical technique—early results usually don't sound too wonderful, so initially there is not much to encourage you. Improvisation is quite a different skill from reading music. You can't read it. You have to create it. An instant synergy between the mind's ear and playing what you hear has to occur. Developing this facility can be humbling; it takes time. There is no shortcut. For me the process of improving was often its own reward and the leap into new ideas usually brought me lasting pleasure and energy. I sensed this was the time and place for me to take that leap.

I was off the road for good, I thought. No more Ted Lewis stuff. No more corny music. Or Texas dance hall brawls. No more trying to sleep every other night in luggage racks on one-nighter buses. No more schlepping luggage and horns into cheap hotels, checking out half asleep, forgetting socks, underwear, razors, alarm clocks, toothbrushes, and wallet—once even a watch. And no more separations from my family.

My kids hardly knew me anymore. I thought when I returned from the road I could resume being a father and husband right from where I left off. But it wasn't so easy. My children were confused. They constantly deferred to their mother. I became impatient and would yell at them out of frustration. I never used to do that. "You're mean, Daddy," one of my daughters once said when I told her, "No more television, it's time to go to bed," not knowing it was a special program for her.

"Be patient, Gene," my wife said, "they have to get used to you being home again. It'll take a little time."

I understood. But it hurt. My poor little male ego was in crisis. I was no longer the *Grand Fromage* and didn't like the minor role that I had been newly assigned. I'm home now. And I'm staying. I'm their father. Don't they understand? I knew I would make progress toward being a better father if I slowed down and let things happen naturally. So I did. However, the matter of my career would never leave my head.

During the next eight years I worked full time for WICC Radio as an account executive, a euphemism for commercial time salesman. Not that I thought of myself as a salesman. Nor did I think of radio as a career. I was a musician, always looking for ways to make music my life's work. It was dishonest, I admit.

I couldn't commit to the station job the way the owners had a right to expect.

When I signed up a new account on my first day in the field, they told me I could move up quickly in this industry. The prospects of a career in radio, however, while more interesting than retailing, didn't seem to promise the same personal fulfillment as music. So along with learning how to be successful on the job, I knew I needed to continue developing my musical skills.

On weekends I played club dates and weddings—sometimes I'd have three or four small bands working under my name on a Saturday night. I'd make the rounds, play a set here, shake hands there, and collect the checks. In the meantime I kept cultivating New York City contacts, once in a while getting calls to play record dates with fine musicians like Doc Severinsen, Ron Carter, Richard Davis, Clark Terry, Herbie Hancock, Urbie Green, Gato Barbieri, Angelo DiPippo, Jerome Richardson, Steve Lacey, Randy Brecker, Mike Mantler, Carla Bley, and Ed Shaunessey. Studies with Joe Allard in New York continued, as well as practicing my horns two hours each day. I wrote and recorded a TV score for a feature cartoon pilot called Billy Bounce. It was good. I liked it. The producers did too. The pilot didn't get sold. We were getting by ... barely.

During this decade, I also substituted occasionally on replacement gigs with traveling name bands like Billy May, Duke Ellington, Buddy Morrow and Ralph Marterie. I heard about Thursday night jam sessions at the Bridgeport Colored Musicians Union located on South Main Street, and went there to learn by listening to other musicians and sitting in with them. In jam sessions you can tell right away where your weaknesses are.

When Tiny asked me to play there regularly with the house band, I told him I'd love to.

"Pays twelve to fifteen, depending on how many door admissions that night," he said. "Admission is a dollar." Obviously money was not the motivation for me playing there — although every little bit helped. As Duke Ellington wrote, "It Don't Mean a Thing If It Ain't Got That Swing." And that's what this place was all about. No waltzes or polkas or country club music. Just straight up blues and jazz.

In the 1950s the American Federation of Musicians was still a segregated union. In Bridgeport the white Local, #63, had a spacious hall downtown, where they held monthly meetings, lots of card games ... and no jam sessions. The union collected a ten percent traveling tax from all musicians and bands that came into the city's jurisdiction to play, even for one night, as did most locals at that time.

If you were a professional, you had to belong to the union or you couldn't work. A few older cronies who mostly played poker and smoked cigars in the meeting hall ran our Local. Sure, they had instruments, but didn't play them much any more, except maybe for a Labor Day band concert in the park. I was a young rebel and didn't respect them. As far as I was concerned, the local union was not about music. It was a club.

The Colored Local on the other hand, as everyone, even its own members, called it, had this funky, quasi-nightclub meeting hall called the Musicians Club.

The club was a third floor walk-up over a wholesale plumbing supply store in the industrial end of town. A wide, double flight of wooden stairs with a landing halfway up was the only way to get there. I once counted the steps—thirty-eight. The hike was always worth it.

The club had swinging music three nights a week and after-hours jam sessions on a fourth night. The club featured a shot-and-a-beer bar for the drinkers and attracted the most relaxed collection of partiers I'd ever seen. But mostly the scene was about the music.

Customers, no matter what ethnicity, dressed up. Even the musicians wore jackets and sometimes ties. The place itself was rather stark, with linoleum floors and fluorescent light fixtures covered with red crepe paper. The small wooden dance floor had been painted red, obviously often; a fresh coat was added when the floor became scuffed and faded. If paint had ever been applied to the walls, it had long since retreated into the pores of the wallboard. Not a mirror or a picture was hung to interrupt the drabness.

None of that mattered to the folks who came there, because the club was theirs. It was their place to hang out, where they could make as much noise as they wanted, enjoy the music they liked, and raise friendly hell when they so chose. This unpretentious place was a musical Mecca for musicians interested in developing improvisation abilities.

The club had a capacity of about 150 people. It was dark, and sexy in a way, though pretty loud at times. A dozen or so wooden tables and chairs surrounded the dance floor. Little racial animosity was shown toward its few white patrons, and none to musicians. Nobody bothered you. Once in a rare while, police came to break up a fight, or because occasionally somebody got quietly knifed "a little"—usually in a dispute over whose mistress was with whom. "He be dancing so close she be on the other side of him, that's why I cut him."

Every night a different group played, usually four or five guys, most of whom belonged to the Colored Union. A few of us grays went up there on Thursdays to sit in and jam and enjoy the usually joyous, rockin', swinging, straight-ahead music. The place was cool, especially if you could really play.

If you were a fake, however, and tried to pass yourself off as a player, even if you managed to blow a few flashy licks you copped off a Charlie Parker or Cannonball Adderley record, they'd know it soon enough. They'd figure you were trying to be *in* with the folks. It didn't work.

For instance, you could wear the coolest suit and hippest tie and have the latest shades on, and sling phrases around like, "Yeah, man, I'm hip," or "Like, crazy, man." But if what came out of your horn when you played didn't live up to your affectations, then watch out. These folks knew good notes from bad notes. It was their thing. They listened. Music mattered. Even if couples were dancing wrapped around each other like ficus plants, they'd still be listening to the band.

One night I was playing at Guest Night, standing alongside Ray Duseki, a white musician sitting in on tenor sax for a set. We were on the slightly elevated bandstand at one end of the room, opposite the bar. The narrow platform was about ten feet long and six feet deep. Behind it were large floor-to-ceiling windows, covered with heavy brown paper, facing the street below. A couple of small red spotlights, screwed into the ceiling in front of the mini stage, were aimed at the bandstand.

I finished playing a few choruses on "Walkin' the Blues" — played it simple and uncomplicated, trying to make it swing. I would have played more impressively if I could have. But hell, that was why I was there. When I finished, there were a few modest comments from nearby dancers ... "All right", "Uh-huh", "I hear you". I felt good about that. I knew I was getting there.

I was making progress. Or maybe they were just being kind. Then it was Ray's turn. He proceeded to blow at least fifteen choruses on his tenor, one after the other, each of which seemed to be filled with a thousand notes. He was dressed in a gray sharkskin, double-breasted suit with a blue shirt and black knit tie and pointed black shoes, looking like he was a serious cat. He had all the right moves—the swaying, eyes shut, elbows flapping, horn raised up toward the ceiling for a few bars, and yes, the climactic knee squats, denoting special emotional involvement at certain highlights of his solo—all of which supposedly added to his image as a heavy player. Man, he looked like the real thing. But what he was playing didn't swing. Just notes were coming out. And everyone knew it. Except maybe Ray. He didn't stop soloing.

The dancers stopped dancing and started grumbling. That was the first time I ever heard *"sh-it"* pronounced as a two-syllable word. I liked it. Usually, if a guy didn't cut it when he sat in, no one said anything. They would just glare at him until he got the message.

This time wide-man Tiny decided it was just too much. While the drummer and pianist kept playing, he put down his bass and bulged up to Ray. "Whoa, man," he said, "You know what your problem is? You so hip, you hoppin' over what's happenin'. Take a break, man."

Tiny's remark wasn't sensitive. I felt bad for Ray. But Tiny's integrity was on the line with the folks who were watching. He probably figured that if he didn't act then, they'd let him know about it later.

Nobody else said anything. Ray put his horn in his case and walked to the door, sensing, I'm sure, the chill he was getting from the crowd. He couldn't seem to get out of there fast enough.

It wasn't that Ray's playing was unimpressive—some people don't play well. But because he came on with all the accoutrements and attitude of an important dude, then didn't play well, the crowd marked him as a jive-ass, honky no-talent. It was *vox populi*. Thumbs down. An instantaneous judgment. Tiny would probably dis-invite him if he ever showed up again.

After Ray left, Tiny turned to me, as if to apologize, and said, "The man thinks flashy playing is jazz."

I nodded in agreement.

In this place music was a meritocracy. As in sports, the best players got the most respect. Bad ones didn't get any. I figured I was just a utility player in this league.

And then there was Hank Conroy—everyone knew him as Zeke—the piano player who played the gig most nights. Zeke was white, tall, lanky, and brown-haired, wore glasses and played great. He'd been around and had street savvy.

One night I was in the middle of playing "Misty" on the alto, a nice slow ballad, trying to make it sound warm and sexy and honest. Folks on the floor were dancing belly to belly. I had shut my eyes. I was into it. "Play Sweet Georgia Brown," I heard a gruff voice say.

I opened my eyes. Several people were close to the bandstand. I couldn't tell who spoke. We kept playing and I looked over at Zeke. He shrugged, like he couldn't care less who was requesting what. I resumed playing "Misty" and closed my eyes again doing my reverie thing. I heard the voice again, this time louder.

"Play Sweet Georgia Brown." I looked up and there was this tall, thin, woozy, red-eyed guy with stinking breath swaying right in front of my face. He had no eyelashes, and his eyes seemed to be focused somewhere between here and Tuesday. He was drunk or drugged up, or both.

Damn it, I thought, drunk or not this guy is way out of line. I was there to play real music and not to contend with jerks. Besides, since I had a few friends around the club who liked me, I decided to handle the situation with acceptable righteous indignation.

"Hey, man, be cool," I said. "We'll play your tune right after this one." That sounded reasonable to me. Maybe I did have a bit of attitude showing. But hey, what's right is right. The guy should have been straightened out. And I figured it was up to me to do it.

I stopped playing, backed away and shot him some rays. Right away Zeke picked up the melody I had abandoned. He played it beautifully on the beat-up upright piano, the thumb and little finger of his right hand spreading out to play the melody in octaves, as if Errol Garner were there in person. I loved listening to Zeke.

The next thing I knew, a five-inch switchblade knife clicked out from the guy's hand and assumed a strategic position just below Zeke's left ear. "Play Sweet Georgia Brown," the geek said to the back of Zeke's head. The blade caught the light just so, and for a moment flashed like a mirror. I didn't know what to do. Dumbfounded, I didn't move.

Zeke froze. The geek plunged the knife into Zeke's shoulder. Blood spilled like a slow garden hose. Zeke fell to the floor. The knifer turned to me, waved the bloody blade. I jumped back, grabbed a folding chair from the bandstand and threw it at him. He lost his balance for a moment. One of the dancers jumped on his back. Dragged him to the floor. More piled on, punching him, kicking him mercilessly. A nurse in the crowd first-aided Zeke, who by then was sitting up, dazed, wondering what had happened. He looked at the floor, shook his head slowly, and managed to say weakly, "I never did like that tune." Police came, arrested and cuffed the assailant and took him away. Zeke was taken to the hospital in a police car. The musicians and I packed up our instruments and left. Zeke recovered.

*

Gene, would you mind replaying that knife scene? This time with film in the camera?

(Okaaaay, so it didn't happen quite like that.)

The blade caught the light just so, and for an instant flashed like a mirror. I didn't know what to do. Dumbfounded, I froze.

Without missing a beat or even turning around to see who said it, Zeke immediately aborted "Misty" and ripped into an up tempo stride piano version of "Sweet Georgia Brown," as loud as he could play it—sounding like a mechanical piano in a shooting gallery. Satisfied, the man nodded, walked away, and mingled in with the crowd. The rest of us joined in and jammed out on the newly selected tune.

I was a little shaken up. I could have been slashed, or worse—and I knew it. I forgot where I was. I was a guest here. I should have been more careful. I could just see the newspapers, "Local Musician, Father of Four, Stabbed in Musicians Club over Sweet Georgia Brown."

Zeke's quick thinking averted what could have been a messy situation. We all forced a laugh when we finished the song and took a break. Zeke said, "Where'd he go?"

"You shoulda' listened to the man," Tiny said to me casually.

"Sh-it!" I said. "If that guy ever comes in here again and asks for a tune, I'll give him a 'Yes, sir' so fast he'll think he's God *and* Charlie Parker."

They laughed. I laughed, too. But I was serious. I never thought music could be so important that I might get stabbed over it. I guess there's more than one way to get your favorite tune played.

I learned a lot about concepts of swing and time and honest notes at the Musicians Club, which is what I set out to do. I also learned that jazz is a lot like life—if you don't have anything to say, shut up.

Since those days, whenever my mouth is about to get me into trouble, I try humming a few bars of "Sweet Georgia Brown." Sometimes it helps … but not very often.

**

12

WHITE FLASH

"You mean Katherine Hepburn? *The* Katherine Hepburn?" I asked.

"That's right," said lean Mike Donato (not his real name), the theater's musician contractor. "Now would you play this cadenza?" He wasn't asking.

A symphony clarinetist might have known the passage, but I had never seen it. So I just plowed straight ahead and played the notes, sight-reading fairly accurately, but not yet fully understanding its flow and how it should be phrased. I knew I could do much better with a second crack at it. "Let me try that again," I said apologetically, yet with enough enthusiasm to show my confidence.

"No, that won't be necessary." He quickly removed the music from the stand. "Now play some of this Mozart Concerto. Start at the *con brio* section, right here." He pointed to a place on the music he had just opened up. "Ready?" Again, it wasn't a question. Without hesitating, he began conducting using a pencil as a baton.

The tempo seemed fast, even for a *con brio* marking. Too fast. Too many notes. Damn. I'm making too many mistakes. What is this, a race?

Mike stopped me before I got through half a page and gave me a narrow look, pursing his lips, rolling his eyes, arching his overgrown brows, and putting on a plebian expression—as if I had tried to tell him a tired joke. I let it pass. This was not the time to take issue, though his attitude did gall me. He was a symphony musician, and he knew I wasn't. To him I was, therefore, not up to his standards. For some reason he was out to prove the point. He didn't know what he didn't know.

The theater's 1958 season required an alto saxophonist who could double A-flat and B-flat clarinets and flute for its pit orchestra. Since I was the most accomplished multi-reed player in the area, and was asked to audition, I figured the audition was more or less a formality.

After I played the Mozart, however, Donato put on a labored, I-told-you-so smirk and inclined his condescension to the other fellow on the audition committee, violist Louie Capucci.

Affable Louie, content in his caloricly challenged physique, shrugged at Donato, as if to say, "So he didn't play it perfectly, but it really wasn't bad."

"Gene," Louie said, "try the cadenza again? And this time relax. Take your time with it."

I played it with more understanding of its proper phrasing, not just producing correct notes. It flowed. I liked it.

"Good," he said, "now take the beginning of the Mozart again, not quite so fast."

It was much better than the first time.

"Okay. Now, play a tune you know on the sax, anything you like, something that shows your tone and phasing."

"Sure," delivering a confident, if slightly slurpy, version of Duke's "I Got It Bad And That Ain't Good" á la Johnny Hodges, the foremost exponent of the gushy romantic style. *Ah, this is more my element. I'm sounding real good now.*

Louie was smiling. Three quarters of the way through, he stopped me and said, "That's fine, Gene."

The two of them got up and walked to the far side of the room, conferring.

"So Katherine Hepburn's going to be in the cast, huh?" I called over to them, trying to divert their attention from dwelling on my mistakes. They didn't respond.

When they came back Donato offered dismissively, "Actually, she's the star."

"My God, that's incredible. I mean ... she's a great actress. And she's coming here to do the plays this season? Wow. How great." *Am I talking too much? I need this job. I don't want to blow it. I can cut it, if they just give me a chance.*

"She's already here. The cast has been rehearsing for two weeks," said Donato with an indifferent tone.

"But how come you're auditioning musicians? Is the play a musical? I never heard of Shakespeare done as a musical."

"No, this is legit Shakespeare," said Louie. "The music is incidental stuff, segues between scenes, at the end of acts, transition music, and a few original songs. Virgil Thompson wrote the score. He'll be here in person to rehearse the orchestra."

"Virgil Thompson?" I hadn't a clue.

"The producers commissioned him to compose it. They want the productions to be extra special this season," Louie said.

"I guess. Well, like, cool, man." What a nice guy, I thought.

Donato grimaced. "Hmm. Look, Gene," indicating he was in charge again, thank you, "we think you can probably handle the music. So you've got the job. It pays scale. Don't forget you need to double both clarinets—B flat and A—and alto sax, of course.

"There are also a few flute and piccolo parts, but Claude Monteux is the principal flutist." He pronounced the name *Cloed,* as the French say it, instead of *Clawed,* like they might say it in Bridgeport. For a moment I didn't get it.

"Who?" I said.

"Cloed Monteux ... from the Concertgebouw?"

"Oh, the Concertgebouw?"

"The symphony orchestra of Amsterdam," Louie offered.

"Oh, right." Again I was clueless. In those days I was into conductors like Stan Kenton, Count Basie, Woody Herman, Dizzy, Duke, and Quincy Jones, and maybe Leonard Bernstein and Toscanini.

"Rehearsals start Wednesday next week," Donato said. "11:00 a.m. sharp." It was more like a challenge than an announcement.

"Right on, man. I'll be here. Thanks, guys."

And so I was hired to play in the orchestral ensemble for the summer/fall season at the American Shakespeare Festival Theater in Stratford, Connecticut, little realizing what would happen to me there. But first let me give you a picture of the place.

By every standard, the theater was elegant. Designed as a modern interpretation of a classic olde theatre, it had a majestic gray teak façade, decorated with flying pennants, coat of arms plaques and highlighted by several red-door entrances.

Nestled on twelve wooded acres amid tall elms on the banks of the Housatonic River in Stratford, about sixty-five miles from New York City, it was a handsome, full-stage, multi-purpose theatrical house, dedicated to performing works of Shakespeare.

Soon it captured the fancy of the American theatrical community from Broadway to Hollywood. Everyone wanted to be associated with it. A formidable cadre of famous actors and directors was assembled to develop and produce high-standard theater.

This year's acting company of over twenty principals included Katherine Hepburn, Alfred Drake — star of "Kismet" on Broadway — and Maurice Carnovski whose sensitive portrayal of Shylock left audiences breathless, plus two renowned directors: John Houseman—fresh from directing *Lust For Life* in Hollywood with Kirk Douglas and who later would direct and star in television's long-running, successful series *The Paper Chase*—and Broadway's Jack Landau.

Without a doubt, however, Katherine Hepburn was the star. Her formidable charisma and artistry were the catalysts that ultimately established the theater's artistic standard—not to mention her considerable draw at the box office.

The stage was different from others I had seen up to then. It was raked in the tradition of an Elizabethan theatre, slanted downward toward the audience. The orchestra was situated under the stage in a dark place I called the dungeon, unseen by the audience. From this location the music could be heard clearly throughout the house, and musicians could hear the stage action. It was possible to walk out from the dungeon into the pit, and watch the performers, unseen by the audience and unnoticed, I believed, by the actors on stage.

The dungeon itself was unlit, except for music stand lights and a single blue light that allowed us to find our places in the darkness. A small, red cue-light would go on at precisely ten seconds before the next music cue so we could prepare.

In a week I settled into a routine. The music was easy and fun to play. But the long waits between cues began to be boring. To pass the time musicians would tinker with their instruments, replace a reed or a string, oil a key or read by the light of the music stands. Sometimes during these lulls, I would go over the fingering of a challenging clarinet passage. But most of the time

I'd just sit there listening to the audience responding to whatever the actors stomping across the stage above were doing.

Eventually, I could identify the actors by the sound of their footsteps. In *Much Ado About Nothing* Larry Gates, who played Dogberry the Constable, had a heavy, slow, kalomp-kalomp-heelskuff walk. I could tell Alfred Drake as Benedick right away as he moved across the stage with his confident, heel-toe strut that never seemed in a hurry. As for Miss Hepburn, who portrayed the feisty Beatrice, her shoes clicked as she walked, with the studied confidence of a woman who was clever, witty and self-assured. At the same time her steps seemed to have a girlish, buoyant quality, as if she were politely deferring to Benedick, yet demonstrating her independence from him. How did she do that? Listening, without seeing the actor's movements, gave me an appreciation of the footstep aspect of acting I would never have noticed.

After several performances, I had my fill of recognizing the sound of actors' feet. I used the minibreaks to go out into the pit and watch snippets of the show, hidden from the audience by the wall that separates the pit from the house. What a rare opportunity to observe Miss Hepburn on stage, so close I could almost touch her. She was enchanting.

Every gesture, every accent, every movement seemed to shape her performance with precise nuance. It was always a masterful example of acting craftsmanship.

After a few nights of this, I found that by timing it just right and watching for the red cue light, I could remain watching the action from the pit until the last possible moment, then run back underneath the stage to my music stand, take up the instrument, just in time to play the next cue.

Donato didn't like my routine at all. "Hey, Hotshot, you better not miss a cue. You're not here to watch the plays."

He was right, of course. *But, oh Donato, you're so dull. You're only thirty-nine, and already you're an old man. While you're* reading *newspapers in the interludes between cues, I'm getting a once-in-a-lifetime theater education. Get a life.*

Three plays were selected for production that season: *Othello, The Merchant of Venice,* in which Miss Hepburn's Portia was extraordinary, and *Much Ado About Nothing,* easily the audience's favorite. *Othello* and *Merchant* were staged in traditional, period Shakespearian costumes. In John Houseman's version of *Much Ado,* set in the American Southwest during the mid-1800s, the actors wore peasant tunics, sombreros, elegant Caballero outfits, boots, shawls, sandals, colorful flowing Mexican skirts, and pastel lace dresses.

What made his direction particularly interesting for the musicians was that we had to be on stage in crowd scenes, once to play for the courtyard entrance of Don Pedro's army, and again in the beginning of the Finale to play for the cast waltz scene.

We were costumed in baggy white muslin peasant pants, white muslin tunics with long, full sleeves, white neckerchiefs, sandals, and white rope ties for belts. Some of us wore sombreros.

Each day, before the day's performances, we arrived an hour early to apply moustaches, sideburns, or beards, with makeup gum, and get into full costume. The extras, including musicians, had lines in one of the scenes—well, more accurately, cheering and yelling "Yea, yeah, yea, hur-ray," thus creating the effect of a boisterous, happy crowd. For serious musicians, who often seek refuge behind their instruments when required to be on-stage, this was heady stuff. They shied away from even the most basic acting attempts. They were uncomfortable with being on stage. Some of them froze when it was time to get into character, even as anonymous members of a Mexican crowd. Of course the audience was always focused on Katherine Hepburn or Alfred Drake, but the self-conscious musicians felt that everyone was looking at them. Naturally.

It was understandable, considering musicians spend years practicing their instruments umpteen hours a day, taking lessons, classes, studying, rehearsing, listening, schooling, and performing. They tend to take themselves seriously as artists. This was true with jazz players I had encountered along the way. Even serious college musicians hated to be in the school's marching band. But I found that professional classical musicians were even more fragile.

I understood the rationale. Their logic might have proposed, would a brain surgeon be required to sing "The Very Thought Of You" to nurses while he was performing a frontal lobotomy? Would a university bio-physicist be expected to break out in a tap dance for his students in the lecture hall? So why should an accomplished musician be asked to act?

Personally, I loved the performing aspect. In fact, I really got into it. As rehearsals proceeded, John Houseman could see my natural-born ham-ism coming out and made me the front guy in the crowd. Maybe because I was the shortest? Naw.

Katherine Hepburn had propelled the company's performances to a high artistic level with much acclaim. You would think someone with such influence and fame might be affected and difficult to deal with. But not Miss Hepburn. Between acts, and for an hour or so before curtain, and sometimes thereafter, there was usually a large, friendly, backstage poker game for quarters. Often she would sit in, smoke a cigarillo, and play a few hands with the stagehands and actors. She was fun to watch. No airs or attitude. Since I was not really part of the acting community, I would stand off a bit and observe, marveling at her one-of-the-guys rapport.

Just before the end of Scene iii, Act I, she had a brilliant soliloquy, which she delivered downstage center. I would leave the dungeon and go out into the pit to watch her. It was a pivotal point in the plot, when, overhearing others say that Benedick loved her deeply, Beatrice believes she has grossly misjudged him and decides to devote herself to him completely.

Her delivery of the speech stopped the show with applause every night. But try as I might to stay until the very end, I could not. The transition music to the next scene had to be played right after her soliloquy. So I would watch her till the last possible second before I'd dart back to play the cue.

There was a problem with my nightly trips into the pit. And it wasn't with Donato.

Sailors allude to a phenomenon called the green flash. In subtropical climates, a green light sometimes appears mysteriously on the horizon just as the sun sets. It's rare, but many people have seen it. However, as far as I know, only one person has ever seen the *white flash*—Katherine Hepburn. Let me explain.

One night during her monologue, I decided I would stay pit-watching her to the last split second before I had to get back to my music stand. This time I did manage to catch one more phrase or so before I had to make a run for it.

After the play, when the lights went up and the house was emptying, I put my horns in their cases and strolled into the backstage lounge to watch the fun. The stagehands and some of the actors were already ensconced in a lively hand of poker. Several of the cast were milling about, doing whatever actors do backstage after a performance, chatting, flirting, laughing, changing.

Suddenly Miss Hepburn came storming into the area in full costume, her eyes blazing, and demanded, "Who *the hell* is that in the pit when I'm doing the soliloquy?"

The room hushed. The poker game froze. Jokes suspended in mid punch lines. The musicians knew I was the one. No one breathed. Miss Hepburn searched faces around the room.

"Well?"

At length, a barely audible voice emerged from a far corner. "It's me. I'm the one." It was my voice. But I didn't recognize it.

She stomped over to where I was standing in my white tunic, white pants, white rope belt and white neckerchief. "Well, just what *the hell* are you doing there?"

Even when she was mad—and she was—I loved the clipped way she separated her words and the nasal sound of her voice.

Everyone was looking at me. I saw Donato sneer at me, with an I-told-you-so, dumb-ass smirk. I deserved it. I wasn't feeling too smart then.

"I'm watching you do the soliloquy," I croaked.

"Yes, I gather that. What's your name?"

"Gene."

"Well damn it, Gene, if you're watching me why are you running back under the stage just when I'm getting close to the end of the piece? Don't you realize that breaks my concentration? Every night, just as I'm building to the climax, I see this *white flash* in my peripheral vision, practically under my nose, dashing back under the stage.

Oh my God, a white flash. Shit, I've been caught. And by Miss Hepburn, the star herself. She's talking at me and she's mad. I'll be fired. What'll I do? Please let me disappear right now.

"Do you have any idea of how terribly distracting that is?" Why on earth arc you doing that?"

"I, I'm so sorry. I'm fascinated by your speech. I was just trying to see you do the end of it before I have to play the next music cue."

"Hmm, I see."

Then a strange thing happened. I could no longer hear her. She was talking to me. I saw her lips moving. But I was fading away to another place. It must have been the stress. I do know that she took my hand, and we were walking.

Suddenly we were all alone in her dressing room and she was standing in costume right in front of me. "Now listen," she said," then declaimed, in character, the ending lines of the noted soliloquy:

> *"And Benedick, love on; I will requite thee,*
> *Taming my wild heart to thy loving hand.*
> *if thou dost love, my kindness shall incite thee*
>
> *To bind our loves up in a holy band.*
> *For others say thou dost deserve, and I*
> *Believe it better than reportingly."*

"Will that do, Gene?" She smiled easily right into my eyes.

"Oh my God, yes. Thank you, Miss Hepburn. Thank you. That's so kind of you. I'm such a fan of yours."

"Yes. I can see that."

I'm sure the poker game suspended while the players and everyone else stood amazed, listening through the door, as one of the greatest actresses of our time delivered the impassioned soliloquy of Act I for a private audience composed of one young, cocky musician no one had ever heard of.

What a special moment.

What a special lady.

Curiously, her voice faded back in. I could hear her speaking naturally again. I looked around; I was standing in the cast lounge, Miss Hepburn standing next to me, still holding my hand and talking to me gently now.

"… and so you won't ever do that again, will you, Gene?"

"No, Miss Hepburn, I certainly won't. You can be sure of that," I said, even more confused. Had I moved? Had she acted out the soliloquy for me in her dressing room? No one could tell me.

That night was the last time The White Flash went out into the pit to watch Katherine Hepburn. He continued to listen from the dungeon. But whenever she delivered the soliloquy, he could just see her, spinning a web, spellbinding the audience, consuming them, carrying them to another time and place, a moment of perfect theatre.

**

Kate. Rehearsal break.

American Shakespeare Festival Theatre, Stratford, Ct.
♫ circa **1960**

Katherine Hepburn, John Houseman, Alfred Drake
♫ **1957**
(Courtesy: *Stratford Library Association*)

13

THE JAZZ GIANTS

The Jazz Giants began as a fun project, a rehearsal band of professional musicians who wanted to play interesting big band arrangements. I gathered together ex-professional players from the Connecticut area who shared this desire. We formed a creative ensemble called The Modern Music Workshop. The name helped to create an image of musicians-on-a-mission, rather than just another rehearsal band.

This was a large ensemble, even for a big band: five saxes, five trumpets, five trombones, piano, bass, and drums. And when things got going, it was a freight train roaring right at you. I loved the feeling.

I had been a big band leader in high school and college. But the buzz I got from this one was more intense. Standing in front of it, experiencing the sheer power and energy, I knew I was meant to do this, shape and guide this giant live-music machine, which wouldn't exist without me. The band became my instrument.

Even in those early rehearsals we realized something unique was happening. We were creating musical moments that excited us, made us feel alive, feel necessary, a reward of no small significance for musicians who were working at other jobs to make a living. We needed nothing more to satisfy our love of big band jazz than to come together once a week, play new charts, improve our skills and recharge our spirits.

After a year of rehearsing as a workshop group, and thoroughly enjoying the process, an unexpected situation developed. Duke Ellington wrote "I Got It Bad, And That Ain't Good." We had become good, and that could be bad.

The fun band evolved into something more serious, more polished. We paid attention to detail, rehearsed more intensely—not just running though arrangements and going on to the next. We cared about our sound. And as we raised our standards, the character of the band changed.

We found ever more challenging arrangements to stimulate the musicians' desire to excel. Curiously, satisfying our growing desire for recognition became an even greater challenge. Rehearsals were rewarding but that wasn't enough. As the quality improved, the desire to perform our work for an audience imposed itself into our collective psyche. The guys needed applause. I could well understand that. I had never been one to run from an audience.

We discussed the situation and agreed. Although we were a big band rehearsal workshop, we would prepare for a public concert, charge admission, and see what happened. The goal refocused us.

Our first concert was to be a cultural event, so I was able to rent Central High School's 1500-seat auditorium from the Board of Education for $75.00. We presented our show in the summer of 1958 with an expanded group—five saxes, four trombones, five trumpets and a double rhythm section, twenty of us in all. Ensuring our chances of success, I hired well-known jazz names as guest artists, "Zoot and Al,"—Zoot Sims and Al Cohn, two of the finest saxophonists in jazz.

The concert was a sellout; its success immediately established our prestige in the community. In time, our concerts featured other famous jazz musicians as guest artists. We dropped the name Modern Music Workshop and became popularly known as the Jazz Giants.

The band filled a void, not only for ourselves, but also for thousands of people in the area who loved big band jazz, which was fading in popularity and no longer accessible on a regular basis. Although it took much of my time, and made only a little money for me, the effort to keep the *Jazz Giants* growing was extremely rewarding.

Once a week we rehearsed at Bill's Castle, a friendly, worn, neighborhood bar and sometime restaurant on Route 1-A. On Friday and Saturday nights, however, dinner was served in the adjoining dining room with white linens and full portions of ownership pride. Bill, the owner, helped serve the home-cooked foods himself. Truck driver food, I called it—soups, mashed potatoes and gravy, soups, steaks, ham, roast pork, corned beef and cabbage, and a few delicious Hungarian specialty dishes. He wore a long white butcher's apron and chatted with everyone who came into the place.

A façade of white stucco coated the front of the building. Suspended in the bar window facing the street, a garish red neon sign spelled out *Bill's Castle* in script. Inside, opposite the long, polished wood bar, a row of tables and chairs lined the wall. The large adjoining dining room, unused during the week, had seen better days, but it had a dance floor and a small stage at one end. We had a fine place to spread out rehearse a big band.

When I first met Bill, I proposed that we rehearse free in his unused dining room on Wednesday nights. "It'll be good for your business, Bill. And it won't cost you anything."

A week later he said, "Well, we'll give it a try for a few weeks and see what happens."

We were still there after three years. Friends and fans dropped in to hear us. They'd buy a few drinks and liven up the atmosphere. Bill's Castle became a cheap place to go for the jazz cognoscenti in town—good for Bill and good for us.

The Musicians Union office called me one day and said they knew we were playing for free and that we would have to be paid or stop playing there.

"But we're just rehearsing," I said.

They didn't care. "Sorry. Drinks are served. No pay, no play." They were serious, and they had power to fine me if I didn't comply. Finding a place to rehearse a band that size wasn't easy. Since I hadn't had much love for the union before; this incident didn't exactly raise the barometer of goodwill. They just didn't get it. We were simply trying to make music.

So I made out a contract to Bill's Castle for $500 as "Fee for Services," i.e. public rehearsals. Then Bill made out an invoice to me labeled "Rehearsal Hall Rental, $500."

Each week I sent both signed papers to the union office.

There wasn't much they could do about it, and soon they stopped bothering me. But their interference reminded me that the Musicians Union, at least this one at the time, wasn't about helping musicians create music, but about rules and control.

As our band built a quality reputation in the region, we played more well attended concerts and college dances, averaging about four dates a month. We had developed a creative, professional product that deserved to be more widely recognized. I poured all my energies into the Giants, probably more than I should have, given I was still working full time at WICC and WJZZ-FM Radio. I often wonder now why I didn't just enjoy it and stop pushing. But I just couldn't. I was an alpha with a dream—a classic obsessive-compulsive combination. I kept hoping the Jazz Giants could turn into my big break-though with a recording contract.

We had been together over three years when we hit another critical impasse: boredom. This is a killer for musicians, who, once so afflicted, begin to find fault with everything. Rehearsals turned into U.N. meetings.

"How much does the next job pay?" one of them said.

"I can't make rehearsal next week. Too busy," said another.

"How far do we have to drive to the gig?"

"My wife says I'm spending too much time doing this."

"Why are we playing there?"

"What are we playing this chart for?"

We needed an incentive, a new goal, an inspiration, something important, something big, perhaps some kind of event. Day and night I thought about the band. How could I keep us moving forward? How could I boost us over the wall?

Every week I drove from Bridgeport to New York to talk to the best arrangers, looking for that special chart that would take us "up front" and be noticed. I met with agents, managers, promoters, venue owners and record companies. I sent out brochures, flyers, letters, copies of newspaper reviews, demo tapes and pictures. More dates came in, but nothing significant. Without a record, promoters wouldn't touch us. Record companies were simply not investing in unknown big jazz bands any more. Even Count Basie, one of the most famous big band leaders, was working with an eight-piece band for a while. Times were changing.

After almost four years of effort, we were on the verge of fizzling out. The band had to keep growing or it would assuredly fade away. I didn't want that to happen. I needed the Jazz Giants and they needed me. I had to find a way to break through with them.

Then it hit me. What's the world's most prestigious jazz event? There was only one: the Newport Jazz Festival, the father of all jazz festivals—like a World Series of jazz, though not a competition. The biggest names played it. And every year it produced a best-selling record album of its concerts. As out of reach as it was, I decided to go for it. If the band was going to survive, I didn't feel I had much choice.

The line to get to George Wein, the Festival's producer, was, figuratively speaking, a mile long in New York. Hundreds of bands wanted in. Without entree it was hopeless. Promotional mail and letters I sent to the Festival office were sent back unopened. My phone messages were not returned. I talked up our band to everyone I knew in the business in New York. No one could offer any advice except, "You've got to get to George Wein." But there seemed to be no way.

Then fate stepped in. I had met Bob Messinger a few years before at Columbia Records in New York, for whom I was recording a flute piece I had written. He liked what he heard. We chatted afterwards and hit it off. Six months later Columbia released the tune, "Pico Peak-A-Boo", named after Pico Peak in Vermont, on a 45 rpm, with a photo and bio of me on the cover.

Bob was an affable, fast-talking, street-smart guy of thirty-five, who had radio station and record distributor contacts. He knew the business of record promotion and knew how to get air-play without paying for it. Those were the days of rampant payola, without which records didn't move. I couldn't pay him, but Bob offered to help.

A few weeks later "Pico Peak-a-Boo" came out at number twenty with a Bullet on the Billboard Top 100 chart, which meant that record stores should watch for it to break out. It got some national airplay, sold a few records, got mild acceptance in record outlets, and then faded to the returns bin. Bob had done all he could. The record died of natural causes, and, I liked to think, lack of payola. But in retrospect, it probably wasn't good enough to have a life of its own after initial exposure in the marketplace. The recording was more like a musical aside, so I was not too disappointed with the sales results.

Two years after that event I recalled Bob saying he worked as stage manager for George Wein each year at the Newport

Festival. It was a long shot, but why not talk to Bob, I thought. He had moved from New York, but I managed to trace him to a small, quiet town in northern New Jersey. He had quit the record promotion business, had married, had a huge dog, and was writing a sports column for the local newspaper. "You still work the Newport Jazz Festival for George Wein?" I asked when I called.

"Sure. Every year," he said.

I told him all about how the Jazz Giants, now four years together, had grown. I asked if he would suggest to George Wein that we play the Festival that year. He laughed and said, "You gotta be kidding. Get in line. George even turned down Stan Kenton this year. It's the Budget."

"I'm serious. Bob," I assured him. "We're good. The band swings. So it's not Kenton. But it's fresh. It's strong. You'd be a hero. Besides, we wouldn't cost nearly as much as Kenton. And we're practically in Newport's backyard."

Probably sensing some logic and certainly the passion in my voice, he said, "Well, send me some stuff and let me look at it. I'll see what I can do."

A week after I sent him all the promotional material I had, plus pictures and a reel tape of our concerts, he called and said, "Hey, I like it. The band is really good. I'm coming up to Connecticut to see a rehearsal." When Bob showed up, I did not mention his arrival to the guys; he watched and listened in the background.

After rehearsal Bob and I discussed possibilities. "Look, Gene, the band is exciting. But you have to understand that Newport is really a long shot. So don't plan on anything. But I do have an idea that might hold some air."

"What do you mean?"

"Every year George books one act for the Festival that's an unknown. You know, he likes to present it as a discovery. It's good for the Festival. Maybe he could see a connection in that way with the Jazz Giants. It might be a story he'd buy into and get promotional mileage out of it. And you said so yourself, you're right in Newport's back yard. How does this sound? Undiscovered New England Territory Jazz Big Band Plays the Famous Newport Jazz Festival in the Heart of New England. "

"How about Brilliant, Undiscovered New England Territory Jazz Big Band?"

"Yeah, sure," Bob chuckled. "George hasn't announced the lineup for the Festival yet. I'll ask him next week when I'm in his office. But remember, Gene, it's a long shot."

"Why don't you call him now? Next week might be too late."

"It won't mean anything until he hears the tape. Be patient."

Be patient? Sure. Easy for him to say. This could be the break-through, the exposure, the record deal. It could change my life. I couldn't sleep. Long-shot or not, I was already counting on it and visualized the Jazz Giants playing on the Newport stage, though I had never seen it.

One evening at rehearsal, just before we called it a night, with the place pretty well emptied out, I said, "Guys, what would you think if we got booked to play at the Newport Jazz Festival this year?"

"Yeah sure, and the World Series, while we're at it," said Joe Daddona, our affable, sometimes acerbic, baritone sax player, a schoolteacher who had played in several name bands.

"How about Carnegie Hall?" called out Bobby Butler, an insurance adjuster by day, and our excellent lead trumpet man—he and I had actually played Carnegie Hall together in Roddy Shull's band when we were sixteen, placing second in *Look Magazine's National Swing Band* contest. Most of the guys laughed and made comments like,

"Any time."

"Newport? Sure, why not?"

"Carnegie Hall."

"The White House."

"Hollywood, here we come."

"Guys, I'm dead serious," I said. "If I could get us booked to play at Newport this coming July, would you all be willing to double up on rehearsals to prepare for it? That's only five months away, and we'd have a ways to go. If we can pull it off, we'd want to be absolutely slick and stone everybody with our music."

"Gene, I don't know if you can really do this," drawled laconic Jack Spake, our North Carolina, jazz-chair trombonist. "But hell, if you can, I for one would work my tired old Southern butt off to see it happen."

Lanky Jack was an easy-going, disheveled-looking ex-GI, a good ole boy, who had been a trombonist in the U.S. Army Band. His slow, easy delivery kept you waiting for the next word to come out, but it was usually worth the wait. He was a true gentleman and the guys respected him.

"Whoa. I don't know if you're pulling our leg or not," said Joe Marzulli, "but remember, we're just a local Bridgeport rehearsal band." Outwardly gruff, Joe was really a sensitive guy, a budding arranger, a trumpeter and a fine high school band director. "Newport is big time," he said. "That's a lot of pressure to put on us. Do we want that, guys?"

I didn't wait for anyone else's opinion. "This is what I think. Each year George Wein, the Festival's producer, presents one unknown jazz group along with his usual array of famous jazz stars."

"Yeah, so?" said Joe.

"The unknowns are from anywhere in the world." I said. "Remember last year? It was the Wreakers from Poland? ... and the year before, the International Youth Band? They were presented as being fresh and new on the scene, and they wound up with record deals. It could be the same sort of opportunity for us. Besides, wouldn't it be fun just to see if we could pull it off? We're good, and you all know it. So why not?"

"But what's the point of wasting time trying for that if we don't get invited?" said saxophonist Ronnie Gebeau.

"The point is this. Why couldn't it be us? Why couldn't we be this year's Newport discovery? We're pretty special. Hell, I've been waiting to be discovered since I was ten years old."

"Me too," said Mickey Walker, our lead jazz trombonist. "Me want fame. Fame mean money. Money make wife happy. Happy wife mean ... well, you know ... Ungawah!" Everyone broke up. "Are you kidding? I'm up for it. It'd be great; and don't ever tell my wife I said that."

Dom Mariconda, another high school band director and trumpeter, who later became Superintendent of Music for Bridgeport Public Schools, said, "Gene, are you just spinning our wheels? Do you even know George Wein?"

"No, I don't. But I've got an idea, and I'm working on it. It could happen. If you guys are willing to commit the time for extra rehearsals, I'll go for it."

"Yeah, sure, fine," was their off-handed response. To most of them the idea was a pipe dream. And that was understandable. You get all worked up about something and then it doesn't happen, and you're left to deal with the disappointment and rejection. It happens a lot in this business. You pump yourself up because of something somebody says they're going to do for you, then ... zilch! These guys just didn't want to set themselves up for a fall.

Even though I was sure they wouldn't even bother telling their wives or girlfriends there was a possibility they might be rehearsing more than one night a week, I knew they would be thrilled if it happened.

Bob Messinger called two weeks later. "George loves the idea. He buys the story. He'd like to do it."

"Fantastic! Incredible! He won't be disappointed."

"HOWEVER, the cost of a big band that size would be heavy for him. And you guys don't exactly have the kind of known name that draws an audience. He figures he'll lose too much money if he books you. Budgets are very tight this year."

"Does that mean no?"

"Probably. BUT ... suppose you guys could sell a few tickets to the festival, if you are booked. You know, to help George offset some of his costs."

"Yeah, then what?"

"THEN ... I think we can make a deal with him."

"You're serious?"

"Yep."

"How much in *costs* do we have to offset?"

"One thousand dollars in tickets."

"How many tickets is that?"

"Less than two hundred at $5.40 each, the best seats."

It sounded fair to me. "Deal. Let's do it. Send me the contract."

"You sure?"

"Are you kidding? Absolutely."

So we made the deal. I committed to selling about two hundred $5.40 tickets, the best seats. I figured we could unload those easily at our local concerts. Besides, we had over eight hundred names on our mailing list and months to go before the Festival.

It was done. It was going to happen. I couldn't believe it. No dream. It was the Big League. I couldn't wait to share the news with the band. They surely would be as ecstatic as I was. But it didn't turn out that way.

A possible Newport performance would be a moment of truth, sink or swim for the band. The reality of it all probably caught them by surprise, sobered them. They had doubts. Were we good at just a local level? Would our band be credible on the national scene? Or maybe we'd be a joke when compared to the famous?

*

So? Nothing is easy. You asked for it. Don't expect any sympathy from me. Remember, Confucius say: "Man who reach too high for star, not see bump on road."

(Oh, give me a break. You're worse than I am.
Are you sure you're me?)

Heh, heh..

**

14

NEWPORT JAZZ FESTIVAL

And so it was official. The Jazz Giants would perform at the Newport Jazz Festival, the world's most prestigious jazz event. Bridgeport people would hardly believe it, once we announced it. Nor would the musicians; they would celebrate, or so I thought. But something strange happened when I told the band a deal had been made. I had expected a roar of excitement and maybe some applause. Instead they were quiet. Too quiet. I could see an uneasy look on their faces.

"Aw, man, I don't know," said one.

"You serious?" another said. A few grumbled. The rest looked down at their music, avoiding my eyes. Their reaction surprised me, confusing me at first. The whole deal would go sour if this was their true feeling. My first thought was Hey you guys, I put this thing together after we all agreed. Remember? Now you're telling me you don't want to do it?

Of course I didn't say that. It would either intimidate them into a weak, "Okay, we'll go," or the band would dissolve. Either way we would lose. I tried to understand their obstinacy. Had I moved too fast? Was it really not a good thing for them?

Or was it in fact put-up-or-shut-up time and they did not think it would ever come to this? Perhaps they were afraid to risk their local reputations on a world stage. Locally, we were important. But were we really as good as we thought? Or would the elite professional music world not take us seriously? By declining, there would be no risk.

I couldn't let the opportunity collapse because of their lack of confidence. I knew we were capable of accomplishing a great deed, one we would be proud of for a long time. But if we were to succeed, the will to do it had to be unanimous. I decided to give it my best shot with a short impassioned speech.

"Come on, guys, this is our chance, a golden opportunity to prove ourselves. We've worked hard for this. Believe in yourselves. You're good. We can do it. I know we can. We'd make a lot of people proud. I think we should go for it. But it's up to you."

With nothing left to say, I waited.

After a long silence, Jack Spake drawled, "Gene, I can't think of a better present than the one you just gave us. It's something I've only dreamed of. Now I can live it."

Jack's comments made the guys think. They pulled out of the negative slump. Chatter started. Doubt was shoved under chairs. Joe Daddona spoke up, "Right. So let's get to work, guys."

Suddenly we were a band with a purpose again. Their new resolve had cheated disaster. It was like a 1940s family movie—the old Mickey Rooney-Judy Garland musicals, where the gang or club saves the day with "let's put on a show in the barn." I guess clichés are based on fact.

Then the contract arrived via Registered Mail. The first clause confirmed we were to open the show on Saturday night, July 7th, with a forty-five minute set. We had not been relegated to some afternoon workshop, which could have happened. This was a prime-time spot. Wow. Bob Messinger, I love you.

The next clause stated we would sell about two hundred $5.40 tickets, which would be sent to us. Fine. Right. But then it went on to say that the $1,000 for the tickets was to be remitted in advance to the Festival office, together with the signed contract, within seven days, or the contract would be null and void. What? A thousand dollars! I can't believe it. Can't be.

I did not have a thousand dollars and had no idea where to get it. In 1962 that kind of money was huge. My wife and I had recently bought a house. Mortgage payments took some doing with seven kids by then. No money, no contract. No way the deal can happen now.

I made several inquiries, not mentioning this snafu to the guys. It might burst their bubble. This issue was about money, not music. I wanted them to stay focused.

By the fifth day I was out of ideas. I could feel Newport slipping away. I had already announced to everyone that we were going. After coming so close, I hurt. I was embarrassed, depressed, even morose. I went to see my friend and family doctor, Mike Cardone, Chief of Staff at St. Vincent's Hospital who had delivered most of my seven children. (Our eighth was born soon after.) Mike was married to Betty Jane, my first cousin.

He listened to the whole story and calmed me down.

"Gene, let me talk to some of the guys our band."

Ironically, Dr. Mike played baritone sax in the Doctors' Big Band. They met every few weeks for fun, to unwind, play a few tunes, drink a few scotches and talk about music and the good old days. Strictly an amateur group, I coached them whenever they rehearsed. It never occurred to me to ask them for help. Dr. Mike called that night. "Don't worry, Gene we'll put up the grand. Pay us back when you sell the tickets. You've done a lot for us. So go, man."

There was a Santa Claus after all. I'll never forget the relief I felt. And I'll never forget Dr. Mike. Without him, Eddie Kochan, Marv Aaron, and Bob Gaffney of the Doctors Big Band, Newport would not have happened for us. The next day I sent out the signed contracts and a cashier's check for $1,000. The tickets arrived by return mail. We were going!

Months zoomed by with extra rehearsals, arrangements being polished, new ones written, PR mailings to hundreds of jazz fans, stories and interviews in local papers, even radio interviews. Interest in us steamrolled. We become a household name in Connecticut. The *Sunday Herald* did a full-page spread with pictures of the Jazz Giants in rehearsal preparing for the Big Day, as did *The Bridgeport Post*, and Hartford and New Haven papers later. I continued to work full time at the radio station, and they were most understanding of the time I gave to this project.

While covering the 1958 national election returns for WICC Radio, I had met U.S. Congressman Don Irwin (D-CT) in his home on Election Night. He was running for re-election. Don was an avid jazz fan and a Jazz Giants supporter. He had written a "Jazz Giants Salute Proclamation Letter" to the newspapers. On the weekend of our performance he led an auto caravan of fans to from Norwalk to Newport, a distance of about a hundred and twenty miles.

Finally, the Fourth-of-July weekend arrived, Newport weekend. We had done everything I could think of to prepare. We were ready. The morning of our evening show we warmed up, in a small local Newport bar room, playing a few tunes, getting loose. Resourceful Bob Messinger had found this dank, neighborhood joint for us. The smell of stale beer permeated the place, as it does most beer joints before they open for business. We didn't mind, we were used to it from Bill's Castle—Bill's *was* a castle compared to this dark kind of bar where, when you bravely stepped out into daylight after a few hours inside, the sun splash makes your couple of beers feel like five.

At eleven o'clock in the morning the place was packed with friends, wives, insiders and touted press who wanted to catch a preview of the Band from Bridgeport. As we finished, Bob came bouncing in, telling me that Russell Procope was ill and wouldn't be able to play with Duke Ellington's band the following night.

Remembering that I had recorded with Ellington and subbed a few times for Johnny Hodges and Procope, he asked if I wanted to play with the band at the Sunday night show.

"You kidding? Twist my arm." Good things come in bunches. Incredible.

At that point I happened to reach into my pocket and found sixty tickets. I realized we hadn't sold all of them. Oops. I had been too busy with all our preparations. I flipped them out and flashed them like a deck of cards. "Ladies," I said to the wives, "can you take care of these?"

"Come on, girls," said Joyce D'Addario, wife of Pete D'Addario, our dynamic drummer, an alumnus of the Sauter-Finegan Orchestra, and owner of a local Bridgeport music store. "Let's go to work." And they did.

Two hours before show time the wives and girl friends of the band spread out between the huge parking lot and the entrance gate, hawking tickets. I don't know if George Wein was ever aware of that scene, but the women sold all the remaining tickets in twenty minutes. We were family.

We kicked off our program at 8:00 p.m. I don't remember a note we played; it went so fast. But I do remember the brass section screaming out into the night with colossal fire. The saxes steamed together like bonded brothers and took their ensemble sound to another level. From our first note, the energy and drive poured over me, almost putting me in a trance. The band was like a locomotive. Get out of the way everybody. Here we come.

The applause was generous from the sell-out crowd who had come expecting to see the famous. We weren't. Joe Marzulli had written an original composition, which he called "Little Big Horn." He didn't think it was good enough to play there, but it was, and we did. And it was a hit. Trumpeter Dom Mariconda's solo was vibrant. Bobby Butler and Tommy Alberts, our two lead trumpets, played brilliantly. As did Mickey Walker. So did saxophone soloists Ronnie Gebeau, Dick Burlant, Al Provenzano, and Steve Royal, who later toured with Woody Herman's band. Dick Burlant, Tony Guzzi and Russ Martino had written some fine arrangements. In reality, almost every player had managed to play close to his best at the same time. A rare moment for us. I was proud to stand up there in front of this real band of brothers, who had laid it out for all to hear. *This is who we are, world.*

Also on the program that night were Charlie Mingus, Toshiko Mariano, the Max Roach Quartet, and Louis Armstrong and his All Stars. From Louis, who watched us backstage from the wings, I could hear loud encouraging grunts of Uh-huhs, whenever something we played particularly pleased him. Audience reception was even more enthusiastic than we had hoped. Famous musicians came up to us later with congratulations. The dream was finally coming true. We were climbing onto the ole' Cloud Nine. Most importantly, we had delivered our best to ourselves. I was proud of each of the men.

Our celebration afterwards was ardent, to say the least. We partied till almost dawn. We had done it. We had gotten the attention of the Jazz world, the press, music critics, and important venue operators. The buzz was genuine. Best of all, the whole Newport four-day event was recorded by Impulse Records. We would finally have a recording as one of the Festival's featured acts. Our teamwork and efforts had paid off.

The band and our entourage of a hundred people or more had stayed Friday and Saturday nights at Newport's Seaview Motel, where we had reserved the entire first floor. Even so, there weren't enough rooms. In some cases we had eight people to a room, crashing wherever they could find space.

At ten Sunday morning the word went around the motel. "Everybody up!" Father Fred, a long time friend and fan, who made the trip with us, arranged to say eleven o'clock Mass in honor of the Jazz Giants at a nearby parish church. Most of us (those who could still walk) attended, no matter what religion or non-religion we professed. It was a brilliant morning—squinting being the alternative to snow blindness. We could hardly keep the proverbial sand out of our eyes. From the amount of moans and groans, I knew some heads were pounding, as if a jungle percussion section were playing inside them.

Father Fred Trumbull had been a handsome, dark-haired, popular Central High School football quarterback in Bridgeport, though he was only 5' 6' and 140 pounds. He was also a talented singer. He had won local Frank Sinatra contests at the Loews Theatre when he was a student. Before enlisting in the U.S. Army he had sung with my high school band. Upon his discharge, he enrolled in a seminary college, became a priest, and served eight years as a missionary in Tanganyika, where he built a hospital. We all loved him.

Midway through the Mass, the pastor turned to the congregation and made a simple announcement. "Today's sermon will be given by a visiting missionary priest who has just returned from the missions in Central Africa, Father Fred Trumbull, of the Holy Ghost Order."

Murmurs followed from the regular parishioners who were well aware, I'm sure, of the bleary-eyed strangers uncharacteristically filling the church on this hot, July Sunday morning. There was a respectful silence as Father Fred stepped up into the pulpit. They were anticipating a talk about the African Missions and possibly an appeal for financial support. After all, here was the out-of-town expert on mission matters, and missions always needed money. As for our contingent, we perked up to hear our guy. And why not? He had partied with us most of the night. He was special to us.

"Good morning, everyone. Ahem." He began, with the serious tone of an important Church dignitary about to share with the faithful the story of the woes and challenges of the African Missions.

"Thank you, Pastor Kiernan, for inviting me to help celebrate Mass here today. Ahem. In deference to those who have labored long and hard through the night, yet have had the strength of character to arise this hot morning and come to this lovely church to give thanks, today's sermon will be short. Love one another. God bless you all. Go in peace. Thank you."

Winking at us, he stepped down from the pulpit. It was, I'm sure, the shortest sermon on record at St. Mary's Church.

Afterward, we all had a picnic lunch together. "Brevity is next to Deity," said Father Fred with a twinkle, as he sipped a welcome orange juice.

That night I played in the Ellington Orchestra. Peabody Park opened at seven for the eight o'clock show. Thousands of people were finding their seats as, one by one, Ellington band members straggled onto the stage for a pre-show rehearsal. I was the first one on stage, anxious and ready to go. I noticed Cat Anderson, Duke's extraordinary lead trumpet player, amble onto the bandstand, sit down at his place, open up his trumpet case and pull out a comic book. He proceeded to place it on his music stand and read with obvious amusement.

There was no curtain. We were in full view of the audience. It was starting to get dark. More musicians arrived. Then the great Thelonious Monk, jazz innovator of the first magnitude, strolled on stage. He received a hug from Duke and sat down at the piano. Monk was, well … Monk, in his tam and goatee, quiet, gentle, friendly as usual, with no need for mundane insincerities like publicly shaking hands. A wave to the musicians would do.

At the piano he pounded a few two-second, three-fingered dissonant chord clusters—Monk chords, I would guess—got up and walked off stage. He never came back. Because Duke's band program ran long that night, Monk performed with the band the following night.

Ten minutes before showtime Duke started passing out parts while Billy Strayhorn was still writing a new arrangement for the band. I kept looking at my watch. When are we going to rehearse? This could be disastrous. But no one else seemed concerned.

Before we had time to play a note of the new charts, or even tune up, it was showtime. Talk about a band being relaxed! As if on automatic pilot, drummer Sam Woodyard kicked into a brief clip of Duke's "Take The A Train" theme, then right into "Satin Doll." After that, Duke called out, "Rockin' In Rhythm, boys." Turning to the audience, he proceeded to deliver one of his famous, splendiferously warm and eloquent greetings, concluding with, "The boys in the band and I want you to know we all Love You Madly." Duke was grandly polite in greeting people, the way men and women of a different era often were. The crowd loved him.

Duke's music library was not numbered; the arrangements were placed alphabetically in each musician's folder, called the book. Well over a hundred arrangements, several of which had more than one version, bulged his book. While he was speaking to the crowd, I opened to the R's, quickly searching for "Rockin' In Rhythm." None of the other saxophone players even bothered to look for music. Evidently they knew the chart from memory. I found "Rockin' In Rhythm," but there were four different arrangements of the same tune!

"Which chart?" I said in a panic to Harry Carney, who was seated beside me.

He laughed a little, like it didn't make any difference, and said, "Man, just start on your high D and follow me." With that the entire sax section arose, Jimmy Hamilton, Johnny Hodges, Paul Gonzalves, Harry Carney, and I. We left our places, and grouped downstage around the mike. Baritone sax player Harry played clarinet on this particular arrangement, doubling the lead alto part exactly, only an octave higher. I played the alto melody by ear, just a fraction of a millisecond behind Harry with an ear glued to him. I fudged notes I wasn't sure of and laid it on strong where I was confident. Duke listened. I didn't get in the way. He was pleased and beamed his ear-to-ear smile.

Later in the program just about everyone in the band soloed a few choruses on an extended blues number, with Duke giving each soloist a grand introduction. "And now," he announced, as the band vamped, "the man whose band from Bridgeport broke it up last night here at Newport, Mr. Gene Hull."

I really don't remember playing the solo. It couldn't have made much sense. I was exhausted by then. The adrenaline that had driven me for the past several months seeped out my seams. I was fading. Late that night my wife and a friend and I drove back to Connecticut. I fell asleep in the backseat and awoke a few hours later as the car pulled into the driveway of our home.

The sense of accomplishment I felt was worth everything it had taken to do it. After all, the Jazz Giants had finally been recorded, and the album would get worldwide distribution. We had finally gotten over the hump.

For weeks we basked in the acclaim. New England papers gave it a big play. The New York Herald Tribune did a glowing article about us, as did the New York Times. Dave Brubeck wrote, "... the best thing to happen to the Newport Jazz Festival." The City of Bridgeport was demonstrably proud. I was asked to join the City Arts Council. The University of Notre Dame Magazine later did a full-page spread with a picture of the band. A white cloth banner—HOME of the JAZZ GIANTS—hung at Bill's Castle. I even got an extension on my bank loan. A minor miracle. Ah, the glory of it all! The $1,000 was repaid to the doctors. Our band was filled with newborn pride.

A month later I got a call from Bob Messinger. "Gene, sit down. I have to tell you something."

"More good news, I hope. You've got a release date for the album?"

"Yeah, it turned out great. Wait till you hear it. Congratulations."

"Yeow!"

Six months later the album of Newport '62 was released featuring the 45-minute program of the Jazz Giants. It sold 500,000 albums worldwide the first year, a huge number for a jazz album. Our future was assured. Back up the truck for the money. I felt vindicated and immensely relieved. Opportunity had been met with preparation. The work, the hours, the planning, the rehearsing and the dedication had been worth it. Luck, the most precious requirement for success in the entertainment business, had smiled on us. Life was indeed good.

*

Oh really? So where's the recording?

(Ah, yes, that little detail, the recording. Okay, the story didn't end in glory. I was just wishing.)

That's why I'm here.

A month later I got a call from Bob Messinger. "Gene, sit down. I have to tell you something."

"More good news, I hope. You've got a release date for the album?"

"No, I'm afraid not," he said. "All of the tapes from the Festival were spoiled by some electronic quirk during the live recording at Newport."

"What? Are you kidding me, man?"

"No one heard it during the tapings in the sound truck, but back here in New York, in the studio mixing session, it's obvious that all the tapes are defective."

"What does that mean, Bob? No Jazz Giants tape? No recording? No album?"

"No recordings of the entire 1962 Newport Jazz Festival! There will be no Festival album this year. It's never happened before. It's a huge blow to George."

"Yeah, I can appreciate that," I said quietly. "Tell him I'm sorry for his bad luck."

"You okay, Gene?"

"Wanna buy a saxophone?" I said in utter disbelief, crushed.

"I'm sorry," he said.

"Me too." What else was there to say?

"But I do have you booked to play Monday nights at Birdland this summer," Bob said.

"With my luck it'll probably close before we get there."

"Gene, did you hear me? Birdland, Broadway and 52nd Street, the Jazz Corner of the World. It's the most famous jazz club on the planet."

"Yeah, I know."

Many bands didn't last as long. We had more than our "fifteen minutes"—eight years in all. Birdland didn't close; we carried the sounds of our music to the Big Apple that summer and the next. It was a special treat. Many famous musicians came to hear us. Years of many good moments followed, performing with movie stars, famous singers, celebrities, and jazz artists, such as Jack Benny, Bob Hope, Mel Torme, Doc Severinson, Sammy Davis, Tony Bennett, The Four Tops, The Temptations, Gloria DeHaven, Dave Brubeck, Art Blakey, Neil Sedaka, Urbie Green, Sonny Stitt, Rosemary Clooney, Bill Evans, and countless others. We created some good notes and had more than our share of fun, fame and glory. But in time, it appeared that the sound of the Jazz Giants would live only in memory. With no *recorded* history, it became a big band dinosaur, extinct before it could be remembered.

SAT IN WITH THE DUKE—Gene Hull joined Duke Ellington's band at the Newport Jazz festival in 1962 when the sax player was hurt in an automobile accident. Producing the jazz sound are, from left, Paul Gonsolves, Jimmy Hamilton, Harry Carney, Gene on the sax, and Johnny Hodges. It was a reunion with the Duke for Gene who was in Newport with his Jazz Giants. He had played and recorded with Ellington in the 50s.

The Providence Journal

JAZZ GIANTS IN ACTION AT NEWPORT—Gene Hull leads the Jazz Giants of a concert before 12,000 jazz enthusiasts at the 1962 Newport Jazz Festival where th recorded their first album "live" for Impulse Records. The Jazz Giants received a array of acclaims from the critics attending the Festival.

The Boston Globe

♫ Newport **1962**

15

LENNIE

"Daddy, the kitten has six toes on its back feet."

"Really? Count 'em again, sweetheart. Cats paws usually have five toes."

"I know that," Becky, our five-year old daughter said. "Look," holding the gangly kitten up to me. "See? One, two, three, four, five, six."

"Well, I'll be. You're right, a cat with twenty-two toes. Whadaya know."

"Please, please, please. Can we keep him, Daddy? Please," said Amy.

"Please, Dad," the others chimed in.

The straggly gray kitten had surprised me that morning, crawling out from under the front seat as I unloaded the band's music and stands from the car. Apparently, the night before it had hidden in the car at Bill's Castle, while I was packing up after an evening rehearsal. There were a couple of stray cats nearby at the time. I was amazed to find this one now. He stretched, looked around and yawned. He was a plain, skinny, alley-variety stray, most likely separated from his mother. When I picked him up he gave me a curious, almost blasé expression that seemed to say, "Okay, I'm here. So what do we do now?" I laughed. He must have been frightened, but he didn't act a bit intimidated. I liked his spunk.

I was not a cat lover, anything but. Our pets were always dogs. Up until that time I had always regarded cats as being of no consequence. After all, if they weren't dogs it was difficult to think of them as man's best friend. But something about this kitten was different. I immediately felt responsible for him, perhaps struck by his personality and air of independence. Yet there was nothing capricious about him.

Willingly, I believe, he joined in with the family flow. The kids took him everywhere. Cyrano, our brown and white Sheltie, a family member for several years, often sleeping sprawled out and content on the floor, tolerated the kitten's impromptu surprise attacks with adult-like forbearance. The kitten loved to play anytime; he wasn't shy or coy. He wouldn't have survived if he had been. A family of eight energetic children is not the place for anyone shy, especially a pet.

Weeks passed. The kitten grew, but, strangely, remained unnamed. The kids could not agree on what to call him. It was that kind of a family. They suggested their own favorite name: Cuddles, Tiger, Mouser, Pussy, Lion, Bitty Kitty, Honey, Killer, Fang, Big Foot, Rabbit. I referred to him as Jazz Giant Cat. After all, it was after a Jazz Giants rehearsal that the kitten had stowed away in my car and come into our lives.

One day, at my son Matthew's suggestion, the appropriate name seemed to be unanimous. There could be no other name. It was solved. Everyone agreed. As bubbly and crazy as the cat was at times, bounding over furniture, friends and fences, as if possessed, he had a more curious and most distinctive habit, unlike any animal I have ever known.

At that time, we were in the habit of watching Leonard Bernstein's "Young People's Concerts with the New York Philharmonic" telecasts live on Saturdays. Bernstein demonstrated the sounds of various instruments, and in his mellifluous tones, rich, deep and pleasant, he told stories about the music and composers. The family loved the program. We'd gather in the living room, settling on couches or sprawling out on the carpet in front of the Philco console black and white TV.

But it was not only the children who enjoyed Leonard Bernstein and the music. The cat watched too, and right next to the screen. Whenever there was a close-up of Bernstein speaking into the camera, the cat would get closer to the TV screen and focus wide-eyed on his every movement. If he raised his hand or gestured or nodded, the cat was right with him. Clearly, the cat was fascinated.

On the day Bernstein narrated *Peter and the Wolf* our new feline started nodding and dipping. He began to follow Bernstein's hand and baton all around the screen, back and forth. The cat was one with Bernstein.

That's all it took. Some of the kids huddled then swarmed around us. "Mom! Dad! Matt's got the name, the cat's name. It's perfect."

"Leonard Catstein," said Matthew, matter-of-factly. And so it was. We all laughed. What could be more fitting for a cat who loved the Philharmonic's famous conductor? From that day, we called him Leonard Catstein. When the girls scolded him for stealing a sock or swiping a toothbrush, they called him Leonard, as in "LEONARD, you naughty kitty, come back here with that sock right now!" The boys sometime called him Lennie. But of course we always introduced him to our friends by his full name.

Ironically, the following summer, 1963, the Jazz Giants band was invited to play a lawn concert at the home of Leonard Bernstein in Fairfield, Connecticut, for a Sunday afternoon Norwalk NAACP benefit. Several well-known jazz artists including the Billy Taylor Trio, Morgana King, and Dizzy Gillespie were also performing.

The stage was set up on a gently sloped, tree-surrounded lawn not far from his large white clapboard, brick-chimneyed country house. Several hundred people attended, sportily accoutered in typical Fairfield County dressy-casual attire appropriate for a garden event. Chairs were set up on the lawn that beautiful, clear, crisp August afternoon. Smells of grass and flowers scented the air; trees were peppered with an audience of feathered chirpers. An idyllic setting.

Between acts, the audience mixed and mingled, had cocktails, and socialized. Bernstein was an affable host, shaking hands and chatting with many friends. It was an informal yet elegant day.

The Jazz Giants performed a fifty-minute program and were warmly received. Near the end of our allotted time, I went to the microphone and thanked Mr. Bernstein for inviting us. Then, before introducing a jazz version of "Something's Coming" from Bernstein's *West Side Story*, I decided to chat a bit with the audience. I told them the story of a little stray, twenty-two-toed kitten that had lived in an alley behind the nightclub, where the Jazz Giants rehearsed, and how he had hidden in my car one night.

I noticed Bernstein, standing in back, break away from a conversation in order to listen. I went on to tell how the kitten was truly fascinated by Mr. Bernstein's close-ups on television, and how as a result, the kids named him Leonard Catstein, or Lennie for short. I thanked Mr. Bernstein for inspiring the name and for solving a family dilemma.

Bernstein seemed to enjoy the story. The crowd laughed and applauded. But in the audience, my mother shrank in embarrassment, even though it was the kind of relaxed, informal setting in which the story seemed appropriate … in my view at least.

Afterward, as I stood next to the bandstand, greeting various patrons of the arts, my mother (all four feet ten inches of her) approached me stern-faced. Usually smiling and congratulatory after one of our concerts, she waited until the people had trickled away from me, then scolded, "How could you tell that story, Gene? A *cat*, yet. It was rude and very disrespectful to Mr. Bernstein. You should know better than that." She thought the world of Bernstein and was seriously displeased with me, perhaps for the first time in her life, though I really couldn't say for sure.

"Aw, come on Marge, it was all in fun. The crowd enjoyed it, and I'm sure Mr. Bernstein did, too."

Suddenly Bernstein approached, appearing upset. "Listen. buddy, why don't you take your cat and band and leave. This isn't a back alley with stray cats. This is my home. Who do you think you are?"

I was amazed at his indignation. I didn't know what to say. It was just a little fun, an entertaining story, I thought. Evidently, he didn't think so. He was nothing like he was on the children's TV concerts.

Marge looked at me. "See, I told you that was in bad taste." Facing Bernstein she said, "I'm so sorry, Mr. Bernstein. My son should have known better."

"Hmm," he said, turned and walked away.

I never watched the Philharmonic again after that, nor did my kids. As far as the cat was concerned, we started calling him Elvis.

*

Cute. But I've got to say this now. Liar, liar, house on fire!
Bernstein was a true gentleman. He would have never done that.

(Jeez, I thought I'd just spice it up a bit. Okay, okay. Actually, the conversation after the concert went like this:)

"Aw, come on Marge, it was all in fun. The crowd enjoyed it and I'm sure Mr. Bernstein did, too." Suddenly Bernstein approached, grinning.

"Yes, I did, Gene," he said. "It was a fun story. I've never heard anything like that before. Does Lennie play piano, too?" He chuckled. "I mean something besides 'Kitten on the Keys'"? He really amused himself with that one. The gravelly timbre of his voice sounded as if he just woke up.

I laughed at his pun.

My mother was slack-jaw speechless. HE was there. Bernstein, HIMSELF.

"Mr. Bernstein, this is my mother, Marge," I said. "She really hates cats, but she loves you and your music," which was true.

Warmly he shook her hand. "So nice to meet you, Mrs. Hull."

My mother gulped and gathered herself together in less time than it took to introduce her. With restored composure, her blue eyes twinkling, she gazed up at her idol, smiled sweetly and said, "It's such an honor to meet you, Mr. Bernstein. Isn't my son wonderful?"

**

16

THE ICONS

Basie and Sarah

During the '60s I produced jazz concerts in the Connecticut area, probably more than a hundred in all. Many featured some of the world's best-known jazz artists. On Monday nights, in conjunction with bassist-singer and energetic friend Dan Arcotta, I promoted a monthly Big Band series called "Cocktails and Concert," held in Bridgeport's Stratfield Hotel Ballroom.

Tables were set up cabaret style, like Boston Pops presentations, with a modest admission price of $5.00, a cash bar and table service. We received the admissions and split the bar revenue, after costs, with the hotel. In turn we paid for the talent. The ballroom always sold out on those nights, which meant success for everyone involved. Productions usually ran smoothly with no surprises, that is, until the night we presented "Count Basie and his Orchestra." As usual, every table was filled, every seat taken. As show time approached, the undercurrent of the audience buzz gathered momentum, not unlike the excitement of a grandstand crowd before the start of a horse race. Basie had not played Bridgeport before in a concert setting. For local fans, it was as if they were kids again and the Beatles had come to town.

I was as excited as anyone there. Basie was one of my favorites. Anticipation peaked, until, finally, it was show time. "Ladies and Gentlemen," I announced from the stage, "welcome to another presentation of Cocktails and Concert. I won't keep you waiting any longer. I know you're as anxious as I am to hear this great band. So here he is, The Kid from Redbank, Mr. Count Basie and His Orchestra." With that the marvelous Basie music machine, sixteen men swinging, began to roll, much to the delight of the overflow crowd.

The crowd was indeed into it from the first note. Excitement spiraled; applause greeted each soloist, clapping in time, whistling, and cheering the band. It was as if the audience were *in* the band, a spontaneous symbiotic bonding. These were rare moments to live for.

Count Basie was the kind of person who seemed to know just where he was. A short, heavy-set, friendly man, he had stuck with his band's uncomplicated, unique, driving style, because it was natural and fun and people loved it. He never seemed out to prove anything, except perhaps there could be no real big-band jazz without a solid, unified musical groove. As a result, his arrangements were relatively simple, conceptualized to let the band swing, and it did so with amazing impact. The ensemble sound he created was the cra's standard for musical power and simplicity, a sound that could lift you and rock you and force you to feel alive. If his band didn't get to you, you were dead.

During intermission, Sarah Vaughn approached me and asked if she could sing a few tunes with Basie. I hadn't realized she was in the audience. Her sister lived in Bridgeport, and Sarah had just happened to come up from New York for a visit. I had recorded with her in the past and was surprised and delighted to see her now. What a coup for our production: Sarah

Vaughn, truly one of the greatest jazz singers ever, here at our presentation. I never felt like a star-struck fan before.

Up on stage I spoke to Basie just before the start of the second set. He was already seated at the piano. "Count, you sound ferociously terrific tonight," I said. "I've got a little surprise. Sarah is here and would like to sit in with you and sing a few tunes." I tried to sound matter of fact about it, as if it were nothing unusual. But inside I was bubbling up like a circus clown. "Is that okay with you?"

"Sarah is here in Bridgeport?"

"Right. Her sister lives here."

"Hell yes, man. It'd be a ball. Where is she? I'll introduce her.

"Well, if you don't mind, I'd like to present her," I said. "You know, as a surprise guest star."

"Whoa, man. It's my band. I should bring her on. You dig?"

"Sure, of course I do. But, Count, I'm the producer of the show. And it would be really good for my business if I presented her. You understand, don't you?"

"She's never sung with my band here before, man. This is history. I'd like to introduce her."

I was uneasy with his resistance. I knew he had a point, but so did I. I decided to give it one more try before caving in; after all, he was the star. "I'm sure she'll sing with you lots of times in the future, Count. Come on, this is only little old Bridgeport. Make me look good. You can have her next time. Okay?"

Basie gave me a knowing smile, cocked his head a little, as if acknowledging some internal voice, and said, "I see, Gene. I get it. You want to be *the man*. You want to present Sarah. Okay. No problem. Go ahead."

I thanked him for his understanding, but I felt a little guilty as I went to the mike and made the announcement with as much pride and pomp as I could gather.

"Ladies and Gentlemen, it is our most happy pleasure to present tonight's special surprise guest star, the one, the only, THE DIVINE ONE, MISS SARAH VAUGHN!"

Basie, resplendent in his blue tuxedo, got up from the piano bench. Smiling at everyone, he crossed the stage, eased over to the wings and escorted Sarah on stage with great and gracious ceremony, as if he had rehearsed the whole scenario. Any static in the air between us dissolved immediately. The crowd was on its feet screaming with surprised delight. An unexpectedly delicious dessert was topping their musical feast.

Sarah sang beautifully with superb accompaniment from the Basie band. The audience enjoyed a rare moment indeed.

In retrospect, the incident may appear to be much ado about nothing, certainly a minor incident in the course of a life. But it was important to me—a lesson learned. Bill "Count" Basie was an exemplary bandleader; most everyone would agree. He consistently presented his finely disciplined swinging band with relaxed and confident aplomb to great effect. But in the subtle way of a wise man, he demonstrated something else to me. By giving in, he showed he was more *the man* that night than I was. Thanks for the lesson, Bill.

Sir Duke

Of all the dynamic people in the entertainment world Duke Ellington stands out to me like no other. He was in a class by himself: elegant, yet down to earth; famous the world over, yet unaffected; a strong leader, yet gentle and gentlemanly; exceedingly bright, yet unpretentious; patient, warm, and considerate, always effective. He always regarded his marvelously talented band members as people first, musicians second—how unlike many high achievers in the music business.

Always in control, Duke had a certain insouciance about him—gracious, urbane, witty in a friendly way, with a clever sense of humor. During intermission at one of our presentations, he signed autographs on several ladies' girdles, after they had giddily hiked up the side of their skirts for him. (Yes, most women wore girdles in those days.) "Charmed, dahling," he said to each with debonair grace. "I'm never washing this again," I heard more than one young woman say.

I had played in his band a few times as a substitute saxophonist on occasions when Russell Procope or Johnny Hodges, his two regular alto saxophonists, were unavailable, and again at the 1962 Newport Jazz Festival. I had also recorded with him some time before in Chicago at a session for Universal Records, which featured Betty Roche singing "Love You Madly." Years later I produced Duke in our Cocktails and Concert series. In all that time I had never once seen him angry or outwardly upset; he remained a true artist, an exemplary bandleader, and a gentleman.

Duke was known for his habit of not reacting when provoked. His philosophy was that reactive knee jerking just caused him pain. As a result, he wouldn't let himself become needlessly agitated. It was often said he refused to be drawn into any kind of verbal confrontation. I once witnessed an example of this first hand.

Duke had done excellent business for us when we presented him in our Cocktails and Concert show in Bridgeport. The following month we presented him in Meriden, Connecticut, in the ballroom of the Holiday Inn in the same format.

On the day of the concert, I arrived in Meriden at five in the afternoon to help get things organized. The band had already set up for the eight o'clock show.

As I hurried through the door, an agitated Joe Sully, Duke's road manager, greeted me with, "Gene, can you please do something about that radio station guy? He's been talking to Duke for forty-five minutes now. He's being rude and insulting."

"What radio guy?" I said.

Apparently a local radio representative was interviewing Duke with a Wollensak tape recorder in the cocktail lounge.

"They're over there in that booth," said Sully. "He just asked Duke how it feels to be a black man in a white man's world. He's deliberately trying to provoke him. "

"What!" I said. "Let me at him."

After listening to the interview for just a few moments, I saw red. The guy was a complete ass.

"Do you find white women attractive, Duke?" he said.

"Do you?" Duke responded politely.

I was totally embarrassed. Worse, I felt responsible that some jerk was belittling one of the world's greatest musicians. Duke gently parried with the man, who in my view deserved a smack. But all the while Duke maintained his composure. You would never have known from Duke's demeanor that the *radio guy* was an offensive lout.

Finally, it had gone far enough. "Excuse me," I said, looking the interviewer in the eye. "Who are you anyway?"

"I'm the local radio D.J. on the morning show."

"I don't recognize you. What station?" I said.

"The Meriden one." I knew everyone at the station. He wasn't on the pass list.

"Let me see your ID and press pass," I said.

"Who are you?" he challenged.

"I'm the producer and you are not authorized to be here. What do you think you're doing?"

"Oh man, listen, I'm not really in radio," he said with a sheepish grin, like he was caught with his hand in the proverbial jar. "But I love to get celebrities on tape. It's my hobby." Like that should make a difference?

"Give me the tape and get the hell out of here," I said. "And NOW."

After he left, I turned to Duke, feeling like two cents ... make it one. "I am so sorry, Duke. That should never have happened. I'm really ashamed. I don't know how that guy got in here."

"Oh, Gene, don't give it another thought," he said. "It's a short life and we have to be nice to the phonies too."

His statement amazed me. Duke had known all along that the guy was a fake.

If not losing your cool when pressed is a mark of true class, then "Sir Duke" certainly had no peers in his realm.

Stan Kenton

Those who knew Stan Kenton, a tall, gangly man with a warm, almost Lincolnesque appeal, regarded him as an out-spoken, hard-working gentleman, who took the ups and downs of the band business in stride. He had a purist's dedication to his music and was respected in the business as a dedicated and no-nonsense leader. Kenton had strong, if controversial, opinions about music, and, if provoked, did not hesitate to express them. He maintained jazz didn't always have to "swing," that it could have more harmonic texture and not necessarily be captive to rhythm all the time. His approach to composition and orchestration was decidedly heavy. As a result, his music was serious and dramatic, and immediately recognizable as Kentonesque.

Watching him present his music was stimulating. He often stood at the piano conducting his orchestra with sweeping movements of his long arms, his face adopting masks of expressions—pain, joy, exuberance, encouragement, crescendo, fire—totally involved in the moment.

I especially admired Stan and his band because they produced musical fireworks. Sooner or later, in every arrangement, the music would climax in blazing brass fusillades and dynamic rhythmic intensity. He consistently showcased an amazing array of exceptional soloists like Maynard Ferguson, Shelly Manne, Art Pepper, Frank Rossilino, Mel Lewis, Shorty Rogers, Kai Winding, Bill Harris, Vido Musso, Lee Konitz, Charlie Mariano and singers Anita O'Day and June Christy.

We played Kenton to a sell-out crowd in Bridgeport at our Cocktails and Concert venue, our biggest crowd to date. The audience loved his unique, screaming big brass sound and the broad reach of the involved, almost Wagnerian arrangements. It was a fine show for Kenton fans and a huge crowd turned out. Our net profit from the show was $1,200. I was delighted.

The next night we had rented the Hartford Bushnell Auditorium to present our second Kenton concert—without cocktails of course—in the theater.

When driving up the Merritt Parkway to Hartford with Kenton in Bill Goglin's red, four-door Toronado, the conversation got around to the styles of various bands. I mentioned how well Basie and his ever-popular group had done with the crowd when he had played our Cocktails and Concert night. "He has a great outfit, don't you think, Stan?" I said. "It swings so naturally."

Critics sometimes faulted Kenton for what they regarded as his heavy-handed orchestral approach, which may have inhibited the band's swing factor, though the sound always did generate excitement. He must have been sensitive about it, because when I mentioned Basie, he grimaced slightly, like a contemplating Beethoven, as if he were pained by my comments. He hesitated before answering, looking out the window at the spring-budding Connecticut countryside whizzing by. Then he said quietly, but quite sincerely, "You know, Gene, once you get past that incredible, awesome, unbelievable swing, they're really playing Little Bo Peep."

I understood his point completely.

We lost exactly $1,200 on the Hartford concert. Serious money for me in those days.

Woody

On a late night flight from Pittsburgh to New York I happened to sit sitting across the aisle from Woody Herman. Free Spirit, my showband, was playing a three-week engagement at a large club in Greentree near Pittsburgh. I was heading back to Connecticut, aboard the Capitol Airlines red-eye for my day off.

I had produced Woody in concert several times and always found him to be unaffected and extremely approachable. We chatted small talk. He asked what I was doing with the *Jazz Giants*. Almost ashamed to admit it, I told him the Giants had died of natural causes, but that Free Spirit was currently very successful commercially.

"Great, Gene. Glad to hear it. I'm sure it's good. Keep playing."

Throughout the years Woody's bands were consistently of the highest caliber. His commitment to big band jazz was unmistakable. His bands had fire, originality, precision and energy. He had the ability to attract the finest players and hone them into an incredibly effective team, understanding them, developing them both personally and musically. Stan Getz, Zoot Sims, Al Cohn, Bill Harris, Ralph Burns, Shorty Rogers, Neal Hefti, Urby and Jack Green, Terry Gibbs, Jake Hanna, Carl Fontana, Kai Winding, Bob Brookmeyer, Sonny Costanzo, Sal Nistico, Nat Pierce. Nick Brignola, Red Rodney, Richie Kamuca and Steve Royal were a few of the jazz greats who played in Herman Herds.

Woody knew what he wanted, and with extraordinary leadership he always seemed to attain it. He chose excellent musicians, then insisted on their best performances every moment. He wasn't a nitpicker, but he wouldn't stand for sloppiness. He set and maintained high standards, producing some of the most brilliant big jazz bands the world has ever heard.

To me, along with Kenton, Basie and Duke, Woody was in an exclusive class of men who were superb leaders in the golden age of big-band jazz. He earned most every jazz musician's respect, much the same as Dave Brubeck has by those who have been privileged to know him. No one, as far as I know, has ever had a negative word to say about Woody's integrity or musicianship.

On our flight that night I complimented him on the many wonderful big bands he had over the years. One Herman Herd always seemed to surpass the previous edition with fresh energy and excitement … and even finer soloists.

"How do you decide on the sound and style for your bands, Woody?" I asked. "Each has had a different sound, yet they're always immediately identifiable as Woody Herman."

He smiled. "I just listen to Ellington and Basie and take what's left."

"Come on, Woody, really, your bands are always powerhouses, always dynamic, always unique. They swing like hell."

"No secret. That's what I do. Take what's left."

A few years later, I saw his band at a Chicago jazz club on my group's night off during our engagement at the Bonaventure Hotel on North Michigan Avenue. His band was ripping it up, playing brilliant big-band jazz. Bill Chase, the bull-like lead trumpeter, led the charge. Other new, young, super talents had recently joined the band. When we spoke that night, I said, "Every musician wants to work with you, Woody. How do you always get all these incredibly talented young guys to go out on the road and blow their brains out for you?"

"Gene," he said quietly, and quite sincerely, "What do I know? I'm just a dumb Polack."

It struck me that for one of the greatest jazz bandleaders ever to grace the world stage, egotism had no voice. His love of music and body of work spoke for him. I could only envy such a state of mind ... and such a man.

Brubeck

The musicians I respected most had all been leaders of big bands, men who had paid their dues and succeeded in bringing the world great big-band jazz. As far as I was concerned, they never lost their self-respect or the respect of others. All were consummate musicians. Each heard the sound of their own concepts and persisted with them through all the vicissitudes of the music business. Each knew the unique challenge and joy of organizing and sustaining a successful big band.

One man I've always respected as much, if not more, is one *not* noted for being a big band leader, although at one time he was. His fame is appropriately associated with his unique quartet.

Pianist and composer Dave Brubeck is an extraordinary man, one who never compromised his musical or personal values. He became known throughout the world performing jazz the way he heard it. During times when most jazz musicians were involved primarily in established duple and triple-meter time signatures—4/4, 3/4 and 6/8, Dave's *Time Out* album, which successfully experimented in less common jazz time signatures, was, and is today, one of the largest selling jazz records of all time. Notable among its many hits was "Take Five" in 5/4 time.

Brubeck recorded over one hundred albums and still records and tours at this writing. Juxtaposed with mainstream jazz, he is truly an innovator, a genuine, original American music icon. His *Time Out* album of 1958 is a music milestone.

But there's more to the Brubeck story. Something else sets him apart from others. Not only is he a man of rare integrity, he is a consummate father and family man. He and his multi-talented wife Iola raised six children—five boys and one girl, several of whom are professional musicians in their own right and who have recorded with Dave. The couple managed to keep their family together through all the difficult early years of traveling, moving, insecurities, lack of money, separations and doubt. Not a simple challenge in the entertainment business. Dave never seemed to put his music before family, yet he achieved enormous success and popularity. His was a doubly difficult task, yet he has been hugely successful on both fronts.

Another front affected his life, and in a certain way brought us together. During World War II, Brubeck was a young GI in Europe. German forces had broken through the American lines in a massive, last-ditch, counter offensive at Bastogne, Belgium. Swift moving German Panzer tanks and thousands of troops had "pincered" the trapped American forces in the famous Battle of the Bulge. For six weeks in frigid cold and snow the battle raged. Losses were heavy on both sides—over 100,000 casualties, the largest single American Army battle of the War.

Dave and his men managed to emerge unharmed. Eventually the Germans were turned back, which reversed the tide of the war, sealing Hitler's fate a few months later.

Deeply affected, Dave was inspired to write a composition called "Hymn for Conquest," which he arranged with the famous Stan Kenton band in mind. Later Dave approached him with the arrangement.

At that time the Kenton band was recording Pete Rugulo compositions, and Stan was more or less enamored with his work. It was the style he wanted for his band then. So Kenton told Dave, an unknown ex-GI, he wasn't interested. "Sorry, but no thanks," and refused to take the arrangement. The score stayed packed away in Brubeck's footlocker for many years.

I asked Stan about the incident. He said he didn't recall it. "Who knew?" he said. After all, Brubeck was an unknown at the time his arrangement was offered to Kenton. "I'm sure that was just another one of my more stupid mistakes," Kenton told me.

In the spring of 1964 my band, the eighteen-piece Jazz Giants was to perform a major concert at the Shakespeare Theatre with the famous Brubeck Quartet, Dave on piano, saxophonist Paul Desmond, drummer Joe Morello and bassist Eugene Wright. Some months before, I had read an interview about Dave in which he told of the Kenton incident. I called him and asked if he still had the arrangement. He did. Since our concert together was coming up in a few months, I asked if he'd like us to play it. He said he'd be honored, so we rehearsed the score.

When Dave conducted the piece at our joint concert, he lit up like a kid. As far as I know it was the first time he had heard "Hymn for Conquest" played publicly, almost twenty years after he had written it—a somewhat delayed world premier.

For several years I worked for a jazz radio station in Connecticut, WJZZ-FM, as sales manager; Dave was the Advising Music Director. It was a PR labor of love for him, a living for me. In all the times we encountered each other—on stage, at rehearsals, visits to his home in nearby Wilton, at the office, or whenever I said hello to him backstage after one of his concerts—he never changed. He was always a graceful, soft-spoken man with humorous sensibilities.

Several years later, I hurried into his large dressing room after one of his sold-out concerts at Tanglewood, in Lenox, Massachusetts. He was standing at the door unassumingly, quietly greeting everyone. I hadn't noticed him as I hurried past into the crowded room. I thought the tall, friendly slim person in the white dinner jacket I noticed peripherally as I entered was a guard or a friend or someone of no consequence. I never looked up to see who it was. I said hello to Iola, looked about and asked, "Where's Dave?"

"Right here, Gene," a voice at the door said, as I turned around. "Just waiting for you to say hello."

In 2008 I went backstage to visit him after his performance at the Sunrise Theater in Fort Pierce, Florida. "Gene, where have you been?"

"Dave, you never have sounded better," I said. And I meant it,

"Wait till next year," he said with a twinkle.

Hello Dave, wherever you are. I am proud to call you friend.

Woody, Sarah, Kenton, Basie, Ellington, and Brubeck – you told it like it was. See? You don't have to streeeeetch things. Congratulations.

(Thank you. You can trust me from now on.)

Oh, really?

**

Note:

As of this writing Dave Brubeck, now eighty-eighty, was recovering at his home in Wilton, Connecticut, from a serious illness and planning to resume a full tour with his group this year.

17

"FATHER OF EIGHT OD's"

I held on to the bathroom sink, fighting the blurs. In the mirror I could just about make out the shape of a head. In place of a face was an amorphous mass, a fuzzy, unrecognizable blob. Was it moisture obscuring the image? I swiped the mirror with my hand. No change. Where was my face? This was like one of those real-life TV police chases where the camera blurs out the face of the captured felon so you can't tell who it is. I opened my eyes as wide as I could. Brighter, but no focus. Eyeballs throbbed, assaulted by light.

In a cold sweat, I leaned against the sink and splashed cold water on my face, splattering my shirt, still not able to focus. My head pulsed like an automobile tire with a bulge in it thumps.

Pulse weak. Heart racing. Legs rubbery. Hands numb. How did I get here? What's happening to me? Am I dying? Am I drugged? Never having taken any kind of drugs before, I had no idea what effect an overdose might produce, but this might be it. Swallowing and gulping air as if my lungs were a sieve, desperate not to pass out, I slumped to the floor and fought to remain awake.

As I sat there, the imagined headlines of my hometown newspaper flashed across my mind: *NOTED LOCAL MUSICIAN, FATHER OF EIGHT, OD's IN NEW YORK CITY DRUG DEN.* It shocked me into consciousness. What would my family think? How could I let this happen? I should have seen it coming.

By 1972, Free Spirit, my six-person showband, was regularly booked at resorts in the Bahamas and Florida during the winter months. The booking dates indicated our success with engagements in the south during the winter months and up north during summers. In the early years of the group it had been just the opposite.

During one of these tours, Steve, our drummer at the time, met a particularly interesting young woman, Diane. We were appearing in the Tradewinds Lounge at Nassau's Loews Paradise Island Hotel, a resort that has since been assimilated into part of the present day Atlantis Resort complex.

Diane was a vacationing guest, a striking figure of a woman, about thirty, athletic, dark-haired with a shag cut. A sophisticated NYU graduate, she had a responsible position as Sports Equipment Buyer for Macy's in New York. Everyone liked her. She and Steve hit it off well, laughing at private jokes between themselves, partying at night after the job, and frequently spending afternoons snorkeling together. She was an excellent swimmer, a winsome, alert, All-American girl. At least that was my perception of her. But as I've indicated, at times I could be a bit naïve.

A week or so after we had returned from the Nassau engagement, Steve called me at my home in Connecticut. Explaining that he was visiting Diane at her New York apartment, he suggested that the next time I came into The City I should stop in, say hello, and have a drink with them on my way home. They'd love to see me. I agreed to meet them the following week.

During those times, between extended traveling engagements, I'd drive into New York City once a week from home, make the rounds of music agents and contacts and have a saxophone or flute lesson with Joe Allard in mid-town Manhattan before heading back to Connecticut.

The day I planned to meet them became a full one. I had played a three-hour recording session backing a singer with Clark Terry, Milt Hinton, Jerome Richardson and Herbie Hancock, had my sax lesson, and later endured a long but necessary meeting with my manager, Dick Towers. I called Steve to say that since it was already eight o'clock and I had a ninety-minute drive back to Stratford, I would have to beg off on coming to visit them. I'd try another time.

He insisted, however. "Aw, come on boss. We're opening a special bottle of wine just for you. You don't have to stay long. Diane is looking forward to it."

About thirty minutes later I found the upper West Side address on Riverside Drive, an older but well appointed fifteen-story gray brick apartment building with large windows. It was the kind of building that appears to govern its corner like a big-brother centurion of old New York. I wondered how many thousands of self-absorbed people had inhabited its recesses, walked its halls, painted its apartments, ridden its elevators, screamed, laughed, made love, cried, and died there. New York renews itself so often. If only the building could tell what they have seen. Tonight would be another moment in this one's silent memory.

The apartment building crested a higher elevation. It faced the park below, the darkened Hudson River beyond, and in the distance across the river, the nighttime twinkling of the Palisades.

I parked on the street, put my sax case in the trunk and locked the car. The doorman let me into the building and buzzed upstairs to let the occupants of 6 C know their guest had arrived. Very efficient. The elevator hummed up to the sixth floor.

"Welcome, Gene. Come on in." Diane greeted me with a hug and wet kiss on my cheek. "Good to see you again. You're just in time. This is my younger sister, Clare. And Steve is here helping us celebrate my birthday." Extra smiles all around. Their eyes looked particularly mellow and dilated to me. *Hmm.*

"Nice to meet you, Clare. Happy Birthday, Diane. I didn't know it was your special day. I would have brought flowers."

She laughed. With an inviting smile she said, "Oh, it was last month, but it's a good excuse for a party."

For a musician who had been around a bit, my street savvy was not exactly world class, a result of my vanilla up-bringing, most likely. But it didn't take a wizard to figure out this scene. "Steve, can I talk to you a minute?" I said. We walked into the small kitchen. "You guys are obviously partying. And that's fine. But I'm really not into it. Besides, it's late, and I'm tired. Time for me to go home."

"Aw, come on, boss, loosen up. Don't be so uptight. Have a glass of wine and a few nibbles. You're here. Relax for a little while. Don't rush off."

"Okay, but only for a few minutes."

I sat on a large upholstered couch, the old soft kind; if you don't sit upright and forward, you sink way back into it. I ate a handful of peanuts, a couple of chunks of cheese, a bite of pastry and sipped about half a glass of red wine. The wine didn't seem like anything special, but it was relaxing. On the walls of the dimmed, high-ceilinged room hung an eclectic mélange of prints and collected artifacts—from Klimpt to Wyeth to Warhol to African masks and woodcarvings, to Mexican clay figurines. The stereo produced appropriate soft-jazz musical wallpaper, resonating warmly off the polished hardwood floor.

Diane and Steve sat next to me. Clare, the well-designed tawny-haired sister, sat opposite me on a leather easy chair with her legs folded under her. She exuded the restrained confidence of a sensual woman who has a model's looks and knows it. The three of them were chatting, snacking, laughing. I enjoyed my wine and told them about the recording session that day with some true jazz greats. They seemed impressed. The atmosphere was convivial, and I was beginning to loosen up. *Maybe I'll stay for a half hour.*

Suddenly Diane reached over and snapped open a vial under my nose. It looked like a smelling salts container.

Steve said, "Breathe in, Gene. You'll like it." He and Diane were giggling. Her sister watched without expression.

"What is it?" I said.

"Go ahead," said Steve. "Take a good whiff. Smell it."

I did so, repeatedly, with big long whiffs. "So? What's the big deal?" Then everything started to whirl around me. What was happening? "I don't feel so good," I muttered, falling back deep into the couch, eyes closing. I tried to get up. Legs and arms leadened. I couldn't move.

"You'll be fine, man," Steve said, laughing. "It'll wear off in a few minutes."

Clare could see my face. She must have realized I was in trouble, because, as she told me later, I was turning gray. Obviously, I was about to pass out. She stood me up and walked me across the large room to the bathroom. I could hardly move. "Just splash some cold water on your face," she said. "Take your time. Don't worry, you'll be all right."

The other two were now laughing. They had turned on a square to his first and only experience with an *amy*—amyl nitrate —a drug sometimes utilized to revive angina heart patients, a popular toy of sophisticates who were into recreational drugs.

Unfortunately, since it dilates the blood vessels, one of the side effects can be to lower the body's blood pressure dramatically. I didn't know it at the time, but I was already in the throes of blood pressure problems. As a result, the usually mild drug hit me like a sledgehammer. For some strange reason, at that moment I imagined the façade of the building looking at me, frowning, shaking its head like an animated cartoon. I must have been hallucinating.

Red-eyed, confused, weakened and absolutely panicked, I slumped onto the bathroom floor. I don't know how long I stayed there. But I knew I had to get up. I couldn't let myself pass out, couldn't die like this. Maybe out on the street or in my car. But not here. Certainly not here. The headlines were still flashing in my mind. What would my family and friends think? This wasn't what my life was supposed to be.

I reached up to the sink with both hands and pulled as hard as I could. *Come on. Push up.* My head bumped into the sink. I hit the floor again. Got to get out of here. An ambulance may come. Or maybe the police. Oh, no.

I tried again. Standing, resolving not to fall, I looked into the mirror, eyes not seeing clearly yet, my face still a blotch. I forced myself to bump out of the bathroom, wobbling, shirt soaked, feeling blood from a cut on my head trickling down my cheek like the beginning of a warm brook.

"I have to go home. I think I'm dying. What, what did you do to me?"

"Jesus, Gene, you look like shit," Steve said. "It's only supposed to give you a quick little high. It doesn't last long. Don't worry." But the sound of his voice told me he was alarmed. I was too. *Got to get out of here.*

Fortunately, Clare came to the rescue again, supporting me under the shoulders.

"Come on, Gene, we're going to walk it off." Next: into the elevator, out onto the sidewalk, across the street, down an embankment into Riverside Park. We sat on a bench, while I breathed deeply trying to recover from the panic. Then she walked me back and forth for an hour or so, never letting go of my arm. I noticed the façade of the building again and imagined it was watching the whole scene, keeping score on some invisible tablet, dispassionate, indifferent, but not missing anything. The other buildings would know soon, I was sure.

For a long time I couldn't speak. When I did, I asked Clare what I had inhaled so freely. She told me it was an *amy* and that I had had an unusual reaction.

"Yeah, I guess." So much for the all-American girl and the urbane drummer. Wait till I get my hands on Steve. "An *amy*, huh? Some joke." I was too weak to vent my anger. I just wanted to get away from there.

My head cleared gradually as I drove cautiously up the West Side Highway, onto the Hutchinson River Parkway and connected to the Merritt Parkway; fifty more miles to Stratford. A roadside cantina's black coffee zapped my brain and revived me further. The more my mind cleared, the more outraged I became. How the hell could Steve have done that to me? What kind of a smart stunt did he think he was pulling? What were they thinking? Years later I learned that for those with blood pressure problems, Amyl Nitrate can sometimes cause death.

I got home at three in the early morning, kissed my sleeping children and wife gratefully and slipped into bed feeling lucky to be alive.

"How did it go today?" she mumbled.

"Oh, fine," I said.

Scary stuff. You were lucky. Too serious to kid about.
I'm going back to sleep now.

(Good night.)

**

18

_____

_____

SOMETIMES I HATED LYRICS

In the seventies, Free Spirit, our premier musical lounge group, played modified pop music and a little jazz, and covered many of the better current MOR (middle-of-the-road) top-forty hits. It was the time when many such show groups were touring the nation's clubs, hotels and resorts,

One feature that distinguished us from the pack was our excerpt vignettes from Broadway musicals, which we customized into the highlights of our shows. Our sound was unique, too. We integrated voices and instruments in a way that produced an effect of a much larger ensemble than six people. This was before electronic enhancements became *de rigueur* in traveling bands.

The group was a far cry from the Jazz Giants big-band sound of former years, so it marked a considerable switch in my musical direction. Survival had dictated a change of religion. I was weaning myself from the altar of jazz. Steady money, as the musicians called it, had become the necessary goal. One can give for art's sake just so long. As my friend Tiny from the Musicians Club used to say, "Jazz don't pay the rent."

Free Spirit was designed to entertain nightclub audiences with humor, clever arrangements and solid showmanship by first-rate musicians. Though not a jazz group in any way, it did present a valid variety of music with jazz-flavored arrangements. The fact that our disparate music pleased so many people—paying to see us perform—confirmed my belief in the project. There is nothing like paying customers to confirm one's validity as a performer.

Before Free Spirit, I hadn't paid much attention to much of the day's pop music. In fact, as a semi-snobbish, discerning (I liked to think) musician, I had gradually developed a somewhat fuzzy credo that maintained, if a pop song had words, it probably was because the music wasn't good enough to stand on its own. How ridiculous. Of course, that didn't include the great standard tunes of the era, but it did embrace most of the shallow tunes of the day.

As if that weren't enough, vocalists had gradually replaced big bands in popularity, much to my chagrin. Many of the major pop singers were lacking in anything I could call artistic sensitivity. Honestly, I resented the success of some of the minimally talented ones who were getting rich singing drivel. I felt let down and insulted, as if my musical training had been a waste. As far as I was concerned, most pop singers weren't even musicians. I cringed every time I heard Eddie Fisher drop a beat, or add an extra one, or sing out of tune. To make matters worse, it was the silly ditty songs that often became the big hits. I was appalled by the declining taste of the mass American market.

Frankly, as far as I was concerned, '50s music was mostly crap, and I never paid much attention to it. The ballads were often insipid: "How Much is that Doggy in the Window?" Bouncy tunes were mostly repetitive nonsense: "Rock Around The Clock," a case in point. And as for the Doo-Wop style, my prejudice ran so deep that I just about tuned out that whole decade of pop music and its lyrics. To my mind, most of the music of that era appealed to the lowest common denominator of musical taste and set popular music back to a simplistic level. I had spent a lifetime trying to cultivate an appreciation for excellence in music, so I wasn't buying any of it.

In retrospect, I realize that it was just fun — a harmless lightweight distraction that helped many people feel good. But back then, music was just too serious to me to see it screwed up like that.

Given the limits of taste I had placed about me to guard against such aural insults, it wasn't until 1964, when my young teenage son David had me listen to a new English group that I came back to being interested in pop music and contemporary lyrics again. The Beatles' *a cappella* arrangement of "Because," in particular, is a work of sheer beauty, as are "Eleanor Rigby" and "Yesterday." I became a Bealtles fan, not of their antics, but of their music. They pushed out the parameters of popular song, both in content and form.

Broadway musicals weren't high on my list of hits for a time either. In fact, I was down on most songs with words, as I have said, but not the work of great lyricists, like Cole Porter, Jerome Kern, Ira Gershwin, Harold Arlen, and other fine writers. In my opinion lyrics were generally ditties for people who didn't understand jazz, which of course I presumed I did. So that made me a musical authority.

Musical snobbery is second only to intellectual snobbery on the snob chart. I was right up there with the best, or worst, of them. I reasoned that if pop music had no room for improvisation or swing, it was inherently inferior.

Fortunately for me, by the time Free Spirit was formed in the '70s, I had outgrown some of my ignorance. The infectious, incredible funk of Motown music stimulated me. And hot horn groups like Blood Sweat and Tears, and Chicago had a cross-over influence on the pop music scene and on me as well. At the same time I learned featured songs from *Music Man* and *Fiddler on the Roof,* studied the lyrics, and went to see many Broadway musical theater performances for the first time. You might say it was my time of pop music and Broadway enlightenment.

My narrow perception of what constituted valid musical art began to expand significantly when I discovered that Broadway didn't have to be corny, but could be a rich source of good music. So many more people could immediately appreciate musical theater. I liked that.

One of the highlights of our shows each night was a ten-minute mini-revue of a Broadway highlight. In Meredith Wilson's *The Music Man,* I became Professor Harold Hill for a few minutes, delivering his famous *pièce de résistance,* "Trouble in River City." It was a wonderful number. Certainly it challenged me. I was intrigued by the words, the construction of the music and the way it built to a believable climax. It was a musical vehicle for Harold Hill to persuade the Iowa town's folks to counter the "evil influence" of the local pool hall by starting a community marching band. Hill would of course sell them the instruments, after which he planned to skip town.

Once I started performing these kinds of pieces, I loved them, though I often had difficulty remembering the exact lyrics, never, as I have said, having been much of a word man. It wasn't a major problem, however. When I forgot them, I just made them up.

Occasionally, my memory decided to take a walk, which more often than not was the case when I performed "Trouble in River City". This number has more words than any other Broadway piece. The others in the band poised themselves with eager anticipation, just waiting to hear what verbal entanglement I would get myself into, and then delight in seeing how I could get out of it.

I always made it through the piece, with the aid of some creative manipulation of instant rhyme and an occasional bit of double talk. I figured that what I lacked in accuracy, I could make up with dramatic sense and performance skills. After all, they were only words; it wasn't as if I made a mistake in the music. Besides, I was the bandleader.

I didn't experience a personal commitment to the power of lyrics with the same feeling that the music could communicate to me. Though sometimes very strong, words weren't real for me, so they couldn't be as important as the music.

Then one night something tragic happened that changed how I viewed life. Quite unexpectedly, the impossible, the unreasonable, the unbelievable plopped itself in my life, as if a wall of steel was suddenly lowered on the road ahead—immoveable, non-negotiable—forcing me to stop and face a trauma I was powerless to avoid.

Free Spirit was playing a return, month-long engagement in New York at Shepheard's, the swank, very *in* supper club at Park Avenue's Drake Hotel. People dressed to be seen there. The entertainment format featured a contemporary showband alternating its show-sets with a top DJ's dance music. That policy was on the leading edge of sophisticated club entertainment in those days. One night at one o'clock, when we were just about to go on for our third show, the last one of the evening, a telephone call came backstage from my wife in Connecticut.

"What's up? " I said, surprised. "You okay? Kids all right?"

"Gene, listen carefully. I have to tell you something," she said quietly. "Your sister's had a coronary."

"What's that?" I said. My wife was a nurse, so I expected a technical explanation.

"A heart attack."

"Oh, my God. Is she okay? Is it serious?"

"She didn't make it," she said.

"Didn't make it? You mean she's dying?"

"She's gone."

"Barbara? It can't be. She's never even been sick."

"I'm so sorry," Connie said. She knew my sister and I were close.

The third show was just about to start. The club was packed. It was Saturday night. There wasn't much choice but to go on stage. "Ladies and Gentleman, Free Spirit." The show began.

The first several numbers I played and sang the music, as always, but this time without hearing any of it. In my mind's eye I kept seeing my sister and me when we were youngsters performing as a professional juvenile ballroom dance team. We swirled across the dance floor in increasingly rapid turns, did spins and lifts and dips and danced many Astaire-Rogers steps, I in my black tails and white tie, Barbara in a white satin gown. She was careful and somewhat timid; I was the one who was always loaded with confidence. And now I could hear her saying to me so clearly, as she sometimes did when I prepared to lift her for an arabesque or spin in one of our routines, "Genie, don't drop me."

I'd laugh and say, "Don't worry, I won't."

It was happening again on Shepheard's dance floor. Only this time I couldn't protect her.

The moment came for our musical vignette of *Fiddler on the Roof,* in which I, as Tevya, sang and acted "If I Were a Rich Man." I made it through most of the piece, until the last few lines, when Tevya looks up to heaven and says, "Oh God, who made the lion and the lamb ..."

I got as far as saying, "Oh, God," and stopped.

I looked down. Paused. Breathed deeply. Lifted my head. "Oh, God," I said again. I wasn't performing then. I was talking to God. And I meant it.

The band stopped. The audience was quiet. I remember thinking in that hole of silence, "You rat, how could you do this? How could you snatch away my sister like that, a forty-one year-old mother of four young children? It isn't fair." After a long pause, I finished the song and the show, then drove back to Connecticut.

I was angry at God for the first time in my life. Even if we had differences in the past, my belief was never threatened. But this was different. I didn't talk to Him—or Her—for many years after that. As a matter of fact, our relationship hasn't been quite the same since.

At Barbara's funeral three days later, I didn't shed a tear. I was too angry to cry. Her husband and four young teenagers survived her. My mother was heart-broken but stoic. This was the saddest day of her life.

Four years later, after a concert performance in a summer theater tent near Boston as conductor for the Sandler and Young show, I came to terms with the grief I was carrying around and bawled all night long in my hotel room. For three days the gushing flowed. And then it was over.

Much later I realized that when the tragedy of Barbara's death hit me so hard that night at Shepheard's, I wanted to stop and quit the show and go home. But curiously, because of the lyrics I was singing, I was able to show my anger at the peak of fury, speak one-on-one with God, in a way, and tell him how pissed I was with Him. I hadn't ever done that before, probably because there had been no reason to.

In retrospect, I tried to make some sense of what had happened. There didn't seem to be any. Ironically, the words of a song had become the vehicle for me to vent. Through the words, I was able to show my anger, albeit silently, to the Main Man. Those lyrics helped me recognize and focus feelings, forced me to confront the cruel reality of sudden death of a loved one and deal with it; she was my best friend.

Now I'm a true appreciator of musical theater. As for lyrics, I don't hate them anymore, no matter what stories they tell. In fact, I've listened to them carefully ever since and just let the words speak for themselves.

Peace.

**

The Dance Team, Barbara and Gene, ♫ ages 9 and 10

19

————————

—————

THE BAND PLAYED ON

Think of your fellow man.
Lend him a helping hand.
Put a little love in your heart.

Jackie DeShannon, 1969.

"Gene Hull, you stink!" snarled the thin, red-faced, forty-ish woman in the black dress, spaghetti straps askew, hair disheveled, "and so does your music!"

There was nothing I could say. It was New Year's Eve. Some people just do not handle celebrations well, I guessed.

1972 had been an eventful year. Israeli athletes had been killed by terrorists at the Munich Olympic Games, foreshadowing dire events for decades to come. Nixon had harvested a landside victory, winning his second term, and with it the seeds of Watergate had probably been sown. The war in Vietnam was still intense.

But happier news speckled that year as well, events of much less significance—only blips on the record of the times—but nonetheless of interest to some. For instance, sixteen-year-old

Ulrike Meyfarth of West Germany won the Olympic Gold Medal in the Women's High Jump, the youngest female ever to do so. The Stratford, Connecticut, *Raybestos Cardinals* won the United States Fast Pitch Men's Softball Championship for the third time. And Free Spirit was booked to play a New Years Eve engagement at the downtown Holiday Inn in Bridgeport, Connecticut. I'm sure if you participated in one of these events, you would remember it. I do.

I was the leader and saxophonist of Free Spirit, by now a national touring show band, and rather well known in Bridgeport in the '70s. I guess we were the closest thing to active musical celebrities that city had. The six-person group—guitarist, drummer, bassist, trumpet player, a featured female singer, and myself on saxophone—seldom performed in the local area. The rare occasions, when we did, usually meant good business for the venue operator.

This New Year's Eve event was promoted as "Gene Hull and Free Spirit, Home for the Holidays," a dinner dance to bring in the New Year. I looked forward to playing in my hometown for New Year's, since it meant I could spend extra time with family. Granted, Bridgeport was not exactly the garden spot of the world then, still isn't—actor Paul Newman later referred to it as the world's armpit—but the booking was really important to me. For the father of four boys and four girls, being home for the holidays was a special treat.

Many Connecticut people remembered me from the Jazz Giants, which had brought us modest local fame and even some national press. As a result, local interest in my musical doings sustained, and the new group quickly developed a strong following.

The Holiday Inn charged heavily that night for the "Dinner, Dance and Show"—$25 per couple, which was rather steep for Bridgeport in the '70s. In keeping with show business standards of the times, Free Spirit always dressed in fancy, color-coordinated, custom-made, designer outfits. We presented ourselves in the elegant attire expected of quality performers in those days. That night the band wore black, white, and silver brocaded vests with black satin lapels, white silk "pirate" shirts, and black tuxedo pants. Lenore SanAngelo (now Lenore Mascar), our dark-haired singer wore a glamorous looking, long white sequined gown. It definitely wasn't the street wear worn by today's performing groups. Ours was an uptown act with an uptown look that usually played some of the best venues in the country. This particular engagement, however, was different.

The event was sold out. In fact, it was oversold. And that was the problem. The ballroom, where we were set up, had a banquet capacity of seven hundred. But, judging from the crowd, tickets had apparently been sold for nearly a thousand.

Our first set, at 10:00 p.m., lasted an hour. By eleven o'clock, many people still did not have tables. Temporary places had been set up in hallways, foyers and an adjoining cocktail lounge. There still wasn't enough room. Many of those who had been seated weren't getting their dinners on time, or weren't served them hot, if they got them at all. Bizarre as it seems, some people were taking others' tables when they'd get up to dance, even stealing each others' dinners. Part-time waitresses, hired for the night, were quitting on the spot because of the abuse they were getting, which only made the situation worse.

Obviously, some people sensed they were getting ripped off, and apparently feeling entitled to get even, justified their conclusion with outrageous behavior. I felt helpless watching the scene from the bandstand.

After the opening set, people I didn't know came up to me and said things like:

"Gene, this is awful."

"Can't you do something?"

"You should know better."

"This is an insult," invected a large woman in a frilly red dress.

"We never would have come here if we had known it would be like this," said another woman.

"You ought to be ashamed of yourself," still another.

Many thought I had handled the promotion and blamed me for the chaos. I tried to explain, but I could tell from their cynical looks that any attempt to set the record straight would do little to calm the seas. I could understand. After all, they had paid out good money to have a special New Year's Eve, and it was turning into a disaster. They were in pain.

It didn't take a wizard to figure out the hotel manager was a sleaze. He probably thought he could wing it with smooth talk and gloss over temporary inconveniences to customers. But it wasn't working out that way.

When I suggested to him that since people were getting downright hostile he might want to put the overflow crowd into the back lounge at the far end of the hotel and set folks up with a complimentary drink, possibly accompanied with an apology, he told me to mind my own business.

His response didn't exactly thrill me. "Sure, no problem," I said, "if that's the way you want it." But in view of his attitude and the ruse he was trying to pull off, and considering all that was going on in the ballroom, something told me I'd better ask him right then for our money. I hesitated to do so. Even though it was so stipulated in my contract, I knew it would be unpleasant, and I didn't enjoy confrontations.

"I'd like to be paid now," I said, "if you don't mind. It's intermission. And we have to drive to the airport immediately after the job to catch an early morning flight to Florida. It would save time if we took care of business now."

"Are you nuts?" he said. "'Can't you see I'm busy? See me when the night's over."

"Nope. Sorry. Pay us the balance you owe us now in this intermission, like it calls for in our contract, or we pack up and leave … now." (I remembered what happened when I was a kid playing at the White Eagles Hall.) I could see by his expression that he knew I would. He also knew that if that happened, handling the crowd would be even more difficult for him.

We went into his office. He gave me a snarly glare that said, You sonovabitch, and paid me in cash. Grumbling. Surly. Sour-faced. Swearing. But he paid.

"You'll never work here again," he said. Like, I'd want to. I liked him even less.

There wasn't much we could do about the situation except play our music, entertain the best we knew how, and try to help some of the people have a good time. A few minutes before midnight we played the usual "What Are You Doing New Year's Eve," a slow ballad, which our Lenore sang smoothly, expecting people to get warm and cuddly. Couples jammed the dance floor but soon were packed together to a point of immobility. Many couldn't get there and danced next to their tables.

Then came the traditional dramatic countdown: "Ten, Nine, Eight, Seven, Six, … "HAP-PY NEW YEAR!" after which we went into a loud, ceremonial rendition of "Auld Lang Syne." Lenore was the only one who knew all the words. I still don't know what they mean. There wasn't much hugging and gentle midnight kissing at the traditional big moment on the dance floor. Couples bumped into each other for more space. Butts smacked into butts. Elbows poked backs. Shoulders jarred off-balance couples that were attempting semi-fancy terpsichorean moves. Heels purposed onto nearby feet, seemingly bent on inflicting un-neighborly discomfort.

Yet through it all, a few inseparably dedicated kissers took it all in stride, clinging, hugging, slurping, standing in place, not missing a single moment of the opportunity for full-body contact in a public place. One embracing young couple was jostled to the floor, a tall thin young man and a short, well-built dark-haired miss. They never stopped kissing. From what I could see, the back of the young woman's gold lame blouse had deserted the area of her black velvet slacks and was heading toward her neck. Impossible to tell if this were a "wardrobe malfunction" or if the blouse's trip had help from her partner. However, I don't think they were even aware they were in a prone position. Most people were definitely not in such an affectionate mood.

We quickly segued into the usual New Year's Eve ritual of merry nonsense songs like "Pop Goes The Weasel," "The Mexican Hat Dance," "Hokey Pokey," etc., to lighten things up. But with all the pushing and shoving that was going on, and the grumbling around us getting louder, we could sense an undercurrent boiling up. Things were about to blow.

We didn't dare stop playing. Instead we began to perform our medley of message songs from the flower-children era of the '60s—the *sine qua non* of every self-contained show band touring the country at the time—with their bright, peppy beat and innocent, if naïve, peace and love message. Vainly we gave it the full evangelical treatment in hopes this would influence the prevailing agitation. The medley was one of our signature numbers, an extended showy-dance piece that built like the "Twelve Days of Christmas" with each of us singing a verse, and the whole group pouncing on the hook-line, *Put a Little Love In Your Heart.*

Our intention was that the good vibes we were sending out so sincerely, all the while smiling our winsome best would soothe the crowd and help them overlook what was, after all, a minor inconvenience compared to the larger picture of World Peace and Brotherhood of Man. It was worth a try, I thought. But my understanding of human-nature-under-stress proved to be somewhat lacking in reality.

Of course, there was a time when certain songs could have a quelling effect on unruly crowds … like playing the national anthem did back in the era when reverence for the anthem really mattered to people in America. But those days had evidently passed.

Anyway, that was just about when a fight broke out somewhere in the back of the ballroom. There were so many people on the dance floor we could not to see what was happening, but we could hear the commotion. In a few minutes, as the shouting got louder and screams more penetrating, we realized this was more than a usual New Year's Eve shoving duel between two drunks.

Stepping up the fervor factor, we fairly bellowed out the song's punch line (no pun intended), "Put a Little Love In Your Heart."

Then ... CRRRASSSSH! We heard a banquet table fall. Dishes and glasses shattered to the floor. A rotund, rosy-cheeked woman, bedecked in costume jewelry, screamed as her husband took a wild swing at a tablemate.

Did we honestly think the crowd would kiss and make up? Or get all warm and fuzzy because of our love medley? Talk about naiveté.

Still, we persisted.

"Come on you people now.
Smile on your brother.
Everybody get together.
Try to love one another right now"

More screams. Punches thrown. Tables collapsing. Women pushing. A football-player-type young man shoved two tussling drunks away from his girlfriend, sprawling them into a falling table. We didn't stop playing or singing. And the crowd didn't stop swinging—fists, handbags, chairs—pulling hair, kicking shins and smashing tables.

Nobody was dancing any longer. Certainly nobody was listening to the music. In the interest of personal safety we moved as far back on the bandstand as we could, where, appreciating the irony of the moment, John Iafrate, our young guitarist, couldn't contain his feelings and doubled over in a spastic fit of laughter. Yet he still managed to keep on playing. British drummer, Cliff Page—clearly relishing the scene, not wanting to miss any of the Fellini-esque action—stood up behind his drums and continued to play. Unrestrained full-belly laughs punctuated his attempts to sing. Jerry Merliani, our trumpet player and I were doing our best to get our horns away from the bumping and pushing. I could swear bassist Gary Fineberg was yelling, "Go man, sock 'em." Almost convulsed with laughter, we continued to play. Hell, what else could we do?

As we moved back, Jerry and I managed to take up protective positions in front of Lenore who never stopped singing the verses—protecting her from any stray attack. It was then that chairs began to fly and bottles went on the wing.

"That's it, guys," I yelled, "let's get out of here … fast." While we were packing up, the New Year's Eve celebrators continued altercations, oblivious to the world around them. People were mad as hell and apparently intent on destroying the place. I could hardly believe it. A man was hanging onto a low chandelier and kicking at anyone unlucky enough to be pushed near him. More sensible patrons were streaming for the exits—out into the freezing First-of-January morning.

This wasn't happening like it had several years before, when I had been playing with the Tex Beneke band on a hot summer Saturday night in the Texas boonies. This was Connecticut, supposedly more sophisticated than the Wild West, and in Bridgeport, my hometown, where most of the crowd knew me and knew Free Spirit. I was surprised and deflated. So much for the fleeting glory of over-rated local fame.

But we had no time to philosophize. We scurried off the platform, grabbed our horns and secured them in the back room. We disassembled other equipment, our portable Shure sound system, and black-pearl drum set. Within ten minutes we had loaded everything into the two cars and U-Haul trailer waiting for us outside the back door.

Some of the remaining crowd had quieted down. But others were still going at it. The place was now half empty.

Just then the manager noticed we were about to leave. "Where the hell are you going?' he demanded.

"Florida," I said, "and quick."

"Listen, Hull, you were contracted to play until 2:00 a.m. It's only 12:40." It was a weightless protest, as far as I was concerned.

Suddenly, a nearby drunk yelled to another, "Let's see how you like a chair in your face, buddy" as he swung wildly, missed his target and crashed against a wall.

"It's not safe in here," I said, just in case the manager hadn't noticed. "We don't want to get hurt."

"You might if you don't finish playing the dance."

I ignored the implied threat. "There is no dance. It's a brawl. Don't you get it?" At that moment an irate woman in a black dress, who apparently knew he was the manager, approached and blind-sided him with her loaded handbag, a full swing to his head. WHUMP! The blow staggered him, knocking him back against a table.

"You snake," she said, her eyes flashing venom. She looked over at me, steadied herself and yelled, "Gene Hull, you stink! *Hic.* And so does your music." With that she turned and kicked a nearby chair over, before swaying back though the crowded ballroom, bouncing off people like a pinball. She was ticked and tanked.

As I tried to help the manager up, he pulled a revolver from his inside jacket pocket and pointed it at me. He got to his feet, shoved it into my ribs and ordered, "Get into my office, NOW." I guessed he wanted the money back. Nobody noticed us; there was so much confusion.

"Come on, Henry, you nuts or something?' Hundreds of people are here," I said.

"Get going and keep your hands down."

I did as I was told, walking a step or two in front of him. The crowd grew wilder and noisier. We made our way through the lounge, passed the bar. "Look out, Henry!" I yelled, as I pointed across the room with my left arm. He turned his head for a second. As he did, I tightened my body and with all my strength rammed my shoulder full into him.

The force caught him in the ribs and threw him off balance. He tumbled back onto the floor. As he did, the gun fired, probably into the ceiling. The crowd panicked and with terrified screams stampeded for exits and windows.

I ran for the back door, dodging obstacles as I did, jumped into the car—the band already there—and drove away. It was a New Year's Eve I'd never forget.

*

Gun? Oh, give me a break!

(It sounds more exciting like that. Besides, you were asleep. Okay, so there was no gun.)

Tsk, tsk.

With that she turned and kicked a nearby chair over, before swaying back though the crowded ballroom, bouncing off people like a pinball. She was ticked and tanked. There was nothing I could say. She stumbled off; the manager was still smarting from her attack.

I turned, quickly left the building, and got into the car. We drove to Bradley International Airport in Windsor Locks, sixty patchy-ice miles north on I-95. We arrived around four in the morning, emotionally drained, freezing in ten-degree weather, but relieved to be going to sunny Florida. It wasn't until after we began thawing out with hot chocolates, coffee and donuts in the almost empty airport lounge that we started to relax.

A delighted John Iafrate, our young guitarist, still giddy from the excitement of the night, dramatically toasted a cup of coffee. "HAP-PY NEW YEAR, EVERYBODY! I hope they're all as good this one!"

**

FREE SPIRIT

♫ Circa **1974**

(L – R) Front, Phil Orr . Back, Claude Berardi, Lenore SanAngelo,
Danny Boswell, Gene, Jimmy Carson.
(Not pictured: former members Cliff Page, John Iafrate, Gary Fineberg,
Jerry Merliani, and George Perillo.

The end of a era ...

For several years after the New Years Eve brawl—when love didn't conquer all—if I heard the song, "Put A little Love In Your Heart," I wouldn't have been too surprised to see a chair come sailing by, or a bottle boomeranging through the air. My contingency plan was always: get paid early, and, whatever it takes, protect my horns.

Eventually, the Holiday Inn closed. As in so many other cities, the downtown areas of Bridgeport became less safe at night. When the Inn reopened the following year with new owners, a chain link fence surrounded the property and a guard monitored its gated access. A few years later, the building was demolished for a municipal parking lot.

To me, the Inn's demise meant another vestige of the age of politeness, fun, and working class respect for authority had passed inexorably into history, much like the demise of the Ritz Ballroom after the big band era faded, whose ignominious end came in a disastrous fire.

The oncoming social evolution of "me-ism" would have its effect on the music business. The majority of the better clubs and lounges in North America evolved from featuring jazz, to presenting showbands (like ours), to booking Top-40 dance bands, to local rock/pop cover-groups, until eventually becoming discos with no live music. Many succumbed to the avalanche of I-wanna-do-it-myself-ism, changing into Karaoke bars. Lounge entertainment devolved into audience interactions, which, as entertainment, were usually mediocre, but apparently, were good for the folks. Pop-culture had morphed again, and the golden age of showbands gradually passed into musical history.

During the transition, however, Free Spirit performed profitably for four more years. We had a great ride while the wave lasted. I was grateful. After all, I had already learned how to duck flying bottles successfully.

20

LAS VEGAS

"Every show band wants to play Vegas," said Ted Purcell, our agent.

"So does Free Spirit," I said. "Why don't you get us a booking there?"

"It's not that easy. Competition is tough." Teddy was always upbeat and effusive when selling to clients. But to the acts he represented, when it came time to field the oft-repeated question thrown at him, "Why aren't we playing Vegas?" he adopted a grim and whiney demeanor.

He'd shake his head slowly—as if he were about to explain that a dear friend had died—before coming out with one of his stock answers to put us off. "Business isn't that good," he'd say. "I'm trying. You don't know how hard it is. Vegas is a tough nut to crack. Be patient." Then he always added, "You know I always want the best for you, you *know* that."

We knew what that meant ... no Vegas booking that year again.

We could only hope that someday we'd land a booking at the Mecca of live entertainment.

We had had a resounding success when impresario Irvin Arthur booked us to open Playboy's new Great Gorge Hotel for four weeks. We were held over for seventeen weeks. But in the '60s and '70s a Las Vegas booking was the high-watermark, a badge of accomplishment for groups that did not have national recordings. This usually established them as having the right stuff and had the prestige to boost careers almost immediately. Lounge acts, in particular, craved the exposure only a Vegas engagement could offer. I wanted that for Free Spirit. Being the Type-A that I became as I grew up, always setting goals and focusing exclusively on them, I started gearing up for Las Vegas soon after Free Spirit was formed in 1971.

Although we gave it an all-out effort in our five years together, and had our share of successes, Free Spirit just did not seem to be what Vegas needed at the time. I didn't have the contacts, the in, the juice, the connections to get us there. It was totally frustrating and the five-year effort drained me.

Faced with the realization that Free Spirit was approaching a standstill and had probably attained its potential, I considered getting out of the music business and developing a new career. But the odds of not succeeding were getting longer; I would have to start over again at something new and was not exactly in the prime of my life.

I decided to give it one more try, this time with a different group. Not an easy decision. Free Spirit members had shared a dream. Disbanding the group would mean more to us than just a loss of money. We were close friends and would have to separate. I felt I just couldn't take us where I thought we should be going and time was running out. Our moment was over. I had to move on.

I weighed the pluses of creating a "record act" with music that satisfied the public, as well as my own tastes, against the advantages of developing a unique performing ensemble that might also have recording potential. The second option seemed preferable because, if successful, it could generate much more revenue. During the next six months I worked on an idea based on what I had learned about the business over the years. I needed to try one more time.

The envisioned group had to be dynamic, visually appealing, have a distinctive sound, be musically interesting, and be commercially viable enough to record for the popular marketplace. Excellent musicianship was a pre-requisite. The goal was to be a Vegas act for main rooms, not lounges.

This criteria distilled into a concept: an all-female string quartet—two violins, viola, and cello—a female singer, four men in the rhythm section composed of bass, drums, keyboards, and guitar, and myself playing saxes and electric flute, ten people in all. The repertoire would be mainstream, disco-jazz-pop, music with a recognizable musical signature sound. Its visual hook, would be the five young women, four string players and the singer.

The project had to have originality, style, looks, and dance appeal in order to sell records and have successful personal engagements. The group's look and sound should be exclusive enough to get noticed, I reasoned. The rest would follow.

Conceptualizing was one thing; putting it together was quite another. I contacted university and conservatory music departments, posted notices in union halls, placed ads in music publications and followed up on personal recommendations. I received letters from hopefuls all across the country, and auditioned many candidates. I found that most of the string players were not yet musically flexible enough, that is, their interpretation of pop music was too stiff. They couldn't swing, or if they could, they were not attractive enough to be show people in a Vegas ensemble. In the surprisingly long process I eventually settled on four excellent classically trained musicians who were beauties, if a bit reticent about being regarded as such: Karen Karlsrud, Ethel Abelson, Mabel Wong and Joan Spergel.

I remember the day I heard Joan. She had followed up on an ad and sent a tape and her picture as requested. I went to her residence on New York's Upper West Side one afternoon. As I entered the red brick apartment building walk-up, I heard a full rich sound, like a French horn, careening through the halls. Or perhaps it was a trombone. It evoked the unmistakable assertion of a strong middle-range brass instrument. As I came closer to her fourth floor apartment, I realized the sound was actually a cello, reverberating with colossal presence through the empty halls. I decided to hire her at that moment, before even seeing her.

None of the four women had played in a pop music group before; all were intrigued by the idea. They were nice people and serious musicians, willing to put in the rehearsal time necessary to prepare. Of course most of them didn't wear make-up, or shave their legs, or style their hair much. After all, they were classical music devotees. Fashion, unless functional, seemed rather shallow and silly to them. But they were very attractive, and as I have said, wonderful musicians. And that meant possibilities for the new group.

I had borrowed $10,000 from my bank, with no collateral but my name, to finance the project: uniforms, gowns, equipment, instruments, sound system, orchestrations, rehearsal costs. I commissioned various writers to do original arrangements that would capture the musical potential of the group. All appeared to be progressing well, except the project was taking too long to put together. Six months without steady income was difficult. In the interim, I played as many casual gigs as I could find.

Finally, we were ready to begin rehearsals, the first time I would actually hear *the sound*. I loved what the arrangers had done. They managed to capture the essence of the group—distinctive, contemporary, vibrant. I thought this could be it. It will make a statement. I named the group "Music

Maximus". But agents often referred to it as "Gene's string thing."

To get us booked and off-and-running, I asked Larry Spellman, the dynamic former Vice President of the William Morris Agency, then head of Complex Four together with Marvin Schnayer, Dick Towers, and Dick Grass, to listen to us at a rehearsal. Larry recognized the potential immediately and called Joe Scandori, Vic Damone's manager. Vic's career was in slow motion at the time and Joe was looking for some new vehicle to help take Vic with some flourish to the main room stages again.

Handsome, dark-haired, fifty-ish Damone was certainly one of the top singers in America. He had had a million-seller record when still a teenager, a rarity in those days. He recorded many best,-selling albums and possessed one of the most perfect baritone voices ever heard—some say the best.

Vic, who was appearing at a Long Island venue at the time, drove up to Bridgeport on a cold March Sunday afternoon to hear us. We dressed the four "string girls" in long red sheath gowns with spaghetti straps and pearl necklaces. For some reason, they were reluctant to shave their legs. It was just an audition to them. Shaving legs seemed dishonest to them, I guess. But we did get them to wear a little lipstick and makeup. They looked *and sounded* stunning.

Our plan was to stage them grouped around Vic. For the audition, Lenore, dressed in a white beaded gown, sang counter parts with Vic on some of his songs. Our rhythm section wore black suits and black shirts without ties. I wore a three-piece white suit.

It worked. Damone was impressed. Apparently we had the look, energy, and sound that felt right to him. Three months later we were booked into the Congo Room, the main showroom at the Sahara Hotel in Las Vegas together with Damone and another headliner, Don Rickles.

We opened a few days before July 4, 1976, the year of the Bi-Centennial, a time when overt patriotism was in fashion. This was a once-in-a-lifetime month to be in Vegas, a city without nuances and always over the top in the flag-waving department.

On the day of opening night, Vic personally brought the four string girls and Lenore to a beauty salon, which catered primarily to theatrical people; there they were given complete star-treatment makeovers—haircuts, styling, manicures, facials and professional makeup. They were knockouts when they appeared on stage that night. The attention they received from then on, from house-band members to audiences, was enough to convince them the time had come for a lifestyle change. Glamour did not have to compromise their integrity as classically trained musicians.

Opening night was a smash success. The blend of Damone and the group was extraordinary. Newspaper reviews glowed with praise for Damone's new look and the sound of the "Gene Hull Strings". The Strip buzzed with inside talk. Cab drivers pitched the show to tourists. Something new had hit Vegas. All agreed that Vic never sounded better. Vic was in demand again. New bookings flowed in.

Wherever we went, people seemed to know us. At times they would pay for our drinks or meals. We felt like celebrities, smothered in the praise and complements that Vegas awards its stars.

I played in a pro-celebrity charity tennis tournament at the Riviera with David Jansen, Hugh O'Brien, Abby Dalton, Juliet Prowse, Rod Laver, Poncho Gonzales and others. John Wayne's wife, Pia, was my partner; we lost.

This was show business nirvana to me, an awesome high, confirming in grand style the attainment of a goal. But the most fun was yet to come.

The third week of our engagement at the Sahara, my mother, Marge, then in her seventies, flew out to Vegas to see us.

We talked backstage about the Benny Goodman stage show she had taken me to so many years ago at the Lyric Theatre. Chidingly, I told her I would never forgive her for getting me hooked on a horn that day.

This was a particularly great night for her to see our show, Las Vegas Hotel Employees Night. I introduced her to many of the celebrities backstage who performed in the special after-hours late show. Lounge entertainers, headliners, movie stars, musicians, hotel workers, taxi drivers, agents, producers from all over the Strip came for the annual FREE big bash. Backstage was like a huge party, packed with stars that were performing. Booze was flowing, jokes were rolling, and Lenore and the rest of my group were in a state of thrall, mingling with Wayne Newton, Neil Diamond, Rich Little, Arlene Dahl, Olivia Newton, Don Rickles, Paul Anka, Foster Brooks, Dick Shawn, Jerry Vale, Joey Heatherton, Joey Bishop, Redd Foxx, Johnny Cash, Red Buttons, Robert Goulet, Roy Clark, Andy Williams, and many more. Overload excitement. All these years trying to get a booking in a Vegas Lounge; and now, here we were on a main room stage on the biggest night of the year. Feelings I cannot describe flooded me. Maybe gratefulness comes closest.

Many of the male performers used my backstage dressing room that night. Except for Rip Taylor; he used Lenore's.

"Dahling," he said to her as he came out of her bathroom rearranging his wig, "Thank you so much for letting me come in. It's so crowded in Gene's dressing room, you know." Rip's comedy routine about a gay astronaut, who refused to be launched at lift-off without his crayons, was always a showstopper.

During the show Red Buttons far exceeded his allotted time on stage. As he was doing his stand-up routine, Rickles came out from the wings with a broom, wearing a red apron, and started sweeping up behind Red. The audience loved it. Red got the message. Rickles, despite his acerbic public persona, is a sweet and gentle man. I worked with him several times after that.

Later in the program, when Vic sang the romantic "And I Love You So" with our string quartet grouped around him, Rickles again came out on stage, this time with Redd Foxx and Foster Brooks. The three of them pretended to sing backup, complete with overt gestures and body language. The crowd of hotel workers roared with delight.

Vic didn't get it until he turned around and saw Don and the other two on stage in back of him. Discovered, Rickles ran up to the mike, knelt down on one knee with feigned sincerity, and began kissing Vic's pant leg, pleading, "Please don't tell Frank."

After conducting Vic's show, I went back to my dressing room and walked in on Dick Shawn "talking" to a young cocktail waitress on the couch. Both were in a diminished state of dress. I turned around and left immediately. I hate interrupting important conversations.

Where else but in Vegas could this happen? My name as musical director was in lights on a Strip marquee—my mother took a picture of it—and my group was appearing on a main stage. Our Sahara engagement was an unqualified success. Each show earned standing ovations. I conducted the Sahara's regular eighteen-musician house band, augmented by our string group. Vic seemed totally comfortable and never sounded better. The "Lady Strings," as the local press referred to them, were "a treat for eye and ear," as were Vic's duets with Lenore.

The only exception apparently was Vic's lovely young wife Becky, who didn't think Vic needed Lenore and the girls around him on stage. I figured the ensemble was so successful Vic would overlook the fact that Becky wasn't too keen on it.

The package, indeed, was on the mark. Vic was immediately rebooked at a later date to co-star with Lena Horne, who was a delight to work with. A consummate perfectionist, she didn't walk through rehearsals; she sang each note full out, rehearsing each musical nuance, every stage movement, even gestures.

Not too many years before, when Vegas was a segregated town, Lena was forced to use the kitchen entrance of the Riviera hotel, where she was performing but was not permitted to stay. On a return engagement, however, her two children stayed in the hotel with her. After the kids used the swimming pool, important hotel guests demanded that management drain and refill the pool before the guest's white family would use it. Management complied. I can only imagine how Lena must have felt.

Damone's career was on a roll again. And as far as I was concerned, a milestone had been reached. It hadn't come easily, but it was worth the effort. It seemed we had finally put together the right thing at the right time. We had conquered the mountain; I started making plans for all the money I would earn.

The gamble had paid off. But show business being what it is, something told me not to get too comfortable.

**

Do I detect clouds of change approaching?

Vic Damone with **Music Maximus**, Sahara Hotel, Las Vegas ♫ 1976

Karen Karlsrud, Joan Spergel, Mabel Wong, Lenore SanAngelo
Seated: Ethel Abelson, Vic Damone

21

_____

___

MEETING ELVIS

Don't move to Rochester, New York, in the wintertime unless you really enjoy cold, brutal cold. Snow pounces on the place in piles, driven by frigid winds that swoop off Lake Erie. Okay, so it's not as bad as Buffalo. Still, you grimace and scrunch up in your coat, scarf, gloves and boots, wishing you were in L.A. or Florida.

Summers there display quite a different palette - soothing warm breezes, glorious flowers, trees clothed in green foliage, lovers strolling in parks, and the general attitude of an apparently relieved populace. It is interesting how the revived citizenry seems to enjoy the shared esprit of having endured another winter. The beast has passed. Once again Rochester is beautiful.

The tour with Vic Damone took us to Rochester, NY during the summer of 1976, performing for a week at the Town Casino Dinner Theater. I couldn't help but appreciate the verdant blanket of the whole area, especially after having spent several weeks in Las Vegas surrounded by its scrubby deserts, rock-and-dirt mountains, all baked in dry, extreme July heat. So, Rochester was easy on the eyes, especially for those of us who missed the greenery of the Northeast. After Vegas, I quickly found it easy to relax in this winsome environment, especially after our Vegas gig had been so highly charged.

We arrived at the dinner theater in late afternoon and had a brief rehearsal, mainly to adjust the sound system to Vic's tastes. Each of our string players was amplified with a contact microphone attached to their instrument. As a result, sound balancing took a little longer; but when properly attenuated, the system allowed the string quartet to sound more like a full string section, one of the keys to the musical success of the group. Vic left this part of the sound check up to me and usually concentrated on getting just the right sound from his mike. He had amazingly sensitive hearing and excellent vocal intonation. He knew just what he wanted to hear, or more precisely what he didn't want to hear.

We opened that night and were well received, even though the sound could have been improved if we had spent more time balancing it. But no matter, we would fine-tune it "tomorrow."

The next morning we returned to the theater, rehearsed and tweaked Vic's mike. I have not met anyone, before or since, more particular than Vic when it came to the quality of the sound system. Once, after the first night of our initial engagement at Dom Bruno's Club at Sylvan Beach near Syracuse, he and I worked until four in the morning testing and adjusting his mike and the sound system until he was satisfied it was the best we could produce. This happened often on subsequent engagements. The process always took longer than expected and Rochester was no exception. So, by the time we got back to the downtown Hilton Hotel from the second day's morning sound check, it was already two in the afternoon.

I had promised the group that the Friday payroll would be ready for them by noon. I rushed up to my room and began counting and recounting the cash for our ten-person group. I was just about to place it into various pay envelopes, when the hotel's fire alarm started blaring non-stop outside my door.

Most anyone who travels often and stays in hotels has been probably through a false alarm or two. I was about to join the club. Upon opening my door and checking for smoke or a sign of disturbance—there was none—I decided to ignore the interruption.

For about twenty minutes I listened to the incessant clanging, then called the front desk.

"Sir, don't you hear the alarm?" someone said. "Everyone has been evacuated from the hotel. You have to get out. You have to get out now!"

I had a few thousand dollars spread out on the bed in counted stacks, and I didn't want to jump up and leave. "What's the problem?" I asked, as calmly as I could.

"There's been a bomb threat. Everyone's left the hotel. You must get out now. And you have to use the stairs." I imagine that a bomb threat in a Rochester hotel in 1976 was a rarity. I mean, this wasn't like kids calling in false alarms at school these days to miss a class or a test. The desk clerk was panicky.

"Do you know what time the bomb threat is supposed to be?" I said.

"Three o'clock!" he yelled.

I looked at my watched. It was five minutes before three. Stuffing the cash into my pockets, I ran down seventeen flights to the lobby, past the glass doors, and outside to join. My watch said 3:05 p.m. Fire trucks and police were everywhere. Search teams were in the hotel searching for "the bomb."

After two hours the incident was declared a hoax.

Elvis was performing a show at the local arena that night and scheduled to stay in the hotel. Apparently someone assumed that if an afternoon bomb threat were called in, everyone would have to evacuate the hotel, including Elvis, and they would get to see him. The police caught the pranksters when a few teenagers in the crowd started yelling, "We want Elvis." Elvis hadn't checked in yet.

Our payday was a little late that Friday. service entrance in back. He hosted an early evening private

Elvis finally did arrive at the hotel, via the underground cocktail reception in his suite prior to his performance that night. Damone knew him and was invited, so some of us went with him to the party to meet The King.

Elvis was already dressed in his cape and famous white suit-of-light when we arrived. His svengali-like manager, Colonel Tom Parker, stood to the side watching Elvis closely. I must admit to being somewhat in awe at the prospect of meeting Elvis, even though I had not been a fan of his. Then suddenly, the man himself, one of the world's most famous, celebrities, approached.

But wait a minute. This was not the vibrant young Elvis I had seen in the movies or on television, the slim-hipped, slow talking, fast moving, karate chopping, dashing lad, who drove millions of women crazy and made lasting fans of men all over the world. This Elvis was obviously overweight, bloated and puffy-faced. Dark circles hollowed his eyes, and he looked completely fatigued. He also seemed to be stuffed into his costume. A massive, three-hundred-pound, six-foot six-ish bodyguard—probably named Bubba, or maybe Tiny, never left his side and appeared to be in charge of guiding him around the room and meeting people.

When Elvis got to Vic, he and Vic hugged warmly. Introductions followed.

"Elvis, this is my conductor and music director, Gene Hull."

With a warm handshake, Elvis said, "Pleased to meet you, Gene. Vic has told me a lot about you and the strings. Sounds great. How 'bout you being my conductor when my man takes a break in a couple of months? Vic will give you some time off, won't you, Vic?"

"Anything for you, Elvis, "said Vic.

"Are you guys serious?" I said.

"For sure," said Elvis.

"Deal," I said. We shook on it. Too bad Elvis died before I could become his music director.

*

Deal? Conductor for Elvis, eh? Hmm.

(Okay. So it was just a little improvement in the story.
The introduction to Elvis actually went like this.)

"Elvis, this is my conductor and music director, Gene Hull." With a warm handshake, a tired Elvis smiled and drew a deep breath, trying to sound upbeat. He looked at me and said in his unmistakable deep, monotone, slurred mumble-jumble something like:

"Heyhiya, Gene.Youthguywiththestringsright?Howyoudoin, man,everythingallright,buddy?"

Wide-eyed, dumbstruck, I thought *What is he saying?* And I wanted to say, "What the hell's happened to you, man? You look terrible." Instead I offered, "Pleased to meet you, Elvis."

We made small talk and he asked how I liked working with his "goomba," Vic.

Later, when people asked me what Elvis said to me when we met, I could only say I really couldn't be sure. But it didn't matter; it was a moment I would never forget.

When Elvis Presley died the following year at age forty-two, weighing 230 pounds, the cause of death was officially announced as a heart attack. It was known that he suffered from anxiety and exhaustion. Subsequent investigations revealed that he abused various stimulant-uppers and depressant-downers prescribed by two different physicians, independent of each other. One doctor admitted to prescribing 5,300 tablets for him in the seven months before he died.

Years later I learned that Colonel Parker was really Andreas van Huijk, from Holland, a man who had never been a legal resident of the U.S., and certainly was no colonel. However, he was a colossal promoter, who had successfully propelled and guided Elvis's phenomenal career. In my opinion, he was also at least partly responsible for his gifted client's tragic death.

I've often thought someone close to Elvis should have managed him more carefully.

**

Music Maximus, first rehearsal – Bridgeport, ♫ January, **1976**

22

IT'S GREAT, BUT ...

One dawn, before darkness had yielded to the
gray of day, I was hurrying along the quiet streets just north of
Chicago's Loop on my way to see Vic Damone. The night before,
at the conclusion of our weeklong appearance at Field's Club in
Cicero, he had asked me to come to his hotel suite early the
following morning for a meeting, an unusual time for us to talk;
it sounded urgent. He explained he needed to catch an early
flight to L.A.

My footsteps echoed in the deserted canyons of concrete
and glass. I began to doubt myself, like a comic might who gets
the blues in advance, fearing the day when the laughter will
stop. I couldn't shake the negative feeling.

I sensed Doctor Doom somewhere ahead, just out of sight.
Was it the atmosphere? Was it intuition? Over the years I
learned to pay attention to gut feelings, so I stepped up the pace
and watched the streets carefully.

Reaching Damone's hotel without incident was a relief—a
welcome haven at the end of an uneasy trek. The surroundings
were impressive. The first thing I noticed in the deserted lobby

was a beautiful arrangement of tall, freshly cut tropical flowers atop an antique table. Several oversized leather chairs on both sides of the area, sat like regal retreats for important bodies, positioned in commanding views.

How luxurious. How tastefully done. This is what you get to afford when you're a star. Must be nice. I smiled *hello* at the desk clerk as I walked past to the elevator. He gave me a perfunctory nod. The purr of the well-maintained lift soothed my ascent to the fifteenth floor. The elevator, with its softly lighted panels of dark red oak and brocaded fabric, must have been a quiet cubicle of comfort for hotel guests engaged in necessary to-ing and fro-ing, as the British like to say. Again, I was impressed.

For a few moments I forgot why I was there. I'd never be able to afford to stay in a place like this.

"Good morning, Gene. Thanks for coming. Come on in, sit down, have some coffee."

I poured a cup from the sterling carafe and added sugar.

"Thanks, Vic. What's up?"

"I want you to know how much I've enjoyed the strings, Gene. Everybody loves them. Lenore and the girls are sweet and talented. And you've handled things very well. I couldn't be more pleased."

"Well, thanks, Vic. We love you, too. I'm glad the whole package is a success." I smiled broadly, as if we were two champions sharing a moment.

"Yes, it's an excellent concept. Looks great, sounds great. But to get right to the point, would you like to be my musical director full time? I mean, without the girls and the group?"

"Huh? I thought you just said you really liked the concept."

"I do," he said. "It's great, but ... well, my financial advisor,"—referring to his third father-in-law, whose daughter, Becky, was not the biggest fan of the group backing Vic— "advises that the package is just too expensive. I'll have to work without a traveling group from now on and contract local musicians wherever I'm booked. But I'd like you to be my music director-conductor-contractor and travel with me. I'll start you at $750 a week and all expenses."

BOOM! The honeymoon was over. Accepting his offer would mean the end of the string group. Nine good people would be out of work. I reflected on the years it had taken to get this far and the effort in developing a successful group like Music Maximus. I thought about the financial investment and about starting over again. I recalled the failures and the phoenix-like successes of some of my other bands. Mostly, I thought about the toll the years had exacted from me and from my family.

I wanted to tell Vic to forget it. I wanted to blame him and tell him to take a flying leap. Instead I sipped my coffee. He was only doing what he felt was right for him. And I was feeling sorry for myself and for the group.

I told him I needed to think about it and would let him know the next day. True, $750 a week was attractive to me in the mid-1970s. But my gut ached when I left the hotel room, knowing I had to make a decision I didn't want to make.

Would I be selling out if I accepted his offer? Would I be letting down the others in the group who believed in me and depended on me and had worked so hard? Yes, of course. I couldn't deny it. But truthfully, I was running out of gas. Leading and managing a ten-piece act on the road, trying to find bookings when we weren't playing with Vic, was more than I could deal with any longer. The years had piled up faster than I could shovel.

During the night, weighing pros and cons, the same answer came up consistently. It would be best to get off the moving train before it stopped completely. I decided to disband Music Maximus, give up the long-shot dream of recording and headlining in Vegas and lay-up, as golfers say, play it safe and become Damone's musical director exclusively. The security of the job outweighed the unknowns of starting over again.

The end was near. I explained the reasons to the musicians and reminded them of my financial responsibilities. Without hitching our wagon to Damone, the future would be too uncertain. There wasn't much choice. A few of them were really disappointed. Most shrugged it off and said, "That's the business." They were gritty young people who were realistic about life. But I felt bad for them ... and me.

Before Music Maximus was dissolved several months later, we played the many dates already booked with Damone, and some without him. Prominent among these was our performance in concert with Mel Torme at Philadelphia's Academy of Music, home of the Philadelphia Orchestra. Unfortunately there were not enough of these extraordinary moments to sustain the group. And so it was over.

For the first time since I was a kid, I was no longer a bandleader. I was lucky, however. Conducting for Vic proved to be good for me. I had the skills and was good at it. It was what I needed at the time. I toured as musical director with Damone, Sandler and Young, and other celebrity acts for almost three years throughout the United States, Canada, and Europe, as well as playing many of the most popular network variety television programs and talk shows.

This job entailed reduced daily responsibilities for me. I didn't have to worry about bookings, transportation, maintaining a payroll, managing personnel, procuring arrangements, uniforms, equipment, and being the boss. Living was easy for a change. I just had to make sure the new orchestras in whatever cities we were booked were rehearsed by me and properly prepared to play the celebrity's shows.

Merely conducting, without the responsibilities I had been used to for so long, was fun and actually kind of a heady experience. I could to concentrate on the music. Working with famous performers was a privilege, and I met many fine people. This period proved to be an invaluable life course in dealing with performer personalities. But the cost was great. My marriage had failed. Or more precisely, I had failed my marriage. Too many separations. Too long away from home. Too much time spent losing touch, trying to catch the brass ring. Divorce would follow a few years later. I blamed myself for pursuing a music career, which had given me reason for being, yet had demanded a commensurate payback.

Eventually I had enough of conducting for celebrities. Steady work was always at their whim. Often they took time off, sometimes several weeks at a time. The conductor was expected to fend for himself. There was no real security. Of course, if security had been my primary concern I should have gotten a job at the Post Office. The road was still the road, a circle that eventually returns to your starting point. I couldn't build a future on it, especially in my situation with a family to support. As my son David later heard national treasure *Dr. John* (Mac Rebenneck) say to the father of an aspiring musician, "As a line of work, I don't recommend it."

A Peggy Lee song came to mind, "Is That All There Is?" And I thought, as Cy Coleman wrote for *Sweet Charity*, "There's Gotta Be Something Better Than This."

Conducting for an established touring show that worked steadily, rather than for a single artist, seemed to be the answer. At that time the Ice Capades was the most established and successful touring ice show, booked a solid forty weeks a year. They carried a conductor and a nucleus of fine musicians. I had heard that the conductor's salary was well over a thousand a week and that the work was steady. It seemed logical to target Ice Capades for a job. I took aim at a new goal, little realizing the path would lead to something quite different from what I expected, the exit from a career as a professional musician. The time-to-change clock had ticked again.

I see you're getting honest again. And the plot is thickening.

(Of course I'm honest. And yes, it is.)

Hmm.

**

23

_____

_____

SEGUE

Where: New York City
Place: The Waldorf Astoria Hotel
             John Kluge's ten-room penthouse suite
Time: Late Spring, 1970
Purpose: Meeting with Eric Rill

For several years I had known Eric Rill personally and professionally, and regarded him as a special friend. A high achiever—*wunderkind* comes to mind—Eric became president of Ramada Inns of Canada at twenty-eight. Two years later he was appointed Corporate President of Ramada Inns Worldwide group, with over 600 hotels in all.

Eric knew my work with both Free Spirit and Music Maximus. He was also a friend of John Kluge, one of the world's richest men, among whose many enterprises was ownership of the Ice Capades. Since I had targeted Ice Capades as a possible job opportunity, I called Eric at his Phoenix office to ask a favor.

"Would it be possible to suggest to Kluge that I might be a good conductor for the Ice Capades?"

Fortunately for me, Eric was planning to be in New York the following week and would be staying at Kluge's Waldorf suite. He suggested we meet there, so we could discuss the situation before Kluge returned to town.

When I arrived he showed me around the huge suite—actually, suites—replete with ten elegant bedrooms with adjoining baths, a huge main living room with at least four elegant couches, tapestried full-length windows, and a mahogany dining room table which could easily seat twenty-four. He didn't have to point out the original art tastefully placed and lighted on various walls, Renoirs, Picassos, Monets and others. A Rodin and a pedestaled Henry Moore guarded a couple of corners. It was a different world.

After my gaping jaw returned to normal, we sat down to talk. Eric questioned why I wanted to be the conductor for the Ice Capades. "Aren't you tired of traveling and being on the road all the time?"

"I'm a musician, Eric. I have to make a living wherever I can. It's the nature of the business."

"That's not all you are," he said. "I know you. You manage people well. You're honest, and you take care of business."

"I'm glad you think so. But conducting for the Ice Capades would be a steady, good-paying gig, and I could use one right now."

"How would you feel about relocating to Phoenix and working for me at Ramada Corporate? There's an opening coming up. Key Howard is leaving the company."

"Are you kidding?" I said. "He's the Entertainment Director. He's a legend. Make me an offer." He did, and I accepted a position in Phoenix at Ramada's Headquarters.

Entering the corporate world seemed like a solid move. For the first time in non-performing employment, I didn't regard myself as a musician working a day job while waiting for the next music gig. I immersed myself totally in the business environment and learned as much and as fast as I could. Part of the job was to screen agents from Maine to California, contract bands and plan weekly entertainment schedules a year in advance for each of the sixty-odd hotels that featured live music. DJs worked the lounges of another sixty hotels. I took to the challenge immediately and loved the job, which required that I visit each of the five national zones at least once during the first year. The traveling covered almost every state.

My work was organized, effective, and successful. Smooth going at last. Life was easy again.

The following year I was caught up in a corporate "re-alignment" when Rill left the company. The new president brought in his own key people. With the inevitable sweep that occurred, my hope for a solid career in the hotel industry vanished as quickly as it had appeared. I was out.

Rill left the business world several years later and since has authored two successful foreign intrigue novels and written a third that is looking for a publisher.

Once again it was tap dance time. I moved to Las Vegas to start over. I formed Century Artists Corporation, a small partnership with Dick Towers, formerly of Complex Four, booking and producing shows and acts for Nevada hotels. I liked producing but hated booking acts. It was sales, sales, sales—not my strongest interest. But it paid the rent, a living at best.

Now began a most difficult time, the period in which I hit bottom emotionally. My personal life was in shambles. A relationship had gone bad. My career had dipped to a new low and the future seemed invisible. At forty-eight I was almost broke. Depression clouded every day. Much of my income went for bills and child support. I lived in a town that didn't care for losers, though it did its best to create them. And since my name was no longer on a Strip marquee, I qualified for non-entity status. Anonymity is the last thing a performer needs. This is not a business for the sensitive. For a while I considered going back to performing.

In retrospect, though it was difficult to gather at the moment, this crossroads was a blessing. It came to mark a definitive moment in my life, the beginning of a personal rebuilding process.

As the early dream of a life-long music career faded, it became less and less important to me. I had given all I could. In spite of some notable successes along the way, it was time to move on. A worthwhile, less ephemeral future, and reuniting with my family, became my two priorities.

The moment many performers eventually face had arrived: complete separation from performing. At first, letting go is painful. But the truth is, I never considered myself a greatly gifted musician. Over the years I had worked with many whose natural musical talents far exceeded my own. My ability to lead, and hopefully to inspire people, far surpassed my talents as a player. Perhaps I was a better than average professional player, but I finally understood that this was not enough.

Because of persistent effort, coupled with a driving passion to succeed, I had achieved much, perhaps more than my talent justified. I was grateful for that. But as a young Jamaican woman wisely pointed out to me in Ocho Rios one night after I had won a bottle of rum at a beach party barefoot dance contest with her and was gasping for breath, "You can dance, *mon*, but you ain't gettin' any younger."

She was right, of course. The clock was ticking. It was time to find a path where I did not have to prove my worth by playing a horn. Booking acts and producing, plus the Ramada experience, had given me an inside look at the other side of performing I was ready to make an honest contribution in corporate work, if given the opportunity. I felt I had something unique to offer and I started searching.

In time, an opportunity arose that reached up to me like a shimmering stairway. A new company in the expanding cruise industry, based in Florida, was looking for an entertainment person with "national corporate experience and Las Vegas expertise" to establish and head its entertainment program. Because of my former Ramada position and tenure in Las Vegas, and having accrued years as a musician with hands-on participation in various facets of the entertainment industry, I got the job. What an exhilarating feeling! I was ready and anxious to begin a new life … career number two.

Miami, the largest cruise-ship port in the world, became my new base of operations. Not knowing anyone there meant another beginning, which can in itself be stimulating. Beginnings often combine several factors: hope, desire to succeed, anticipation, discovery of a new place, the attraction of new friends, and finally the ever-present motivating fear of failure. This alone can really concentrate the mind—not unlike the "possibility of hanging," as Dr. Samuel Johnson once wrote.

I arrived shortly after the 1980 Marielito emigration from Cuba. Tens of thousands of Cubans, mostly good people bitterly opposed to Castro, were suddenly allowed to emigrate overnight to the United States—125,000 in all. Castro then emptied the jails and freed the worst criminals, saying that unless they were included with the massive Cuban exodus to the United States, there would be no boatlift. It was all or nothing.

The emigrants left from the port of Mariel, Cuba, evacuated in a massive American boatlift to Key West.

Miami felt like a frontier town after that. Thousands of displaced Latinos poured in. Money, opportunity and crime splashed across south Florida.

Miami Vice became a hit TV show. Cocaine was king and had many slaves. The city undertook massive redevelopment, including voluminous high-rises. Business opportunities seemed unlimited; the economy boomed. Miami became known as the Magic City with dazzling nightlife and a skyline of multiple colors. Latin music resounded in all corners of the area. Latin foods and a vibrant new pulse attracted the world's fun-seekers to Coconut Grove and later to South Beach. Incredible wealth and poverty existed side by side, like city streets abutting sidewalks.

Just because it was on the menu, though, did not mean I had to order it. I could observe the mood without participating. A city was in process, just as I was. I was immersed in a vibrant new world and resolved that whatever it took, I would make the most of this extraordinary opportunity in the burgeoning cruise industry.

Work as Corporate Entertainment Director of Scandinavian World Cruises involved extensive international travel, especially to Denmark, Norway, Germany, England, France, Greece, and Sweden. The job included planning entertainment programs, producing shows, overseeing construction of shipboard showroom refurbishments and new-builds, hiring acts, and establishing the company's shipboard cruise activity programs. The past had prepared me well, and I never looked back.

I was fortunate to have entered an exploding new industry at an opportune time. After three years I became Director of Hotel and Casino Operations. Along with this professional growth, I also reconnected frayed ties with my family, the most important undertaking.

Horn playing dimmed to the distant past. Then one night, as I was traveling on one of our ships, the band's trumpet player took ill just before show time. His part was critical to the show, so a minor panic ensued. When I heard about it, I asked if the tenor sax player had a soprano sax. I borrowed his horn, sat in, and sight-read the show's trumpet parts on soprano. No big deal, considering my experience. But the musicians were surprised. They had no idea that the Entertainment Director was also a musician. From that night on I never had any problem managing ships' musicians.

In 1989 Royal Caribbean International, one the world's largest cruise line companies recruited me. For many years I produced its award-winning stage shows and co-produced its ice shows, all of it the work I now loved best. I had the opportunity to help produce many fine young dancers, singers, and ice skaters.

There were some wonderful surprises, like working with Katarina Witt and other international skating stars. Co-ice show producer, Willy Bietak, a creative, organized, honest and affable man, was a particular joy to work with and is certainly one of the world's most important ice production producers today. As of this writing, Willy had just been inducted into the Ice Skating Hall of Fame, a most high honor.

During my tenure there, I was privileged to work with an amazing array of directors, arrangers, designers, chorographers and technicians, dedicated to their craft: Lenore SanAngelo, a traditional Broadway writer/director extraordinaire; great directors and choreographers Mark Dow, Harrison McEldowney, Sarah Kawahara, Willie Bietak, Vickie Davis, Kathy Steele, Sherie Zunker, Laura Dunlop; Anita Mann, a fine independent producer; brilliant scenic designers Brad Kain, Jerry Hariton, Vickie Baral, Steve Rundle, and Bob Rang; gifted costume designers Pete Menefee, Jordan Ross and Edwin Piekny; creative lighting designers Peter Moore, Mike Pitzer; music producers Mike Lewis and Wade Hubbard, and video graphics entrepreneur John Potts—all of whom were exceptional in their fields—plus a solid team of extraordinary managers: Robin Cahill, Jeff White, ice cast manager Sylvia Froescher, and production cast manager MaryAnn Delany. Costume maker Brenda Bontiere and her dedicated team produced thousands of production costumes, often dealing with stressful deadlines and extruded budgets, yet always managing to spread kindness and goodwill to everyone.

The success of the shipboard development of the program was due in no small part to the company's supportive technical guru, Knut Sheisvoll. He continually found ways to gain the new-building support and footholds needed to accommodate a rapidly expanding entertainment product.

Peter Compton, later Royal Caribbean's Vice President of Entertainment, and I were recruited at the same time. While his mission was more corporate and involved more planning, mine was more hands-on. He was an extraordinary visionary with an entertainment and cruise line background. I was the can-do guy. A symbiotic relationship developed between us that proved extremely beneficial to all. The entertainment product of this cruise line set a standard that became the envy of the industry and remains unequaled today.

Ironically, life added another welcome surprise during this period. A meaningful union developed in 1997. I was fortunate to meet dynamic Beverly Myers in Miami, a career paralegal and divorced mother of three grown boys. After many years of being single, we both seemed to have found the possible missing frosting for our cake. The following year our families attended our wedding in Boston. My four sons were my Best Men; her three sons "gave her away."

The world was new again. And because of the experience gained in the crazy up-and-down years as a musician, I was felt prepared for the new job. Frankly, after the insecurities of a long jazz and pop music career, I often felt giddy receiving a corporate payroll check every two weeks. It always seemed like a gift.

From notes to boats, the transition was complete. Seeing life from a different perspective, I mellowed considerably. I had fthe ideal combination of financial security, companionship and artistic creativity. The new environment proved to be a catalyst for appreciating new interests and providing new challenges.

Royal Caribbean ships were being built in Finland, Germany and France, with refurbishments of older ones undertaken in Portugal, California, Virginia and Florida. Many trips to the shipyards were necessary. I brought out each new ship, fifteen in all, from the European yards as they repositioned to their new market places in America, the Mediterranean and the Pacific. In this new life I had the time and desire to smell the roses, not the least of which was appreciating some of the world's wondrous ocean vistas.

I often think that if it weren't for sensitivities gained as a musician, I wouldn't have appreciated this new life so intensely. It became an extension of music. I listened to it carefully.

Agreeable culture shock – corporate life.
Scandinavian World Cruises, 1981-1988
Royal Caribbean International, 1989-2003.

"And so the serious business of

expanded show production began."

EARLY WIZARDS OF RCI ENTERTAINMENT
Entertainment Director Peter Compton, Senior Producer Gene Hull
Circa ♫ 1995

Oh, yes ... serious business. I can see that.

WILL ROGERS FOLLIES

Shipboard entertainment in the fleet expanded to include in-house production shows, major variety acts, celebrity stars, Big Bands, ensembles. The new mega ships added ice rinks and ice shows

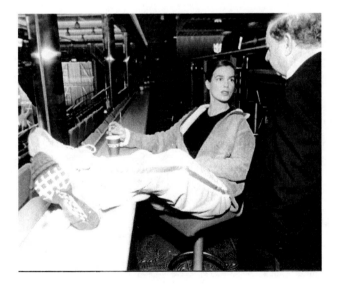

Ice skating diva, **Katarina Witt**, two-time
Olympic Gold Medallist, offered some rehearsal break advice:
"Gene, next time make the ice bigger."

SHOWSTOPPERS
Broadway revues were extremely popular during the 1990s.
This one by Lenore SanAngelo Mascar

Vegas style revues presented a different view.
STARSTRUCK
A **Mark Dow** / **Harrison McEldowney** opus

Many of the shows were staged with
Brad Kain's innovative scenic designs.

Jerry Hariton and Vicky Baral took special effects in shipboard production design to even more sophisticated technical levels.

Ready for passengers

Navigator of the Seas, the world's second mega ship, *twin* of *The Voyager,* sails from Finland to Florida on its initial positioning cruise. ♫ **2002**

24

VOYAGE

For some the fascination of the sea is a fact of life: mesmerizing, like staring into a campfire, or watching a quiet snowfall from a cozy cabin. It has its own special call. Initially, this was not so with me.

During ocean crossings for RCCL my responsibility was to ready the entertainment programs on new ships. When a ship was introduced into passenger service, the entertainment venues, shows and systems were expected to be fully operational. In a sense, then, the ocean existed *outside* the job for me, more of an incidental aspect of the journey. I hardly noticed the sea. My focus and concentration was on preparations and rehearsals. Every moment counted.

By the time of my final voyage as senior producer for RCCL, more than twenty years had passed in a blink. I had become more aware of the sea. The shows and entertainment systems were ahead of schedule. Brad Kain, my talented successor-to-be, who is also a fine scenic designer, was on board and had the project well organized. I was relaxed and kept extensive notes, having the time and inclination to observe more of nature's wonders. This was my twenty-fifth crossing as the producer, in almost as many years in the cruise industry. This last crossing for me began in Turku, Finland.

I arrived in Finland two weeks before the voyage. Unseasonably frigid winter weather for early November, with temperatures dropping to four degrees Fahrenheit, was enough to chill even the Finns. Packed snow and ice covered the ground. Frigid wind slapped at shipyard workers.

In spite of the weather, I felt fortunate: the airlines had NOT lost my luggage on the 23-hour flight to Turku. The trip already seemed successful and bound to have good fortune.

The ship sailed from Masa Yards early that November morning with its crew of 1,200, plus construction contractors, a few guests, and RCCL supervisors like me. Billowing clouds of new snow swirled at us from all directions. It was a beautiful dense, dry snow, though I'm sure the captain didn't care for it. The reduced visibility meant the ship had to inch its way for hours through the early stages of the Finnish archipelago.

Hundreds of small islands, broken off from the mainland, form the archipelago and are scattered for miles into the Baltic Sea. Negotiating a huge ship through the narrow, winding channels at five knots is challenging, especially in blinding snow. The going was slow. Within the ship, theater and ice show rehearsals were slow ride.

I wondered how the ocean crossing would be this time. The *Navigator of the Seas* was the world's largest passenger ship to date, fifteen decks high, a thousand feet long, 144,000 tons displacement, over three times the size of the Titanic, a floating city. Yet, if the seas became unusually rough, we could seem as tiny as a bug on a beach. The massive ocean is unpredictable, rarely calm for very long, sometimes suddenly angry, and always powerful; I was curious to see how our new ship handled it.

After two days the ship reached the beginning of the Baltic Sea at the Atlantic Ocean. A stop was scheduled in Kristiansand, Norway, on the Atlantic coast. There we would disembark travel agents and VIP guests before undertaking the Atlantic crossing. Kristiansand is a refueling place for Baltic and ocean-going cargo ships and tankers. It is also a quaint tourist stop and transfer point for passenger ships.

What a sight when we approached through the fiord-like harbor entrance in semi-darkness that morning. The ship, almost hidden in more blinding snow, crawled through the narrow channel toward the port like a huge white panther stalking an invisible prey, inching ever closer, until suddenly the dock magically appeared close by. Nice job, Captain!

As daylight filtered through, the edge of the town emerged, speckled with wood frame houses perched on nearby hills among tall fir trees, lights twinkling like welcome beacons. Four inches of fresh white stuff had already covered the ground. On the pier below, cabs and buses waited to shuttle our passengers to the airport. No wind. Cold. Quiet, except for the muted sound of falling snow, like a soft ringing in the ears. No hoopla. No horns. No shouting. No confusion. Calm. Organized. Patient. How Norwegian.

Three hours later we were on our way into the North Sea. It was a little rough, but not too bad—twenty-foot seas and winds at twenty knots. A few minor hiccups as the weather punctuated show rehearsals. Due to the heavy, but not violent seas, a few of the sets, as yet unsecured, moved in and out on their tracks making unscheduled stage entrances, not unusual for a new ship. Sometimes, you don't notice unsecured sets until rolling seas quickly tell you which ones are loose. The cast of fourteen and the show installation staff of forty had a good laugh each time a hanging set would glide unannounced onto the stage during the rehearsal; we'd paused to secure it. Excitement and anticipation ran high, knowing we were bringing out the world's largest and newest passenger ship.

During the night the weather cleared and the seas calmed. I woke up at 3:30 a.m., looked out my sliding glass doors and saw several brightly lit North Sea oil rigs about three miles off the starboard side, looming there like ominous, giant machines in a

War of the Worlds film. I couldn't imagine being a rig worker living on those things—miles from nowhere in one of the most turbulent bodies of water on the planet. How gutsy.

On the fourth day we proceeded south through the English Channel, then cleared France and Spain, passing by the Bay of Biscay. The seas were flat. Someone could probably have water-skied off the stern. We were cutting along at about 22 knots, already having covered over 1,500 miles since Finland. All seemed smooth as we headed southwest toward Florida.

One night the captain announced that a large storm was moving toward us from the coast of America. "Too large to avoid by tomorrow." I accelerated our work schedule in the theatre and the ice rink, in the event we had to batten down later.

We managed to avoid the main storm—a huge one, perhaps a thousand miles across. But we had to pass through its outer fringes. I was ready and anxious to see how the big ship handled the weather.

As we got closer to the storm, the seas kept building. By four in the afternoon the waves were 30- to 35-feet, deep swells with a surly chop. Our course took us right into the wind. With gusts kicking in at 40 to 45 knots, our forward speed against this was 15 knots, so the relative wind across the deck was around 60 knots. Not exactly your stroll-around-the-promenade breeze.

It was bumpy. We called off rehearsals. Several of the dancers were already seasick, especially those who were first-time ocean-crossers. It's a miserable feeling. You want to die. Some of them looked close to it.

Every time the huge ship collided with a big swell, the ocean spray kicked up from the impact and flew past my windows in huge billowing white plumes. These reached well above my Deck 6 cabin, about the height of a six-story building—really Kodak-moment stuff.

An hour later, holding tightly to the main stairway railing, I made my way down to the theatre lobby again. At times I was momentarily in space with both feet off the stairs. On Deck 4, closer to the sea, I looked out the glass doors that led to the outside Promenade deck. Several hearty younger folks were in the lobby, "oo-ing and ah-ing" at the huge sea and its spectacular sprays. We were doing our sea-legs thing, bobbing and lurching and shifting weight from one leg to the other, knees flexed, riding the swells like snow skiers, enjoying the elements.

An ominous cloudbank was moving across the water toward us. Stretched out as far as I could see, it looked like one of those summertime squall lines that comes up suddenly and sweeps across Long Island Sound or the Chesapeake. This wasn't as dark as some of these storms; it had more of an eerie opaque gray quality with a definite leading edge. Its distance from the ship closed rapidly, and soon we were enveloped in dense, hard-driving rain.

It pelted the ocean's turbulence with billions of bead-like drops, smothering the white caps, flattening their tops, muting the chop, as if a huge pillow were stifling he waves. All the while, the big rolling swells continued. I stared in awe at it all. The rain was actually beating up on the ocean.

The effect was beautiful and, yet, a little spooky. For a moment I could imagine we were in one of those Twilight Zone Bermuda Triangle TV shows ... you know, where some huge ship is caught in a strange time-warp cloud, mysteriously finding itself back in the middle of World War II.

But that was not to be on this day. The phenomenon lasted fifteen minutes or so. The cloud passed, the rain stopped, and the sea kicked in wildly again, angrier at having been stifled by the rain attack. The fierce chop then resumed, even surlier than before.

A half hour, later an announcement came from the bridge. The captain informed us that the ship had to be stopped.

Everyone was to prepare to hold on securely. All public rooms were closed. Elevators were shut down—the ship had twelve passenger lifts and several for crew. All activities ceased. A ship does not stop in high seas unless it's absolutely necessary. The seas were rough, but nothing close to hurricane force, which this ship could well take. We speculated there might be engine trouble. We hoped not.

Headed into waves and wind, the ship was stopped and began drifting backward. Oddly, things calmed down because we were now floating with the sea. At that rate I figured we'd be swept back to Spain in three days.

Several minutes later we were underway again, making forward speed. The pounding resumed as we again rammed into the seas. We found out later that one of the two stabilizers had fouled in the formidable waves.

Stabilizers are twenty-five-foot-long wings that can be extended out from the sides underwater near the bow to stabilize the ship in rough weather. The only way the captain could retract them was to stop all forward power, drift backwards, reducing resistance, then withdraw the stabilizers. It worked. The wings were retracted for repair, and off we went again, bouncing and jitterbugging across the ocean. Nice ride. Very little damage to the ship. A few bar glasses took a dive, but not much else. A most interesting interlude. The sea was full of surprises.

We made up for the four hours we'd lost in mid-Atlantic rough seas. The ship was making 22 to 23 knots now. Arrival in Miami was scheduled to be on time.

One night near the end of our fourteen-day trip, I woke up at 3:00 a.m. I went outside onto my cabin's balcony. The sea was asleep. We were skimming along like a giant porpoise.

Overhead a dome of millions of stars hovered over us like a huge glowing empyrean, a celestial vault softly illuminating the ocean. There was no ambient light from below; the heavens really lit up. Stars I never knew were there said hello. And the more I stared, the more there were. You just couldn't see them all. It was awesomely peaceful.

The sun finally did its I'm-back thing—the first time in two weeks. Temperatures rose into the 70s, and the steely gray ocean was blue again. We were nearly back to the States. Crew and staff were anticipating our arrival in Miami. Many of them were foreign nationals who had never been to America. Some, especially the young Russian ice skaters, told me they were really excited to see South Beach! Now, that's America.

This had been an excellent voyage for the new behemoth, *The Navigator of the Seas,* as it sailed the 5,000 miles to its new home in Miami. For me, it had been a privilege to be a part of another beginning, one more time. The re-positioning voyage was an eye opener for me in more ways than one.

During my tenure at Royal Caribbean I wrote a second collection of poetry – not very good. but I was determined to write- and published a book of poems about tennis hackers, *Going To Court.* The project allowed me to satisfy a different creative inclination and supported my love for the sport. I was pleased with some aspect of the book, but not all. I was a lousy poet. Later I wrote several short stories, began a memoir, and decided to study creative writing in the Creative Writing Program of Florida International University in Miami when time permitted. I was discovering yet another world.

When I entered the cruise industry, as a former musician, I had not envisioned the new career being so stimulating and productive, both professionally and personally. Frankly, I was amazed at my luck. The golden age of exponential growth of cruising and of building super-colossal ships beyond reasonable imagination—ships four, five, six times the size of the Titanic—was at hand, and I was fortunate to be part of it.

During those stimulating times, I observed a plethora of corporate intrigues and ship adventures. I was able to assist in implementing the vision of RCCL's dynamic CEO at the time, Richard Fain; and before that, Scandinavian World Cruises' quality leader, Niels Eric Lund. Life after music had managed to be most fulfilling. While I had journeyed from Big Band to no band, so to speak, I always felt that knowing music gave me a extra advantage. It's a musician thing, I guess.

Music is more than what you once did; it's a part of you that never dies. An old Greek saying says, "The monks come and go, but the monastery remains." For me, it was, "Ships come and go, but the music never leaves."

*

And so another ocean was crossed. The transition was made to a new life. You were born again. And they all lived happily ever after. Tsk, tsk.

(Oh, give it a rest. Why don't you write your own memoir!)

Huh?

**

Visiting the Masa Yards during the building of RCCL/ RCI ships - Turku, Finland, 1996-2003

Photo: *Nancy Corbin*

Reminiscent of the Music Maximus concept of 1976,
a charming Venetian string ensemble with rhythm section, playing
contemporary music in period costumes, entertains for the Naming
Ceremony reception in the ship's lounge on *The Splendor of the Seas.*
Barcelona, circa ♫ 2001

25

———————

———

CODA

Many classical works of music summarize themes and add new sparks, as the coda, or tail, brings a composition to its finale. With this in mind, I add these thoughts, which tell the tail, or tail the tale, if you prefer.

Driving to the cruise line Miami office one morning in 2000, I heard a local FM jazz station announcer say, "And that was the Duke Ellington Orchestra at the 1962 Newport Jazz Festival."

There had to be a mistake. No recordings of the '62 Festival were ever released, since the master tapes were all defective. I was curious and called the station.

"Yes," they insisted, "that was Duke Ellington at the 1962 Newport Jazz Festival."

"Are you sure it was 1962?"

"Yes sir."

They had apparently picked up the program from a New York City FM outlet. But when I contacted that station, no one seemed to know anything about the Duke Ellington 1962 Newport recording. One person suggested that perhaps the Festival's live overseas broadcast via Armed Forces Radio was recorded and found its way back to the States.

So began a surprising series of events that caught me unaware and unprepared.

Thirty-eight years after the Jazz Giants performance at Newport '62, one of life's ironies that delights in staging capricious appearances, made a surprise entrance. This time the ripple effect morphed into a wave that did not sputter and disappear like a spent flood on a beach.

The search began: verify the radio broadcast.

The trail led to the Rutgers University Institute for Jazz Studies; here I sought information from anyone who would listen to me. At someone's suggestion, I then tried to contact a well-known jazz writer at *Downbeat Magazine*, writing and calling him several times. No response. The trail that had warmed so quickly suddenly cooled.

I gave up the search and set it aside as just another near miss. Though a disappointment, it seemed no tragedy to me. You can't lose what you've never had.

At our annual Christmas-in-Connecticut family reunion that year, I told the story to my family, suggesting that if there were Festival recordings of Ellington in '62, it was possible that the Jazz Giants '62 had been recorded there also.

"Not that it would make any difference now," I said. "But wouldn't it be ironic if the story were true? Oh well, we'll never know." But silently, I mused on what might have happened if the past had been different—if the Jazz Giants had released a best-selling international album back then.

Two years passed. Early in 2003, forty-one years since Newport, Peter, one of my four sons, called me from Connecticut more excited than I had heard him since he was a spirited two-year-old who gleefully discovered the sheer joy of banging pots and pans together in the kitchen at six o'clock in the morning.

I didn't know it at the time, but ever since I had mentioned hearing Duke's live recording, Peter had been quietly trying to track it down. He was on a mission. He had heard part of a

National Public Radio announcement saying the Library of Congress was making available to the public thousands of heretofore inaccessible jazz recordings it had acquired and catalogued. Peter started digging.

Now the wave, almost dissipated a few years before, was building again. This time it would smack into me with an impact I could not have imagined. Phone calls and letters were exchanged, request forms filled out. Peter finally received the answer. No wonder he was excited when he called me. I was amazed.

In addition to Ellington, the Library of Congress had in its archives a tape of the Gene Hull Orchestra—The Jazz Giants—at Newport '62. A single CD could be assembled from the tape and made available with permission of the producer, George Wein. His office staff graciously assisted Peter in his quest, approving a CD for him with their blessing. Apparently the original tape was of a live Armed Forces broadcast, not the damaged recording made by the record company.

"Dad," said Peter, "I'm going to get those recordings for you. It's going to be your birthday present this year."

Not really, I thought, not after all these years. "Thanks for trying. But don't count on it. It's been so long. Anything could happen."

The possibilities startled me. I recalled many forgotten journeys. I tried to convince myself that some history should remain buried, that some things really do not matter after they've been lived. The truth was, I wasn't sure I wanted to hear the recordings for fear they wouldn't live up to my memories. And what difference would it make now anyway? After all, I wasn't a musician any longer, so it really didn't matter to me. Or did it?

Would I be disillusioned when hearing the recordings after so many years? Perhaps our Newport performance was, after all, just another gig along the way. We all choose our memories and the way we want to remember them. I wondered if my memories of Newport would have to be reshaped. I could see the visuals of that day clearly, but the sounds that filled the night had gradually faded.

The Jazz Giants days had been engrossing for me, as were the years spent with my other bands. I was always determined to develop and hone a first-class, professional product. That goal took a colossal amount of time and energy. Sometimes I regretted the commitment. But the early promise to succeed, a promise born of pride and desire for accomplishment, would not tolerate being unachieved. So I persisted.

As I considered these thoughts, Peter continued digging and subsequently received the CD from the Library of Congress.

Finally, in July 2003, Peter chose a family reunion in Hingham, Massachusetts, at my son Matthew's home, to present the recording to me. Many of the family were grouped around the kitchen table to watch the big moment.

Just looking at the packaged CD placed before me gave me a jolt like an electric current. Shivers came right from the stomach. Then I completely lost it.

"Dad," my daughter Amy whispered, "why are you crying? I've never seen you cry."

"I don't know."

But I did know. I was seeing my yesterdays. My grown children as wide-eyed little kids, asking me where I was going. And me telling them, "Straight up." The Jazz Giants rehearsing at Bill's Castle. A boy sitting on a bus on a cold winter night, clutching his first saxophone wrapped in a pillowcase. The Notre Dame years. The jazz concerts the band had played. Katherine Hepburn scolding me. Benny Goodman captivating me. Paul Whiteman berating me. Woody Herman and Duke Ellington praising me, making me feel humble. Las Vegas dazzling and disappointing me. The years with Damone. Elvis greeting me with such honesty. The miles of piled-up travel.

And saying good-bye to a teary-eyed young family and wife on the front porch, as I would leave to seek fame and fortune on yet another road trip.

Being a musician came with a price. Either I hadn't realized the possible collateral damage such dedication could do to my family, or I knew it, and thought I could repair it, once I had succeeded. The goal was a gamble. But at the time the risk seemed reasonable. Such decisions depend on things that live only in your own head.

Crossroad choices are certainly influenced by early-seeded emotions. In my case the need for replenishing a sense of self-worth was the stuff of motivation; it was also curse. The passion becomes not what you want to be, but what you must be. The desire for self-affirmation can drive one to the limit of judicious decisions.

And now it was many years later.

I tried to tell my family that this CD was more than just a recording, that their lives were in it as much as mine. It didn't matter that I couldn't find the words. They knew.

We listened to the CD together. The sound of the band, its energy and musicality, far exceeded the memories I had parked away in an unknown place. The sounds were alive and bright, clearer than ever.

The look on the faces of my family was worth the struggling years. The kids understood at last why the Jazz Giants had been an important holy grail for me. They gathered in the moment and seemed to appreciate what it meant.

David and Chris, both professional musicians, said they had no idea the level of musicianship of the Giants was of that caliber. Matt, a former musician, was wide-eyed at the sound. Becca, Margaret and Sara hugged me with the shared joy only daughters can give their fathers.

Peter, also a musician, personally delivered a copy of the recording to each of the surviving members of the Jazz Giants.

Originally there were twenty musicians. Twelve were still living. He said the response from them in almost every case was initially disbelief, then shock, followed by profuse thanks, and, finally, with tears. Ron Gebeau, clearly surprised, was speechless. He couldn't believe it. Tears invaded his eyes as he kept staring at he CD. Mickey Walker was astonished and clearly overwhelmed. "Are you kidding me, man? This is unbelievable." He telephoned me in Florida to tell me how extraordinary hearing the CD was, and what a wonderful son I had. Bobby Butler praised Peter and proclaimed the CD one of the most appreciated gifts of his lifetime. Danny DeMarco at first was speechless, then, wet-eyed, hardly able to get the words out, said, "Oh man, so many years.... " Freddie Fortunato and Al Provenzano wrote glowing letters of thanks to me. Others voiced similar effusion.

I need to take a moment here to remember the fine young men who were members of the Jazz Giants over the years. Leo Grabinski, Nick Mariconda, Sonny Costanzo, Jeff Leonard, Joe Howard, Tommy Alberts, Glen Zatola, Bobby Zatola, Dick Prestige, Ed Pistey, Claude Berardi, Bobby Harry, Harry Ashmore, Rick Bruno, Jack Corso, Bobby Butler, Dom Mariconda, Joe Marzulli, Danny DeMarco, Danny Acrotta, Peter D'Addario, Tony Guzzi, Fred Fortunato, Mickey Walker, Jack Spake, Bob Nolting, Joe Daddona, Steve Royal, Ronnie Gebeau, Dick Burlant, Al Provenzano, Bruce Wilson, Chic Marchetti, Sheldon Rose, Steve Powers, Marty Rose, Robert Foster, Roland Chirico, Bob Kolb, Ronnie McClure and Bobby Sagnella. And there were probably more.

Gentlemen, you were dedicated. You were the best.

For some of the band members, the Jazz Giants experience was a musical highlight in their lives. I suspect the experience also meant more to the others than they cared to admit at the time. When most of those who played at Newport received the CD package that recaptured a singular musical accomplishment more than forty-one years prior, it was an emotional moment. What they achieved years before still mattered to them, just as it did to me. And that was the most surprising aspect of the whole saga.

The Jazz Giants ♫ circa **1963**
In Concert with Mel Torme and Dave Brubeck
Gene- conducting far left. Piano- Tony Guzzi. Bass- Fred Fortunato.
Drums- Peter D'Addario. Saxophones- (L to R) Steve Royal, Leo Grabinski, Ron Gebeau, Dick Burlant, Joe Daddona. Trombones- Bruce Wilson, Mickey Walker, Sonny Costanzo, Jack Spake.
Trumpets- Dom Mariconda, Bob Butler, Tom, Alberts, Joe Marzulli.
Not pictured- Singer, Dan Arcotta

In writing this memoir I decided to omit darker personal incidents in my life, which cannot be relived. I know that no life is all good or all bad and regrets always accompany memories. But in looking back, which I seldom do—most always focused on the now—I realize I have been one of those lucky ones who has known first-hand the heady experience of communicating real emotions, feelings and ideas through the unique language of music.

No matter how musicians are sometimes regarded by a segment of the Establishment, they know music matters; it always has. Creating it is a gift, without which there would be no … well, that's the point. Can you imagine a world without music? The way I see it, making music is one of life's important endeavors, not to be taken for granted, especially by musicians themselves. Countless musicians, much more accomplished than I, have made lasting contributions to the fabric of our lives. For this, they deserve our thanks.

As for myself, even though I have long since recovered from the fascinating grip of making music, I will always be grateful for the opportunities I have had because of it.

After all, it was music that hooked me and led me to chase the muse that kept saying "One More Time."

And that's the truth, so help me, Charlie Parker.

*

How sweet. Was that a sermon?

(Oh stuff it.)

***

POST SCRIPT ♫ *The Family*

After reading *Hooked On A Horn,* many readers inquired about my children. Though family is mentioned at various times in the preceding pages, I did not write extensively about them. They have, however, always been a vital part of my life. For those who are curious, I offer the following family update in chronological order of birth.

As this book was in preparation, recording producer-composer-bassist David, the oldest son, has completed another tour and other projects with Aerosmith and Joe Perry and is musical director of the James Montgomery Blues Band. He is in the midst of producing his new solo album. A well-known Boston area musician, he has played and recorded with many famous rock and blues groups worldwide. His CD, *Cooneymus Rex,* was recently released, and he has just finished a solo album of his own. His wife, Sally Wright, is the actress-director.

Oldest daughter Margaret, Nurse Practitioner, Vassar graduate and family big sister, has relocated from Hartford to Portland, Oregon.

Peter, avowed avatar for the event, is planning and producing the next "Hull Brothers and Friends Annual Reunion Jam" in Stratford, Connecticut, featuring David, bassist Chris, singer Matt, guitarist Peter and guest artists . . . always a blast. Peter and his wife Robin play host to throngs.

Classically trained pianist Becca is co-chair of the Piano Department at New Hampshire's renowned Concord Community Music School; its multi-talented director is her husband, pianist Calvin Herst.

Matthew, medical I.T. guru, and perennial father of the year to his three kids, is re-limbering up his vocal chords and guitar chops at home in Hingham, Massachusetts after the Hull Brothers Reunion. He and his wife, Mary Jo, and their kids are a tight team. Two of the kids are getting familiar with music via piano and flute.

Multi-talented Amy, resident of Concord, NH, long-time Academic Dean of Boston's New England School of Acupuncture, is developing her new entrepreneurial business ventures.

Christopher, fine bassist and erstwhile Red Sox armchair advisor, proud father and young grandfather, is fully engaged in Boston real estate activities and gigging with his band on weekends.

Sara, the dynamic technical director of The Literacy Project in Greenfield, Massachusetts, where she lives with her husband Kevin, has expanded her invaluable work to five other cities in the western part of the state.

Coda, the loquacious mini-schnauzer, continues to talk avidly—when she isn't sleeping—with anyone in Florida who smells interesting . . . just about everyone.

Guess who?

FAMILY TRIVIA

"A music tree of over one hundred years.
Over ninety thousand song performances.
Over ten million notes played. "

A hundred years of music? 90,000 songs? And how many notes?
Who's your accountant?

(Haven't you gone away yet?)

Never. You need me.

The Music Tree in Pictures follows.

THE MUSIC TREE

Grandfather: Tony Persico, (second from right) ♫ circa **1896**

Mother: Marge Hull and Her Melody Boys, circa ♫ **1932**

When HEP was hip

High School Friday nights at the teen "Hep Club"

♫ **1947-48** (Father) Fred Trumbull, far left (Pg 161), Gene, far right. Paul King, trumpet, standing left. Duane Hull (Gene's brother) trumpet, standing, second from left. Others, John Klotz, Ralph Hillman, Ray Carlson, Bruce Bolye, Dom Squillante, Steve Catendella, Bob Brady, Drums: Dan Parisi, Bass: Clarence Johns, Piano: Henry Tellone.   *Photo: Dick Gavlick*

Saturday nights at the Palais Royale Ballroom, South Bend. Notre Dame, circa ♫ **1950-51.** .
ND Students: Joe Desautels, Jim Hawes, Jack Bradshaw, Jerry Costello, Jack Ross, Gene Hull, Jack FitzPatrick, Jack Totty, Hank Keating, Herb Dir, Dave O'Leary, Ed Vlaun, Rollie Kohlbeck, John Skudris, Art Goldkamp.

Notre Dame, circa ♫ **1949**. *Photo: 1952 ND yearbook*
Background: Don Bebenek, Bass; Ron Myrter, sax.

The Jazz Giants. The Ritz Ballroom, circa ♫ **1961**

The Jazz Giants
Birdland, New York City
♫ 1963

Backstage at Shakespeare Theatre ♫ 1964
The Jazz Giants. In Concert with **Tony Bennett**
(L -R) Bob Butler, Jeff Leonard, Dan Arcotta, **Tony Bennett**
Henny Youngman, Mickey Walker, Gene Hull, Peter D'Addario,
Bob Haray, Bobby Sagnella, Sonny Costanzo

The lost recording
"Live at the Newport Jazz Festival"
♫ 1962

Columbia Records
"Pico Peak A Boo"
♫

The opening of Russian ports to the West

June **1992**
The author "conducts" the welcoming pier-side local band in St.
Petersburg, Russia, greeting the first American cruise ship to enter the
Russian port, marking the fall of the Soviet Union and the end of the
Cold War. An amused passenger from RCCL's *Song of Norway*
shortcuts her return to the ship from a day of city shopping. The tune
being played, believe it or not, was
"When The Saints Go Marching In."

Photo: Lois Greenberg

"42 Street" ♪ circa **1978** (Later renamed "Bad Habit")
Pete Hull   Chris Hull   Matt Hull

"Bad Habit" Reunion ♪ 21 years later, **2009**
Hull Brothers and Friends - *The Windmill, Stratford, Ct*
Pete, Bill Duphiney (drummer), Matt, Chris, George Maher
Not pictured: Keyboardist Glen Masso.

The four Hull Brothers reunion ♫ 2009
Peter,   Matt,   Chris,   David

Matt,   Chris,   Barry Butler
Not seen: drummer, Brian Butler
(The Butler brothers: author's nephews)
Reunion ♫ 2009
Reunion Photos: Patty Duphiney and Robin Hull

"Aerosmith" - David Hull and Steve Tyler take a bow
♫ 2006-07, 09

Becca and Calvin Herst, Four *Hands,* ♫ **1998**
The classical musicians of the family

Amy ♫ during her piano playing days

One final thought ...
Sometimes life in the music business could be dreary.

The Golddiggers (of the Dean Martin Show) with the "Producer"
Phoenix, circa ♫ 1979
Taken just as Peggy Gohl (standing, 2nd from right) grabbed my butt.

Yeah, right, dreary. You cad.

Oh yes, and then there was the time with Joey Heatherton, main showroom, 'The Congo Room,' Sahara Hotel,

Las Vegas ♫ **1977**

The Joey Heatherton Show

Now, wait minute. What about these last two pictures? You've spent a whole book telling how dedicated you were to your career. So, what's with this Golddiggers and dancing with Joey Heatherton stuff?

(Well, you know… sometimes you have to do what you have to do what you have to do. That's showbiz.)

Yeah, right.

ACKNOWLEDGEMENTS

My true thanks to those who helped keep these memoir moments on track during the long draft-and-revision process. I have since added text, revisions, and many photos.

Helpful readers have included Margaret Spencer Hull, Lenore Mascar, Patrick Lennon, Barry Wood, David Hull, Chris Hull, Amy Hull, Becca and Calvin Herst. My special thanks to brilliant Sara Mackay for her expertise and patience in assisting in the layout of the book, to Almut Metzroth for her invaluable editing of this edition, and Patrick Lennon for his patient publishing preparation expertise.

I thank the Stratford Library Association for its assistance and accesses to its archives of the American Shakespeare Festival Theatre, and the Library of Congress and producer George Wein for making available exclusively to me the recording of the Jazz Giants at the 1962 Newport Jazz Festival.

Most importantly, I thank both Marge, the matriarch, and Connie, the dedicated mother of my children for a lifetime of encouragement and goodness. To all of you, and others whom I may have missed, I offer my most sincere gratitude.

Gene

Portrait of an author-musician-to-be at age two.

ABOUT THE AUTHOR

A native of Bridgeport, Connecticut, Gene Hull is a graduate of the University Of Notre Dame with additional studies at the Juilliard School of Music, Fairfield University, and Florida International University's Creative Writing Program.

Since his careers in the music world and the Cruise industry, he has authored four books. He serves as President of the Treasure Coast Writers Guild, moderator of the Morningside Library Writers Workshop, and is a regular contributor to print and online publications. His book reviews have appeared regularly in Scripps Florida Newspapers

A frequent guest speaker for schools, groups and organizations, the author invites inquiries and reader comments at www.genehull.com or genehull@msn.com.

He lives in Fort Pierce, Florida.

*

The *Newport '62* recording of the Jazz Giants, heretofore unavailable and successfully retrieved from the Archives of the Library of Congress (pg. 263) is available exclusively through the author's website.

♪

LaVergne, TN USA
13 February 2011
216347LV00005B/5/P